New Cambridge Advanced English

Student's Book	Leo Jones

CAMBRIDGE
UNIVERSITY PRESS

148743

PUBLISHED BY THE PRESS SYNDICATE OF THE UNIVERSITY OF CAMBRIDGE
The Pitt Building, Trumpington Street, Cambridge, United Kingdom

CAMBRIDGE UNIVERSITY PRESS
The Edinburgh Building, Cambridge CB2 2RU, UK
40 West 20th Street, New York, NY 10011–4211, USA
477 Williamstown Road, Port Melbourne, VIC 3207, Australia
Ruiz de Alarcón 13, 28014 Madrid, Spain
Dock House, The Waterfront, Cape Town 8001, South Africa

http://www.cambridge.org

First published 1991
New edition 1998
Ninth printing 2005

Printed in Dubai by Oriental Press

ISBN 0 521 62939 X Student's Book, paperback
ISBN 0 521 62941 1 Teacher's Book, paperback
ISBN 0 521 62940 3 Class Cassette Set

Contents

I'd like to thank everyone whose hard work, fresh ideas, helpful comments and criticisms have enhanced this book immensely:

The following teachers reported on their experiences using the first edition with their students:

Dolly Irani in France   Chrysoula Georgouli & Fotini Petrou in Greece   Andrea Marschalek in Hungary   Bernardo Santano Moreno in Spain   Anna Kibort in Poland   Peter Tomkin in the UK

Elizabeth Tataraki and Clare West reported on the proposal for a new edition.

Alison McCabe alerted me to some of the problems that face candidates in the Reading paper of the CAE exam.

The following teachers reported on the new material as it was being written:

Christa Kochuyt Temple in Belgium   Katherine Spence in France   Philip Devlin, Ines Laue & Caroline Mears in Germany   Andrea Marschalek in Hungary   David Massey & Mary Nava in Italy   Karina Schymik & Tadeusez Z. Wolanski in Poland   Teresa Corchado in Spain   Sue Gosling, Nick Kenny, Patricia O'Sullivan, Peter Watkins & Martin Wilson in the UK

Liz Sharman set the ball rolling. Charlotte Adams took over and continued to give her encouragement and support, with help from Niki Browne.

Alison Silver edited the book and guided the project efficiently through to publication. I'm very grateful for her insights and meticulous attention to detail. It was, as ever, a pleasure to work with her.

Hilary Fletcher researched the photographs.

Michelle Uniacke Gibson was responsible for text permission.

Celia Witchard did the illustrations.

Ruth Carim was the proofreader.

Paul Wilson of Sage Associates designed the book with the help of Gecko Limited.

Susie Fairfax organised the Interviews and asked all the right questions.

James Richardson produced the recordings. Andy Taylor was the engineer at Studio AVP.

From the first edition

First of all, I'd like to say how grateful I am to:

Jeanne McCarten for her inexhaustible patience, support and encouragement throughout my work on this book,
Alison Silver for her friendly editorial expertise,
Peter Ducker for the design of the book,
and Peter Taylor and Studio AVP for producing the recordings.

Thanks very much also to the following teachers who used the pilot edition with their classes and contributed detailed comments on it and who evaluated and reported on subsequent revised units. Without their help, this book could not have been written:

Pat Biagi, Christ Church College ELTU, Canterbury   Jenny Bradshaw   Sylvie Dawid, Beverly Langsch and Monty Sufrin, Migros Club School, Berne   George Drivas, Moraitis School, Athens   Tim Eyres, Godmer House, Oxford   David Gray   Amanda Hammersley, British School of Monza, Italy   Chris Higgins and staff, Teach In Language and Training Workshop, Rome   Tom Hinton   Roger Hunt, International House, Madrid   Ruth Jimack   Christine Margittai   Laura Matthews, Newnham Language Centre, Cambridge   Joy Morris and staff, British Institute, Barcelona   Jill Mountain and staff, British Institute, Rome   Julia Napier   Patricia Pringle, Université II, Lyon   Lesley Porte and Diann Gruber, ESIEE, Paris   Rachelle Porteous, London School of English   Tom Sagar and colleagues, Collège Rousseau, Geneva   Katy Shaw and colleagues, Eurocentre, Lee Green   Elizabeth Sim and staff, Eurocentre, Cambridge   Lynda Taylor   Kit Woods

Finally, thanks to Sue, Zoë and Thomas for everything.

Introduction

New Cambridge Advanced English will help you to develop all your skills in English: speaking, listening, reading and writing — as well as helping to develop your vocabulary and improve your grammar. You'll find exercises and activities in each unit that concentrate on different skills, helping you to revise and consolidate what you already know, and to develop and extend your knowledge further.

New Cambridge Advanced English is specially designed to be suitable BOTH for students who are preparing for the Cambridge Certificate in Advanced English (CAE) exam AND for students who aren't preparing for this exam, but who want to develop their English for their work, studies and social lives.

Each unit is based on a different topic.

The odd-numbered units are '**Theme units**' and they contain:

· informative **Reading** texts from a variety of authentic sources, with tasks, exercises and activities to improve your reading skills
· **Listening** exercises with tasks and activities to help you improve your listening skills
· **Interviews** with people who have special knowledge of the theme or stories to tell about it
· **Effective writing** exercises to help you develop useful techniques you can use in your writing
· realistic **Creative writing** tasks to give you an opportunity to express yourself in writing

The even-numbered units are '**Language units**' and they contain:

· shorter **Reading** texts or **Listening** exercises, leading to discussion or a writing task
· **Grammar** review: the 'problem areas' of English grammar are revised in a thought-provoking and interesting way
· **Word study** exercises to help you to develop your vocabulary skills
· **Speaking** activities to help you to practise the functional language needed in different situations and improve your pronunciation

Every unit contains:

· exercises on **Vocabulary** connected with the topic of the unit
· opportunities for **Discussion**
· work on **Idioms and collocations** or **Verbs and idioms**, including phrasal verbs

Symbols in the Student's Book:

👥 = Work in pairs

👥👤 = Work in threes

👥👥 = Work in groups

👥→👥 = Join another pair to form a group

(Some of the 👥 activities are **Communication Activities**, where you and your partner(s) are given different information that you have to communicate to each other. These are printed at the end of the book but in random order so that you can't see each other's information.)

🔲 = Recorded material

✎ = Writing task

🖍 = Use a highlighter

Notes like this appear throughout the book. They give you extra advice and study tips.

Enjoy using *New Cambridge Advanced English*!

Leo Jones

Map of the book

	Reading	Interviews	Listening	Word study	Effective writing	Creative writing	Grammar	Speaking & pronunciation	Verbs, idioms & collocations
1 Desert islands	Landings The Castaways	Pen Hadow, survival expert	A year on a desert island		Joining sentences – 1	Writing a narrative			All's well that ends well!
2 Around the world	Japanese beach lovers & Push-button lover		World Music See the world?	Synonyms & opposites – 1		(Informal letter)	The past – 1	Really? That's amazing!	You can't lose!
3 That's show business!	The rage of Rambo	Maev Alexander, actress	One of my favourite films …	Making an emphasis	Punctuation	Planning ahead …		Opinions	At … & by …
4 Enjoy your meal!	Cat canteloupe			Words easily confused		(Instructions + note)	Simple + progressive aspect	Appropriate language	Bring, carry & take
5 Travellers or tourists?	Trouble in paradise Travel writers	Susan Davies, traveller			Making notes	A letter of complaint			High, middle & low
6 It takes all sorts …	Politically correct? Horoscopes		7 descriptions	Synonyms & opposites – 2		Letter of reference	Modal verbs	Describing people	
7 Put it in writing	Different styles The unstoppable Albert Sukoff Spammed & Writing unlimited The secrets of writing business letters	Isabelle Amyes, writer	Handwriting The differences between spoken and written English		Different styles Long & short sentences Formal & personal letters	A tactful letter			In … & out of …
8 Past times	The good old days?		Fourteen ninety-nine In other words …	Forming adjectives		(Descriptions of 2 historical figures)	The past – 2		Get
9 You're as old as you feel	Life begins at 50 The Greys Family life	Geoffrey Smerden, U3A organiser	Granny power		Paragraphs	Letter to the editor			Ages
10 Utopia?	Island The best of all possible worlds Brasilia		An ideal home? The perfect society	Synonyms & opposites – 3		Letter describing a place	Articles	Describing a place	Hard, soft, difficult & easy

One

Desert islands

(1.1) A year on a desert island
Listening and Speaking

A This advertisement appeared in *Time Out*, a London weekly magazine. Discuss these questions:

- What kind of person would place such an advertisement?
- What kind of person would reply to it?
- Why is the word 'wife' in inverted commas?

> **UNINHABITED TROPICAL ISLAND ADVENTURE.**
> Writer wants "wife" for one year.

B It was Gerald Kingsland who placed the advertisement in *Time Out* and Lucy Irvine was the 'wife' who was chosen to accompany him. This is the first page of *Castaway*, her account of their year together. After you've read it through, discuss the questions below.

CHAPTER ONE

Landings

An infinity of sea and sky bluer and more brilliant than in any dream. Our wake made a white streak across the blue so struck with glittering points of light it smarted the eye. We passed islands to our left and to our right; bottle green bosomy mounds frilled about with white sand rising out of that electric world of blue.

Which one of them was to be our home for the next year? Its name, and the fact that it was situated somewhere in the Torres Strait where the Arafura and Coral Seas meet between the northernmost point of Australia and Papua New Guinea, was all we knew about our island.

We were travelling in an aluminium dinghy, resting low in the water under the weight of five people and luggage for the two of us who were to be castaway. Our temporary companions were a young female photographer and the two silent Torres Strait Islanders who were manning the boat. G and I were squashed close together but each clamped stiffly in a separate world of anticipation. The sensation of waiting and the vastness of the sea and sky made the passage seem timeless. We skirted the edge of a reef across a long stretch of open water and then the dinghy made a decisive turn and the boy steering pointed ahead.

'Tuin,' he said simply, the 'u' sound an 'oo'.

The first impression was of a long narrow island with small hills to north and south muffled in dense dark green. Huge boulders, like gigantic molars, stood out in the middle of a wide open bay. There was a long straight beach with light coloured sand. And palm trees.

from Castaway *by Lucy Irvine*

Discuss these questions:

- How did they reach the island?
- Why couldn't they identify their island as they approached it?
- How many people were in the boat with them?
- What colours are mentioned in the first paragraph? What impression does this give you of the place?
- What features of the island are mentioned in the last paragraph? What impression do you get of the island?

C You'll hear a conversation about what happened during their year together.

1 Before you listen to the recording, look at the questions and see which answers you can GUESS, without hearing the conversation.

Was it Lucy (L) or Gerald (G) or both of them (L + G) who . . .

wrote *Castaway* ☐	wrote *The Islander* ☐
was 24 years old ☐	was 51 years old ☐
had lived on another island ☐	had worked in a tax office ☐
caught fish ☐	tried to grow vegetables ☐
did the cooking ☐	was going to write a novel ☐
was bad-tempered ☐	went off for long walks alone ☐
fell in love with the island ☐	wrote a diary ☐
was badly bitten by insects ☐	could hardly walk ☐
lost a lot of weight ☐	had an irritating voice ☐
lost touch with reality ☐	drank salty water ☐
did repairs for local islanders ☐	went to another island for Christmas ☐
wanted to stay longer ☐	wrote a best-selling book ☐

2 Listen to the first part of the recording and note down your answers above. Then compare your answers with a partner's. Which answers have you heard so far and which do you still have to listen out for?

3 Do the same with the second and third parts of the recording.

D Discuss with your partners:

- your reactions to the way Lucy and Gerald behaved
- how YOU would have coped if you'd been Gerald or Lucy's companion
- which of their books you'd like to read — and why?
- whether you'd like to see the film

E 1 Student A should look at **Communication Activity 1** on page 180, student B at **19** on page 186 and C at **35** on page 191. You'll see a summary of one of these stories:

Spend a few minutes studying the summary and then tell the story. Don't just read the summary aloud to your partners — try to MEMORISE the main points. Refer back to the summary only if you lose track of the story.

2 Rewrite ONE of the summaries as a complete story.

(**1.2**) **Joining sentences — 1**
Effective writing

A In a SPOKEN narrative, we usually explain the events of a story in fairly short sentences in the order they happened, using *and* or *then* to join the sentences or clauses together. In a WRITTEN account, longer, more complex sentences tend to be used.

▼ Look at these examples. There are two written versions of each spoken narrative. Highlight the connecting words that are used. Which of the two written versions do you prefer, and why?

> Well, you see, the train was late and we didn't arrive till midnight. Then we were much too late for dinner at the hotel and we had to go to bed hungry. It was awful!

As our train was late we did not arrive till midnight and, because this was too late for dinner at the hotel, we had to go to bed hungry.

We had to go to bed hungry because our train had been delayed, and by the time we reached our hotel at midnight meals were unfortunately no longer being served.

> Well, what happened was that we had a really nice lunch and we had a long chat about old times. And then the bill came and we split it between us and then we went for a lovely walk together beside the lake.

We enjoyed a long, nostalgic conversation while we were having a delicious lunch, followed by a very enjoyable walk beside the lake together after we had agreed to split the bill.

During our lunch, which was delicious, we enjoyed reminiscing about old times and then, after splitting the bill, we went for a delightful walk together beside the lake.

B 1 The events in these stories aren't in chronological order. Decide together on the correct order of events for each story. Take turns to retell each story, using *and, but, so* or *then* to make longer sentences:

1 They managed to swim to a nearby island. Their ship went down in a typhoon. They wanted to attract the attention of passing ships. They lit a fire on the highest point of the island. They were rescued. A passing cruise liner spotted the smoke.

> Their ship went down in a typhoon but they managed to swim to a nearby island. They wanted to attract the attention of passing ships, so they lit a fire on the highest point of the island. A passing cruise liner spotted the smoke and they were rescued.

2 I arrived late for work. I couldn't get the car to start. It was a cold, damp morning. I had to push the car down the hill. I managed to start the engine. I jumped into the car. The car gathered speed.

3 Her interest in politics made her decide to stand for parliament. She won the by-election with a large majority. She gave up politics for good. She lost at the next general election.

4   They got home very late. They spent a long time drinking coffee and talking. They went dancing together. They went to a café together.

5   Our plane didn't take off. The airport was closed because of fog. Many flights were delayed. Inconvenience was caused to hundreds of passengers. We had to spend the night in the departure lounge.

6   The kidnappers were caught by the police. All ports and airports were being watched. The kidnappers were trying to get out of the country. The hostages were released. The ransom money was paid.

2 Rewrite each story in B1 as one or two long sentences. But CHANGE EACH ENDING, substituting a happy end for an unhappy end and vice versa — as in this example:

They managed to swim to a nearby island after their ship had gone down in a typhoon. As they wanted to attract the attention of passing ships, they lit a fire, but their signals went unnoticed and none of them survived.

Use some of the following connecting words and alter some of the verb forms as necessary (e.g. did to had done).

after   although   and then   as   as soon as   because   before   but   by the time   eventually   finally   however   in the end   once   since   so   so that   subsequently   until   when   which   while

C Rewrite these notes in complete sentences, using suitable connecting words:

1   ship went down — hurricane — nearly drowned

They were nearly drowned after their ship had gone down in a hurricane.

2   found driftwood — built bonfire — beach — caught fish — grilled — fire

3   gathered palm leaves — built rough shelter

4   sleepless night — insects — began lose heart

5   made mosquito nets — protect themselves — next night

6   found wild bananas, very glad — hillside — ate them — started look — drinking water

7   couldn't find fresh water — afraid not survive on island

8   hoped collect rainwater — but so little rain — in despair

9   build raft from remaining driftwood — set sail across ocean

10 raft started sink — man-eating sharks began circle ominously round

(1.3) Writing a narrative
Creative writing

A Select just ONE of these opening lines and use it to begin your own desert island story (about 250 words). Make notes of the ideas you would like to include.

I began to swim towards an island on the horizon …
I found myself lying on a sandy, palm-fringed beach …
It was clear to us both that we were alone …
After the plane crash the three of us were the only survivors …

B 1 Write the first part of your narrative on one sheet of paper — but write the LAST PARAGRAPH on a SEPARATE sheet of paper.

2 Show the first page of your story to your partners (WITHOUT the last paragraph). Ask them to suggest what might come next. Do their ideas agree with what you had in mind?

Finally, show them your last paragraph and ask for their comments.

Try to imagine how your target reader(s) will react — will they be intrigued, excited or entertained? How can you keep their interest while they're reading?

The Castaways
Reading

A 1 Ask your partners:

- if life on a desert island would be wonderful – or a nightmare
- why they think desert islands are popular in fiction and movies

2 Fill the gaps in these sentences with suitable words from the list below. Look up any unfamiliar words in a dictionary.

1 As Lucy and Gerald were *resourceful* people they stood a good chance of ＿＿＿＿＿ in difficult ＿＿＿＿＿ . But the longer they were alone together the more the ＿＿＿＿＿ between them grew and they got on each other's ＿＿＿＿＿ .

2 In Shakespeare's *The Tempest* (1610) some sailors are ＿＿＿＿＿ on a ＿＿＿＿＿ island, where the magician Prospero and his daughter Miranda live. Prospero rules the island's natural creatures, including the good spirit Ariel and the evil monster Caliban.

3 In Daniel Defoe's *Robinson Crusoe* (1719) the hero, after living many years in ＿＿＿＿＿ , finds a ＿＿＿＿＿ who becomes his ＿＿＿＿＿ .

4 In Robert Louis Stevenson's *Treasure Island* (1883) a man is ＿＿＿＿＿ after many years on an island where he had been abandoned by ＿＿＿＿＿ .

> circumstances   companion   isolation   lonely   nerves   pirates   remote   rescued   resourceful ✓
> servant   shipwrecked   surviving   tension

B Listen to the recording as you read this poem:

THE CASTAWAYS OR VOTE FOR CALIBAN

The Pacific Ocean –
A blue demi-globe.
Islands like punctuation marks.

A cruising airliner,
Passengers unwrapping pats of butter.
A hurricane arises,
Tosses the plane into the sea.

Five of them, flung on to an island beach,
Survived.
Tom the reporter.
Susan the botanist.
Jim the high-jump champion.
Bill the carpenter.
Mary the eccentric widow.

Tom the reporter sniffed out a stream of drinkable water.
Susan the botanist identified a banana tree.
Jim the high-jump champion jumped up and down and gave them
*   each a bunch.*
Bill the carpenter knocked up a table for their banana supper.
Mary the eccentric widow buried the banana skins,
But only after they had asked her twice.
They all gathered sticks and lit a fire.
There was an incredible sunset.

Next morning they held a committee meeting.
Tom, Susan, Jim and Bill
Voted to make the best of things.
Mary, the eccentric widow, abstained.

Tom the reporter killed several dozen wild pigs.
Tanned their skins into parchment
And printed the Island News *with the ink of squids.*

Susan the botanist developed new strains of banana
Which tasted of chocolate, beefsteak, peanut butter,
Chicken and bootpolish.

Jim the high-jump champion organised organised games
Which he always won easily.

Bill the carpenter constructed a wooden water wheel
And converted the water's energy into electricity.
Using iron ore from the hills, he constructed lampposts.

They all worried about Mary, the eccentric widow,
Her lack of confidence and her –
But there wasn't time to coddle her.

The volcano erupted, but they dug a trench
And diverted the lava into the sea
Where it formed a spectacular pier.
They were attacked by pirates but defeated them
With bamboo bazookas firing
Sea-urchins packed with home-made nitro-glycerine.
They gave the cannibals a dose of their own medicine
And survived an earthquake thanks to their skill in jumping.

Tom had been a court reporter
So he became the magistrate and solved disputes.
Susan the Botanist established
A university which also served as a museum.
Jim the high-jump champion
Was put in charge of law enforcement –
Jumped on them when they were bad.
Bill the carpenter built himself a church,
Preached there every Sunday.

But Mary the eccentric widow . . .
Each evening she wandered down the island's main street,
Past the Stock Exchange, the Houses of Parliament,
The prison and the arsenal.
Past the Prospero Souvenir Shop,
Past the Robert Louis Stevenson Movie Studios,
Past the Daniel Defoe Motel
She nervously wandered and sat on the end of the pier of lava,

Breathing heavily,
As if at a loss,
As if at a lover,
She opened her eyes wide
To the usual incredible sunset.

by Adrian Mitchell

1 Highlight any unfamiliar words using a fluorescent highlighter and, if necessary, look them up in a dictionary.

2 For TWO of the five characters in the poem, make notes on the following points. Begin by using a pencil to mark all the references to your characters in the poem.

- useful things he or she accomplished
- useless or pointless things he or she did
- why you admire or sympathise with him or her (or why you find him or her objectionable or unlikeable)

3 Compare your ideas. Then find out from your partners:

- what their impressions of the poem are
- which character they sympathise with most – and why
- what they think the poem is about, beneath the surface of the narrative

4 Write a paragraph (about 100 words) about your impressions of the poem and explain what you like and/or don't like about it.

Highlighting new words or phrases in the context you first met them will help you to remember them more easily. But highlight just the new word or phrase not the whole sentence.

One Desert islands

13

Survival
Interview

Pen Hadow

 A **You'll hear an interview with Pen Hadow, who leads expeditions to the Arctic. Fill in the missing information by writing a word or phrase in the notes below.**

Pen Hadow enjoys being in the Arctic because one can ₁ _____ oneself — as well as seeing the wildlife and landscape.

He doesn't enjoy ₂ _____ .

He has made two ₃ _____ on the north geographic pole. You can avoid making mistakes under pressure if you are ₄ _____

You're more likely to suffer from hypothermia if you ₅ _____ .

He was crossing the Denmark Strait in a small rubber boat when both their ₆ _____ seized.

They drifted more deeply into the ₇ _____ as the sea became ₈ _____ .

They didn't use their search and rescue beacon because ₉ _____ .

To prevent themselves being swept overboard they ₁₀ _____ .

His colleague was suffering from ₁₁ _____ .

After ₁₂ _____ adrift they found themselves within ₁₃ _____ of their final destination.

Pen Hadow's ideal desert island would be in ₁₄ _____

He'd be perfectly happy surviving there alone for ₁₅ _____ .

B **How would you and your partners cope if you found yourselves together on a desert island in the tropics? Decide together:**

· what useful skills you possess between you, which you could use if you were on a desert island — make a list

· what qualities you would hope for in a fellow castaway — make a list

· what basic supplies you'd need on a desert island as survival rations

· what TEN luxury items you'd like to have with you on the island

(1.6) All's well that ends well!
Idioms and collocations

Each unit in this book has a section on idioms and collocations, or verbs and idioms (including phrasal verbs). These sections introduce you to a range of useful expressions so that, with time, you can incorporate them into your active vocabulary.

(A) **Replace the phrases in red with one of the expressions below.**

1 Taking everything into consideration, I wouldn't like to be a castaway.
   All in all

2 There were palm trees on every part of the island.

3 'If it doesn't matter to you, I'd like to borrow this book.' 'Certainly.'

4 A two-week holiday on Tahiti costs £1499, including everything.

5 They were completely exhausted after swimming to the island.

6 Suddenly and unexpectedly they heard an explosion and the ship started to sink. Miraculously, everyone except the captain survived.

7 If nothing goes wrong my plane will arrive just before lunch.

8 The film wasn't brilliant but it was just about satisfactory, I suppose.

9 'How are you feeling?' 'Much better, I'm feeling fine today, thanks.'

10 I enjoyed the story but nevertheless I felt a little cheated by the ending.

11 There were 187 passengers on board altogether and they tried to get into the lifeboat at the same time.

12 To begin with, in an emergency, remember, this is important, don't panic!

> above all   all at once   all at once   all being well   all but   all in   all in   all in all ✓   all over
> all right   all right   all the same   all told / in all   by all means   first of all   it's all the same

(B) **Fill these gaps with suitable expressions from the list above.**

1 _____ learning new idioms and expressions is worth the effort. Secondly . . .

2 I'll meet you tomorrow evening at 8 o'clock, _____ .

3 If you want to read a book, I don't mind at all: it's _____ to me.

4 Going out on Sunday sounds like a good idea. _____ , I don't think I'll join you.

5 We got caught in the traffic and by the time we arrived it was _____

6 I'd rather do this work by myself, if it's _____ to you.

7 'Would you mind helping me?' ' _____ .'

8 _____ when reading an English text, try to work out the meaning of unfamiliar words from the context before you consult a dictionary.

Highlight any
expressions that
are new
to you.

Two

Around the world

(2.1) United nations
Vocabulary

A 1 What would you call a person from each of these cities?

Algiers *an Algerian* Ankara *a Turk* Bamako *a Malian* Bangkok *a Thai*

Bombay Bratislava Bucharest Budapest Cairo Havana Jakarta Johannesburg

Karachi Kiev Kuala Lumpur Lagos Lima Ljubljana Manila Moscow Oslo

Prague Riyadh São Paulo Seoul Sofia Sydney Toronto Vienna

2 Which countries do these cars come from? What nationality is the driver?

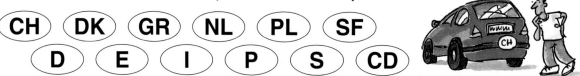

3 Write down the names of FIVE more countries in each of these regions:

B Think of TEN countries which you think are important or interesting — or difficult to
remember in English. Make a chart like this:

Country	nationality	a person	the people	language(s)
Brazil	Brazilian	a Brazilian	the Brazilians	Portuguese
Poland	Polish	a Pole	the Poles	Polish
Switzerland	Swiss	a Swiss	the Swiss	German, French, Italian, Romansch

C Find out which are the FIVE countries in the world which your partners would most like to
visit one day. Ask for their reasons.

(2.2) **World Music**
Listening

DUBBED the Madonna of Mali, Oumou Sangaré is currently the biggest female star in West Africa. From her opening track, *Kun Fe Ko*, Sangaré's voice swoops over the complex, skittish Wassoulou rhythms. She can soothe with soulful intonation or come slamming in with a strong note and impeccable phrasing, her voice a rich counterpoint to the sweet shrillness of the girl chorus. Though she was born in Mali's capital Bamako, 27-year-old Sangaré has taken the traditional sound from her ancestral home, a joyful, declarative style derived from hunting and harvesting dances, mixed it, modernised it and made it her own.

A 1 Read the record review above – does it sound like the kind of music you'd like?

2 You'll hear part of a broadcast about World Music. Match the names of the musicians with their country of origin.

Ali Farka Touré	Algeria
Elio Revé	Brazil
Fong Naam	Chile
Gilberto Gil	Colombia
Inti Illimani	Congo
Joe Arroyo	Cuba
Juan Luis Guerra	Dominican Republic
Khaled	Greece
Ladysmith Black Mambazo	Hungary
Márta Sebestyén	Mali
Nikos Ksidakis	Mali
Nusrat Fateh Ali Khan	Pakistan
Oumou Sangaré	Panama
Papa Wemba	Senegal
Paul Simon	South Africa
Ruben Blades	Thailand
Youssou N'Dour	USA

3 Listen to the recording again and fill the gaps by writing one word in each space:

1 World Music is ▮▮▮▮▮ music from ▮▮▮▮▮ other than Western Europe and the USA.

2 It has been referred to as ▮▮▮▮▮ traditional music – still being ▮▮▮▮▮ and enjoyed, not being ▮▮▮▮▮ or rediscovered.

3 Most modern American popular music is rooted in ▮▮▮▮▮.

4 Anglo-American popular music is more ▮▮▮▮▮ and commercialised – World Music is more alive and ▮▮▮▮▮.

5 Many West African musicians belong to ▮▮▮▮▮ who have been making music for ▮▮▮▮▮.

6 *Soukous* and *salsa* music makes you want to ▮▮▮▮▮.

7 The music of the Andes and Hungary is very ▮▮▮▮▮.

8 Asian music uses different ▮▮▮▮▮ from Western music.

9 The term 'World Music' was ▮▮▮▮▮ by a group of record ▮▮▮▮▮ to help buyers to know where to find such recordings in a record shop.

10 Peter Gabriel's motto is 'High-tech and ▮▮▮▮▮'.

B Ask your partners to describe what kinds of music from foreign countries – including the USA and the UK – they enjoy listening to and why.

REALW●RLD

The past – 1
Grammar

A **Look at these groups of sentences. What's the difference in meaning between the sentences in each group?**

1   *When we heard the song we started singing.*
    When we had heard the song we started singing.

2   *Did you enjoy your holiday?*   *Have you enjoyed your holiday?*

3   *I never enjoyed travelling alone.*   *I've never enjoyed travelling alone.*
    I had never enjoyed travelling alone.   *I never enjoy travelling alone.*

4   *She lived abroad for two years.*   *She has lived abroad for two years.*
    She had lived abroad for two years.   *She still lives abroad after two years.*

B **First, match these MEANINGS (a–f) with the verbs in red in the numbered examples (1–6) and write the letter in the little boxes (1–6) on the right:**

a   The CAUSE of an event or situation that people already know about

b   Actions or events that happened BEFORE a particular past event

c   Recent events that have RESULTS in present time

d   Actions or events that happened within an AS-YET-UNFINISHED period

e   Events or actions that happened at a DEFINITE time in the past

f   REPORTING what someone said or asked about a past event or action

Then fill the *gaps* **in the incomplete sentences.**

Then *Write a similar example of your own for each meaning illustrated.*

Simple past

1   She was born in India and came to Britain when she was 18.   1 | e |

    She   *began*   learning English six years ago when she _____ twelve years old.

    _____ you _____ that programme about Japan on TV last night?

2   Look over there: someone has broken a window. I wonder who did it?   2 | |

    What a lovely photograph! _____ you _____ it yourself?

Present perfect

3   She has worked hard all her life.

    I haven't seen her recently.   3 | |

    _____ you ever _____ to the USA?

    _____ you _____ Lucy Irvine's new book?

4   I've just returned from a long trip, so I don't feel like travelling anywhere.   4 | |

    I heard on the news today that there _____ a terrible earthquake in China

    and thousands of people _____ killed.

Past perfect

5   It was very cold when he got to Moscow because winter had (already) arrived.

    My car wouldn't start this morning because I had left the lights on all night.   5 | |

    He _____ get on the plane because he _____ his passport.

6   She said she had been in Burma in 1988 but that she had never been to India.   6 | |

    We asked him why he _____ to the party the previous weekend.

In some cases the **past perfect** is optional. There's no difference in meaning between:

After I had been to Japan, I spent a week in Korea.

and

After I went to Japan, I spent a week in Korea.

C 1 Look at these examples – the verbs are in red and the time expressions are in blue:

Time expressions

Some time expressions are not normally used with the present perfect but with the SIMPLE PAST (or past perfect):

In 1989 Japan overtook the USA as the world's richest nation.
Did you see that documentary about South Africa on TV the other day?

Some are not normally used with the simple past but with the PRESENT PERFECT (or past perfect):

I haven't been abroad since January.
Have you seen any good TV programmes lately?

Some can be used either with the SIMPLE PAST or the PRESENT PERFECT, depending on the situation:

'Have you ever been to Kenya?' 'Yes, I have. I went there earlier this year.'
'Did you ever go to Mombasa while you were in Kenya?'

A few are normally only used with the PAST PERFECT:

He had booked his tickets a few days before.
We were worried because she hadn't arrived by 11 o'clock.

2 Arrange the time expressions below into four lists:

1 used with SIMPLE PAST   3 used with either SIMPLE PAST or PRESENT PERFECT

2 used with PRESENT PERFECT   4 used with PAST PERFECT

> already   a little while earlier   a long time ago   a moment ago   all my life   always   at midnight
> by midnight   by now   by the end of the year   for two months   in the morning   in 1997   just now
> last year   never   not long ago   not long before that   recently   so far   still   this afternoon
> this week   this year   till now   till midnight   until today   when I was younger   yesterday   yet

3 Write only the BEGINNINGS of four sentences and the ENDINGS of four more sentences, using the time expressions above. Ask your partner to complete them, like this:

When I was younger . . . *I didn't know anything about foreign countries.*

I have wanted to go to the United States **. . . all my life.**

D Underline the mistakes in these sentences and then correct them.

1 How nice to see you again! I <u>didn't see</u> you for ages. *haven't seen*
2 It's six years since their eldest son has been born.
3 What a delicious Indian meal that was – have you cooked it yourself?
4 Where have you got that marvellous Persian rug?
5 I couldn't look up the word because I lost my dictionary.
6 That is the funniest story I ever heard.
7 It was a long time since I wrote to my friends in Mexico.
8 I didn't finish yet, can I have a few more minutes, please?
9 By 1965 most African countries have become independent from colonial rule.
10 He was having three cups of tea by the time I arrived.

E Ask your partners:

- what foreign countries they have travelled to and what their impressions were of the place, the people and the lifestyle
- what they consider to be the most significant international events that have happened during their lifetime, and why
- what the most significant international events this year have been

> Many of the time expressions on this page are also used when referring to the present or future:
> *I'll see you in the morning.*
> *I have a shower in the morning.*
> *Let's meet this afternoon.*
> *I have a meeting this afternoon.*

Really? That's amazing!
Speaking

A You'll hear 15 short extracts, in which people are reacting to a piece of information or news that a friend gives them. Interpret the reactions by noting the number in one of the spaces.

surprised:	☐ ☐	not surprised: ☐
interested:	☐ ☐	uninterested: ☐1☐ ☐
disappointed:	☐	relieved: ☐
annoyed:	☐	excited: ☐2☐ ☐
pleased:	☐	sympathetic: ☐ ☐

B 1 Arrange the phrases in the middle to show which of the eight REACTIONS they would normally express. Some of them can express more than one reaction.

	That's amazing!	How annoying!	
ANNOYANCE	How infuriating!	What a nuisance!	PLEASURE
DISAPPOINTMENT	What a pity!	Phew!	RELIEF
EXCITEMENT	That *is* good news!	Thank heavens!	SURPRISE
INTEREST	Good lord!	I *am* pleased!	SYMPATHY
	Fancy that!	Oh dear!	
	Thank goodness!	Fantastic!!	
	How interesting!	How exciting!	
	Really!	What a shame!	
	That's wonderful!	That's a relief!	

2 Note down some other expressions that express the same reactions.

C Listen to the second part of the recording and imagine that some friends are talking to you. React to each piece of news or information with an appropriate remark.

> Many of the phrases in B can be used sarcastically as well as sincerely.

D 1 Make a list together of some of the following things. Use your imagination to invent some of these if necessary:

- your favourite colour, car, book, TV show, film, writer, song, piece of music, holiday resort, hobby, sport, animal, first name, country
- some things you're looking forward to AND some things you're dreading in the future
- some amazing AND annoying AND disappointing things that have happened recently
- some good news and some bad news
- the main turning points in your lives: what decisions and choices you've made and what happened as a result

2 Join another pair and get them to react to your information and 'news'.

"For me? Ooooooooh! I love surprises!"

(2.5) See the world?
Listening and Reading

A You'll hear a broadcast about theme parks. Note down ONE main attraction of each place in the chart.

Theme park	Main attraction
Tokyo Disneyland	
Huis Ten Bosch, Nagasaki	
Sea Hawk Resort & Hotel, Fukuoka	
Garasunosato, Hiroshima	
Russian Village, Niigata	
Shingo-mura, Aomori Prefecture	
German Happiness Kingdom, Hokkaido	
Canadian World, Hokkaido	
Shakespeare Country, Marayuma	
Tobu World	
Epcot World Showcase, Florida, USA	

B Two of you should look at Communication Activity 2, the others at 20. You'll each see the continuations of these two newspaper articles.

When you've read your article, find out what your partners have discovered by asking them questions. Discuss whether the same ideas could become popular in your country and why (not).

JAPANESE BEACH LOVERS BASK IN THEIR ARTIFICIAL ALL-WEATHER PARADISE

IT IS almost summertime in Japan, which means it is time to head for the beach. Not the gritty stretch that separates Japan from the ocean – a garbage dump and drag-race strip combined, atop dark volcanic sand.

Instead, it is time to head for the indoor beach park, with its predictable waves, clean, rubberised, sandgrained flooring and perfect weather – rain or shine.

"It's the instant noodles of beaches," explains Rie Kato, as she lies under

Push-button lover

WHAT do video cassettes, ice cream, pizzas, whisky and bouquets of flowers all have in common? The answer is that in Japan they can all be bought from a vending machine. Japan boasts more vending machines per person than any other country in the world, with one for every 22 people. America, by contrast, has one for every 46; the European Community only one for every 200.

Japanese vending machines are also more productive. Sales per machine are almost two-thirds higher th

C Find out what your partners know about the people who live in the various countries you talked about in 2.1: their characteristics, habits and behaviour.

- Which countries are supposed to have the friendliest people, the tastiest food, the most beautiful scenery, and the easiest language to learn?
- Which nationalities do you have first-hand personal experience of?

D Write an informal letter to a friend (about 250 words) telling him or her about the country you'd most like to visit and why you'd like to go there. Try to persuade your friend to go there with you during your next summer vacation.

Synonyms and opposites – 1
Word study

If someone asked you this question:

> Would you be afraid if you were about to spend a year on a desert island?

would you reply like this:

> Afraid? No, I'd be absolutely petrified!!

or like this:

> Afraid? No, but I suppose I would be a bit apprehensive.

Ⓐ 1 Some adjectives have similar meanings but have a different 'FORCE'.
Notice how these adjectives have been arranged in the chart to show their force.

AFRAID	anxious apprehensive frightened nervous petrified scared scared stiff terrified uneasy worried

slightly afraid →	afraid →	very afraid →	extremely afraid
anxious	frightened	terrified	petrified
apprehensive	scared		scared stiff
nervous			
uneasy			
worried			

2 Choose THREE of the following groups of adjectives and make similar charts to show the relative FORCE of the adjectives. Then add one more word to each of your charts. (If you need to use a dictionary to look up any words you don't know the meaning of, look carefully at the examples as well as the definitions.)

ANNOYED	cross discontented dissatisfied furious grumpy indignant irritated livid resentful upset
SURPRISED	amazed astonished horrified shocked stunned taken aback
CALM	composed detached impassive indifferent relaxed serene unemotional unmoved unruffled unworried
HAPPY	cheerful delighted exhilarated glad light-hearted on top of the world overjoyed pleased as Punch satisfied thrilled
UNHAPPY	dejected desperate disappointed discontented dissatisfied down in the dumps fed up feeling down feeling low heartbroken inconsolable miserable sorry upset wretched

Ⓑ 1 Make a list of things that might make you feel angry, happy, unhappy, excited, surprised or afraid.

2 Ask your new partners to say how they would feel about the things in your list and ask them why.
Like this:

> How would you feel if you saw a shark while you were swimming?
>
> Why is that?

> I'd be absolutely terrified!
>
> Because I might get eaten by it!

(2.7) You can't lose!
Verbs and idioms

A **Replace each phrase in red with the correct form of one the expressions from the list below.**

1 We didn't have a map and so we couldn't find the right direction. *lost our way*

2 I'm sorry that I panicked when the policeman stopped me, but I didn't know what to say to him.

3 I really enjoy getting thoroughly absorbed in a good book but this one is so dull that I'm no longer interested in it.

4 I'm so glad you're back, we couldn't manage without you.

5 I know you felt humiliated when you had to apologise, but don't worry too much about it.

6 I don't want to stand too near the edge in case I start to fall.

7 70 million people were killed in the First and Second World Wars.

8 The only way to become slimmer is to eat less; it's easy to become discouraged when other people are eating as much as they like.

9 I was going to complain to the manager but in the end I didn't have the courage.

10 We used to correspond regularly but now we are no longer in contact.

11 I couldn't remain calm with her when she refused to listen to my explanation and I quickly got angry with her.

12 He gets so upset when someone else is winning — I can't remember the number of times he has stormed out of the room.

> be at a loss   be a bad loser   be lost without   lose count   lose face   lose heart   lose interest
> lose one's balance   lose one's head   lose one's life   lose one's nerve   lose one's temper with
> lose one's way ✓   lose oneself in   lose patience   lose touch (with)   lose weight
> (not) lose any sleep over

B **Complete each sentence with a suitable expression from the list above:**

1 They were enthusiastic at first, but they soon _____ .

2 Let's write to each other regularly — it would be a shame if we _____ .

3 It's not as difficult as you think, try not to _____ .

4 In some countries people will do anything to avoid _____ .

5 In an emergency don't _____ .

6 I'm sorry I'm late, I'm afraid I _____ .

7 Just because someone doesn't understand, don't _____ .

8 He said he could ski down the slope easily but half-way down he _____

Highlight the most
useful new
expressions (or other
vocabulary) in this
section.

Three

That's show business!

(3.1) **Films, shows and concerts**
Vocabulary and Listening

A 1 Look at the photos and write down ten words that come into your mind when you think about different kinds of entertainment.

2 Find out from your partners how often they:

- go to the cinema — and watch movies on television or on video
- go to the theatre or listen to live music
- listen to music on cassette or CD

3 Fill the gaps with suitable words from the list below (the list includes some words that are not suitable).

> In a movie, the names of the stars, the producer, the person who wrote the _____ and the _____ are given in the opening _____, but you have to wait till the end to see the complete _____ of characters and the actors who _____ them — and the name of every individual member of the film _____. Some films are shot in a _____, others are filmed on _____. Foreign-language films can be shown with _____ or they may be _____.
>
>   A really exciting movie depends on good photography, good _____ (the way the film is cut with perfect timing so that each _____ surprises you), exciting _____ (car chases, fights and falls), _____ (visual techniques which make the fantasy seem like reality), and the _____ (music and sound effects).

> action   award   cartoon   cast   credits   crew   director   dubbed   editing   flashback   list
> location   played   plot   scene   screenplay   sequel   set   shot   soundtrack   special effects
> studio   stunts   subtitles

4 Make a list of the instruments you can hear in a pop or rock band. And make a similar list of some of the instruments that play in a symphony orchestra.

B You'll hear an interview with Maev Alexander, who plays the leading lady in *The Mousetrap*, the world's longest-running play. Complete each of the sentences in the summary opposite with a number or a short phrase.

1 The Mousetrap has been running for ▨▨▨▨▨ years.

2 Maev has played the part of Molly over ▨▨▨▨▨ times. The challenge for her in playing Molly is ▨▨▨▨▨.

3 The skills you need as an actor are: a good ▨▨▨▨▨; to adapt your ▨▨▨▨▨ to the part you're playing; the ▨▨▨▨▨ to stand up on a stage.

4 She became a member of the Royal Shakespeare Company at the age of ▨▨▨▨▨.

5 When the curtain comes down she finds it easy to ▨▨▨▨▨.

6 One night the lights failed. She found it hard to switch back into her role after ▨▨▨▨▨.

7 The audience found it thrilling to be reminded that they were watching ▨▨▨▨▨.

8 Actors don't just need ▨▨▨▨▨, a good ▨▨▨▨▨ and a good ▨▨▨▨▨.

9 Actors have to: ▨▨▨▨▨ to get work; live the life of a ▨▨▨▨▨; be good ▨▨▨▨▨.

10 But she still keeps acting because it's like ▨▨▨▨▨.

Maev Alexander

C Find out from your partners about their tastes in:

music   TV   drama   reading

And ask them to explain WHY they enjoy the things they do.

(3.2) One of my favourite films . . .
Listening and Speaking

A 1 You'll hear four people talking about a film they enjoyed. Match the names of the stars to the movie — and the names of the stars to the characters they played.

Movie	Stars	Characters
Miller's Crossing	Gabriel Byrne	a journalist
	Steve Buscemi	a playwright/scriptwriter
	Charles Durning	a bad guy/thug
Barton Fink	Albert Finney	the police chief
	John Goodman	Charlie Meadows
	Jennifer Jason Leigh	Bernie Birnbaum, a bookie
The Hudsucker Proxy	William H. Macey	Jerry Lundegaard
	Frances McDormond	Leo, a gangster
	Paul Newman	Norville Barnes
Fargo	Tim Robbins	Sydney J. Mussberger
	John Turturro	Tom Reagan
		Waring Hudsucker

2 Listen to the recording again and this time note down ONE memorable scene or feature that each person mentioned about their film.

3 Decide which of the films sounded most entertaining to you. And which sounded the least entertaining?

B Find out from your partners which of all the films they have seen were the most:

exciting   amusing   moving   disappointing   memorable   overrated   underrated

Tell them your own feelings about the films they mention.

Adults only
Reading

A 1 Discuss these questions:

- What was the most violent film you've ever seen?
- How did it make you feel? Do you avoid seeing violent films?
- Should violent and frightening films be banned?
- Have you seen any Sylvester Stallone movies?

2 Read this article. Judging by the tone of the article, do you think the writer is a man or a woman (Christopher or Christine)? Is he or she a fan of Sylvester Stallone?

The rage of *Rambo*

1 AS the most popular adults-only US film ever screened, *Rambo* grossed over $100 million in a few weeks, and was cheered in 2,165 cinemas. *Time* magazine said, "It seems to have perfectly articulated the nation's mood over Vietnam."

2 Articulate? Hardly. Stallone, co-writer of the film, substitutes oafish muttering for dialogue, making that other hero of the genre, Clint Eastwood, seem almost garrulous. Other than the mass murder of foreigners who don't agree with him, Stallone's only preoccupation in the film is exposing his preposterous body. His enormous breasts loom over the screen like Jane Russell in *The Outlaw*. The acting is performed mostly by his biceps.

3 The several hundred killings are perpetrated almost entirely by Rambo alone, although early on he is assisted by a female Vietnamese agent for the US called Co (who is not even played by an Oriental, but Julia Nickson speaking in broken English).

4 Rambo stabs, clubs, shoots, strangles, burns, bombs, drowns, and garrottes his victims, using enough knives to equip a meat market, mostly carried in his boots. As well as a high-tech bow with exploding arrows, he also manages to produce three assorted machine guns, all with inexhaustible ammunition clips.

5 He has no need of a helmet or flak jacket – let alone a shirt – because none of the enemy fire ever hits him, whereas he never misses. Rambo was obviously what the Americans needed before being chased out of Saigon in 1975.

The B-52s might even have remained in Guam, for Rambo is "a human war machine", as his old colonel observes. He becomes Bombo and blows up two dozen bamboo huts, an entire village, a bridge, several vehicles, a monster Russian bomber helicopter, two boats, a rice paddy and about half a battalion.

As an ex-Green Beret, Rambo's task is to find a jungle camp for American MIAs, Missing in Action, photograph any if there, and return "without engaging the enemy". (As this is supposed to be 1985, the incursion is illegal and Vietnam is not an enemy.)

Ignoring his brief from the start, he tells Co that "orders don't matter". His first act is to shoot an arrow through a guard's head, impaling him to a tree. This caused a fellow behind me in a T-shirt marked "USA" in red, white and blue, to shout gleefully "good arrow" as if at a Sunday darts match.

Zombo's final words are the nearest he comes to a full sentence. All he wants, he grunts, is "for our country to love us as much as we love it". Howls of approval from audiences, most of whom, like Mr Stallone, did not actually serve in the real Vietnam either.

The idea that the US did not lose has obvious attractions for an imperial power beaten by a nation of peasants.

Chris Reed

▼ **B** Highlight these words in the article (the ¶ symbol shows the paragraph they are in). Work out their meanings from the context. When you've decided, look them up in a dictionary to check if you were right.

Highlighting the words in context will help you to see the kind of contexts they can be used in and the collocations they are used in.

¶ 1 articulated	confused contradicted expressed	
¶ 2 articulate	athletic interesting speaking clearly violent	
¶ 2 oafish	idiotic inaudible noisy	
¶ 2 garrulous	peace-loving very quiet very talkative violent	
¶ 2 preposterous	enormous muscular ridiculous-looking	
¶ 3 perpetrated	committed enjoyed witnessed	
¶ 4 inexhaustible	incredible never-ending tiring	
¶ 8 brief	instructions report request short	
¶ 8 gleefully	at the top of his voice in dismay joyfully loudly	

Which information in the text helped you to guess the meaning of each word?

C Answer these questions about the article, and find EXAMPLES or QUOTES as evidence for your answers. (Note that the writer uses irony to make some of his points.)

1 What does the writer dislike about the film?
2 What does the writer like about the film?
3 What does the writer dislike about Sylvester Stallone?
4 Which is the most horrifying scene described in the article?
5 What were the reactions of the audience, according to the writer?
6 What kind of people enjoy films like *Rambo*?
7 Why has *Rambo* been such a popular film?
8 Why does the writer misspell Rambo as 'Bombo' and 'Zombo'?

D **1** You'll hear six people talking about the influence of TV. Match the name of the speaker to the opinion he or she expresses.

Andrew	Everyone knows that violence on TV isn't real.
Kate	Family members no longer communicate with each other.
Karen	People become envious of the lifestyle shown on TV.
Melinda	People copy crimes shown or described on TV.
Tim	Violence on TV is bad for children.
Ishia	We don't know what effect violence on TV may have on children.

2 Discuss whose opinions you agree and disagree with and why.

UK film classifications:
Ⓤ = Universal
ⓅⒼ = Parental Guidance
⑫ ⑮ ⑱

Making an emphasis
Word study

A Highlight the words in this paragraph which emphasise or intensify the meaning of the
nouns and adjectives used. What would be the effect of omitting all ten of these words?

> Our class picnic very nearly turned out to be a
> big disappointment because of the heavy rain and
> the large number of people who dropped out at
> the very last minute, but to everyone's total
> amazement it was a great success and we all
> had an extremely enjoyable time. Every single
> one of the people who stayed at home must
> have felt really fed up when we told them
> about it later.

B 1 To add emphasis we can add an EMPHASISING ADVERB, like this:

> It was an *absolutely* appalling performance. ✓   It was a *really* sensational show. ✓

But we DON'T normally say:

> It was *very* awful. ✗   It was *totally* not bad. ✗   It was *terribly* superb. ✗

2 Which of these EMPHASISING ADVERBS would normally be used with each of the adjectives
below? Look at these examples first:

very or *extremely*   *angry   disappointed*
absolutely   *astonished   furious*

> amazed   amazing   brilliant   catastrophic   clever   cross   different   disappointing   disastrous
> enjoyable   fantastic   happy   helpful   idiotic   impressive   marvellous   moving   perfect
> powerful   proud   remarkable   sleepy   superb   surprised   wonderful

C Which of these EMPHASISING ADJECTIVES would normally be used with each of the nouns below?
In cases where there is more than one possibility, just choose one. Look at these examples first:

deep	*admiration sleep*
big	*decision disappointment*
large	*number proportion*
heavy	*rain sleeper*
high	*cost level*
strong	*feeling taste*
absolute/complete/total	*amazement astonishment disaster*
great	*achievement disappointment number success*

> amount   anger   catastrophe   difference   drinker   enjoyment   excitement   failure   fool   friend
> fun   happiness   idiot   improvement   love   nonsense   number   opinion   power   pressure
> price   pride   proportion   quality   quantity   sense of humour   show   sigh   skill   smell   smoker
> snow   speed   strength   success   surprise   traffic   trouble   understanding   wealth

D 1 Write SIX sentences, each containing at least one of the adjectives or
nouns used in B and C. Leave a gap for the appropriate emphasising
adverbs or adjective. Here's one as an example:

> We were . . . . amazed at
> the . . . . number of people who came.

2 Pass your sentences on to another pair and
get them to fill the gaps with suitable
emphasising words.

(3.5) Punctuation
Effective writing

Punctuation is important because if you dont punctuate a sentence correctly it makes it hard for your reader to understand what youre trying to say which may make him or her lose patience and give up

A **Explain the differences in meaning between the sentences in each group:**

1 *He likes his sister's friends and colleagues.*
He likes his sisters' friends and colleagues.
He likes his sisters, friends and colleagues.

2 *Her brother, who works in America, is a film extra.*
Her brother who works in America is a film extra.

3 *Rambo was dreadful.* *'Rambo' was dreadful.*

4 *I don't watch television – much!* *I don't watch television much.*

5 *They said it was marvellous.* *They said it was marvellous?*
They said it was marvellous!! *They <u>said</u> it was marvellous . . .*
They said, "It was marvellous." *<u>They</u> said it was marvellous . . .*

B **Look at these examples. Fill the gaps in sentences 1 to 5, and add the necessary punctuation to sentences 6 to 11.**

Apostrophes (' ' ')

1 *If she's your aunt, she's either your ▨▨▨ ▨▨▨ or your ▨▨▨ ▨▨▨ .*

2 *He was born in '79 and left school in ▨▨▨ .*

3 *It's important to distinguish between ▨▨▨ (= it is) and ▨▨▨ (possessive).*

4 *▨▨▨ and ▨▨▨ are contracted forms of do not and they are.*

Commas (, , ,)

We thought, however, that the music was too loud.
Hello, everyone, my name's Bond, James Bond.
James Dean, who died in 1955, is still greatly admired.
If you enjoyed the show, why didn't you tell me?

5 *My three favourite film stars are: ▨▨▨ , ▨▨▨ and ▨▨▨ .*

6 *When commas are used it makes a long sentence easier to read doesn't it?*

7 *When the film was over we stayed in our seats watching the final credits.*

BUT notice the lack of commas here:

Why didn't you tell me if you enjoyed the show?
The film that we saw yesterday was very enjoyable.
He said that he had enjoyed the show.

Colons (: : :)

I thought it was a good film: the photography was marvellous, the acting was good and the story was exciting.
In the words of the song: 'There's no business like show business.'

8 *There are four members of my family my mother and father my sister and me.*

Quotation marks (" " ' ') can be either single or double.

'A Nightmare on Elm Street' was a scarier film than 'Rambo'.
Rambo is a "human war machine" as his colonel observes.
I was feeling 'down'.
Should it be 'a university' or 'an university'?
"What a lovely day!" he exclaimed. "I feel like taking the day off."

9 *Well that's all thank you very much ladies and gentlemen the lecturer said at the end of the lecture Does anyone have any questions?*

Semi-colons (; ; ;) are used as a kind of 'weak' full stop or 'strong' comma in formal writing; in informal writing a dash is often used instead.

It was a hilarious story; everyone enjoyed it enormously.

10 *'Barton Fink' was a wonderful film the director was Joel Coen.*

A dash (−) is used to add an afterthought − sometimes.

It was an excellent film − apart from the violence.

11 'Fargo' was a great film   we all enjoyed it.

C 1 Rewrite this film review, adding the necessary punctuation: commas, apostrophes, quotation marks, etc.

A *Nightmare on Elm Street* made one experienced journalist scream with terror at the preview screening I went to. The noise frightened me more than the film itself written and directed by Wes Craven an ex professor of humanities. Its all very spooky but not at all bloody says Wes of this teen orientated horror film which has a ghostly and ghastly murderer attacking the children of Elm Street not in their waking hours but in their dreams. John Saxon and Ronee Blakley dont believe all this and he a policeman goes looking for a real madman. But we know better and so does Heather Langenkamp as their daughter. Langenkamp apparently known in America as the worlds most promising Scream Queen screams louder than the journalist. I just cringed. I think Craven has done better though one has to admit that its a good idea followed through with efficiency and state of the art special effects. Perhaps my trouble was that I wanted the Evil One to win. I cant stand those awful kids.

2 The original review was in FOUR separate paragraphs. Decide where to insert the paragraph breaks.

(3.6) Planning ahead . . .
Creative writing

A Here are some guidelines on planning a piece of writing. Rearrange them in the sequence YOU prefer, leaving out any you consider to be irrelevant.

☐ Decide which points are irrelevant and should be left out.
☐ Decide which points are relevant and should be included.
☐ Write a first draft and check it through carefully, correcting any mistakes you notice.
☐ Check the facts and figures: can you spell all the names correctly?
☐ Think of your target reader: what does he or she want to find out from you?
☐ Write down your AIM: what is the main purpose of this piece of writing?
☐ Write an outline in note form.
☐ Make notes of all the points you might want to make.
☐ Decide which points each paragraph will contain.
☐ Decide on your style and layout.
☐ Choose a title or heading, if necessary.
☐ Rearrange the ideas in the order you want to make them in your writing.

Planning what you're going to write may take a few minutes − but it usually saves time in the long run. If you organise your ideas well, your writing will be much easier for a reader to follow than if you just write the ideas down as they occur to you.

B **Look at this piece of writing and decide together what's wrong with it and how it can be improved:**

"Independence Day" is a film I really enjoyed because it was very exciting and the special effects were really impressive. There were no big stars in it but the idea of aliens taking over the planet and destroying New York was exciting. I liked the way the Jeff Goldblum character solved the problems and in the end put a bug in the aliens' computer and saved the world from destruction. I saw it in the cinema but I don't think it would come over very well on TV because you don't get the same impression of size on a small screen. Bill Pullman played the President and Will Smith was good too.

C **Find out what shows or films both of you have seen and can remember reasonably well. Choose one that you share similar views on.**

Make notes on the following aspects:

THE PLOT	Give the reader an idea of the story.
THE PEOPLE	Tell the reader about the characters and the actors.
DESCRIPTION	Help the reader to imagine what it was like – what was particularly remarkable or memorable about it?
YOUR REACTIONS	Explain what you enjoyed and didn't enjoy.

D 1 **Imagine you're writing in a student magazine or a local English-language newspaper. Write a review of a show or film, explaining why you recommend / don't recommend it to the readers (about 250 words).**

2 Show your completed review to another student and ask for comments.

(3.7) *At . . .* and *by . . .*
Idioms

Replace the phrases in red with suitable expressions from the list below:

AT . . .

1 The hero was rescued a moment before it was too late.

2 The show closed because it was running without making a profit.

3 We were talking about different things but didn't realise it.

4 It's impossible to get tickets for such a popular show without previous warning – you need to book no less than six months in advance.

5 She was working much too hard causing harm to her health.

6 When abroad, it's advisable to carry your passport constantly.

7 The winners are selected without any plan by a computer.

8 It was a wonderful show – anyway I enjoyed it.

9 It was a difficult problem and I was uncertain what to do.

10 I'm sure that our friends will arrive very soon – anyway I hope so.

11 If you need to stay overnight, please book a hotel room and we will pay.

12 I could tell by taking one quick look that there had been a mistake.

13 Finally they did arrive, but by that time the show was nearly over.

BY . . .

14 'May I open the window?' 'Certainly!'

15 Incidentally, have you seen the new Coen Brothers film?

16 I wonder if you know what's on at the cinema tonight, perhaps?

17 I know that person from her appearance but not what she's called.

18 I don't like going to the cinema alone.

at a glance   at a loss   at a loss   at all times   at any moment   at any rate   at cross purposes
at least   at least   at long last   at our expense   at random   at short notice   at the expense of
at the last moment   by all means   by any chance   by name   by sight   by the way   by myself

Four

Enjoy your meal!

(4.1) **To whet your appetite . . .**
Vocabulary

A 1 Find out from your partners:

- which of the dishes in the photos they like most – and why
- what they ordered the last time they ate out – and what the other people at their table had
- what dishes they know how to cook
- what they'd cook if they were at home on their own and felt hungry

2 Write down ten words that come into your mind when you think about food and drink.

B Fill the gaps in these paragraphs with suitable words from the list below.

1 If you buy something in a supermarket take a look at the label. The ▒▒▒▒▒▒ tells you how long the product is supposed to ▒▒▒▒▒▒ . It also tells you if it contains any artificial ▒▒▒▒▒▒ . The nutritional information tells you how much fat, ▒▒▒▒▒▒ , ▒▒▒▒▒▒ and how many ▒▒▒▒▒▒ it contains.

2 I'll give you my ▒▒▒▒▒▒ for pasta salad: it's a very easy ▒▒▒▒▒▒ to make if you have the right ▒▒▒▒▒▒ . There's no meat in it, so it's suitable for ▒▒▒▒▒▒ . You can have it as a ▒▒▒▒▒▒ for lunch or supper or as ▒▒▒▒▒▒ between meals if you feel peckish.

3 In a restaurant it's usually better value to have the ▒▒▒▒▒▒ than to choose from the à la carte ▒▒▒▒▒▒ . At the end of the meal, after you've had your ▒▒▒▒▒▒ , you ask for the ▒▒▒▒▒▒ . (In Britain you're expected to give an extra 10% as a ▒▒▒▒▒▒ .)

Thinking about food makes my mouth ▒▒▒▒▒▒ and my tummy starts to ▒▒▒▒▒▒ !

> additives bill/check carbohydrate dessert dish ingredients last/keep loaf main course
> menu protein recipe rumble sandwich sell-by date set meal slice snack
> starter/appetiser tip/service charge vegetarians vitamins water wholemeal

C Find out from your partners:

- what they understand by the term 'good food' – and if it's important to them
- if they 'eat to live' or 'live to eat'
- what kinds of food they consider to be 'healthy' and 'unhealthy'
- what convenience foods, takeaways and junk food they eat

4.2 Favourite foods
Spelling and Punctuation

A In most lines of this text there's either a spelling mistake or a punctuation error. Write the correctly spelled word or show the correct punctuation beside the line — or put a tick if the line is correct.

Cat cantaloupe

We were eating cantaloupe and it was'nt very good. We should have let it ripen a little longer or	1 *wasn't*
maybe it never would have tasted good. Perhaps it was a cantaloupe doomed to fail from the very	2 ✓
beginning but we will really never know because it didn't have a full chance to proof itself.	3 *prove*
When my wife and I finished, feeling vaguely unsatisfied, we put our plates on the floor. I don't	4
know why. We could just as easily have put them on the cofee table.	5
We have a new borowed cat in the house. Because we don't spend the entire year here in Montana,	6
we lure our neighbours cats over with extravagant promises of cat delicacies and all-expenses paid	7
vacations to the Cat Ritz in Paris. We have a lot of mice. The cats never get to Paris. When we leave	8
Montana for California, the cats go back to their original homes with unused passports.	9
Anyway, the new cat walked over to the cantaloupe rinds on the floor and began very carfully	10
examining one of them. The cat gave the cantaloupe an exploring lick. Then the cat: who would	11
never get to use it's French, gave the rind a few more licks, but they were very much more familiar.	12
The cat started eating the cantaloupe. I had never seen a cat eat cantaloupe before. I tried to	13
imagane what the cantaloupe tasted like to the cat. I cannot think of anything that a cat would	14
normally eat that would taste like a cantaloupe?	15
We have to rule out mice, birds, gophers, insects, and eliminate such housecat foods as fish,	16
chicken milk and all stuff that comes in cans, pouches and boxes.	17
What is left that would taste like cantaloupe to a cat.	18
I have not the slightest idee nor will I probably ever have but I know one thing for certain: I will	19
never walk into a grocery store and go to the pet food section and see a can of cat cantaloupe on the shelf.	20

from *The Tokyo-Montana Express* by Richard Brautigan

B Find out from your partners:
- what their favourite meal of the day is — and why
- what their favourite meal of the week is — and why
- what their favourite vegetables, fruit, snacks and desserts are
- what their favourite national dish is — and how they'd explain it to a foreign visitor

C Imagine that when Tim, an English friend, was staying with you in your home there was one particular dish that he very much enjoyed. Now he has written to ask you for the recipe. Send him the instructions for preparing the dish (about 200 words) and a short note (about 50 words) to enclose with it.

Appropriate language
Speaking

A 1 Look at these short conversations and decide which remarks are NOT appropriate to the situations, as you imagine them. Decide what the people SHOULD have said.

Little boy:	Hello.
Adult:	Good afternoon, I wonder if I might have a word with your mother?
	Hello. Is your mummy at home?
	OR *Can I speak to your mummy?*

1 *Shop assistant:* Can I help you?
Customer: No, that's not necessary.

2 *Guest:* The meal wasn't as bad as I expected.
Hostess: Oh, good. I'm so glad you enjoyed it.

3 *Your boss:* Yes, come in.
You: I'm going to come to work half an hour late tomorrow.

4 *Boss:* Do you see what I mean?
New employee: Yes, and I don't agree with you.

5 *Friend:* Would you excuse me, please? I'd very much like to make a phone call.
You: Fine.

6 *Student:* Have you had time to mark my composition?
Teacher: Yes, and I do hope you don't mind my saying this, but you've made one or two tiny mistakes.

7 *Waiter:* Are you ready to order now?
Customer: No, go away.

8 *Wife:* Would you mind assisting me with the washing-up, if you've got a moment?
Husband: Certainly, I'd be delighted to.

9 *Waiter:* Was your meal any good?
Customer: Yes, it was.

10 *Patient:* Good morning, doctor.
Doctor: Oh dear, you look ghastly, what's the matter with you?

2 Compare your ideas with the model conversations.

B 1 The kind of language you might use yourself in different situations depends on who you are talking to, and also how polite, tactful or direct you want to be. There are also different degrees of formality:

VERY FORMAL	*May I say what a pleasure it is to meet you.*
	I owe you a deep debt of gratitude.
FORMAL	*It was a pleasure to meet you.*
	Thank you very much indeed.
NEUTRAL	*Goodbye.*
	Thank you.
INFORMAL	*Bye for now.*
	Thanks a lot.
FAMILIAR	*Bye-bye.*
	See you.
	Cheers!

Using a very formal phrase in an informal situation may sound pompous or sarcastic. Informal language in a formal situation may sound rude or disrespectful — or simply silly!

2 Decide which of the following phrases are:

VERY FORMAL • FORMAL • NEUTRAL • INFORMAL or FAMILIAR

1 *A lot of people like fish and chips.*   *Loads of people like fried chicken.*
  Lots of people like curry.   *Many people enjoy hot dogs.*
  A significant number of people prefer sandwiches.

2 *Good to see you.*   *Hi there.*
  It's a pleasure to make your acquaintance.   *Pleased to meet you.*

3 *I'd like to introduce myself. My name's . . .* *I'm . . . – what's your name?*
  May I introduce myself, I'm . . .   *My name's . . . – who are you?*

4 *Do you feel like a drink?*   *Like a drink?*
  May I offer you a drink?   *Would you like me to get you a drink?*

5 *Can I have tea, please?*   *Tea, please.*
  I'd like a cup of tea, please.   *Would it be possible for me to have some tea?*

6 *One should always try to be polite.*   *You should always try to be polite.*

7 *Give my best wishes to your parents.*   *Give my love to Mary, won't you?*
  Oh, love to Jim, by the way.   *Remember me to your husband.*
  Please give my best regards to your wife.   *Say hello to Sally from me.*

C 1 The vocabulary that we use may also change according to the SITUATION we are in. In most cases this is a question of:

- your ATTITUDE – serious, joking, sarcastic, disparaging, approving, etc.
- WHO you are talking to – someone older, younger, senior, friend, stranger, acquaintance, superior, male, female, etc.
- the SUBJECT you are talking about – food, farming, films, geography, etc.

2 Decide what situations you would use these words or phrases in:

1 children   kids   youngsters   boys and girls

2 people   men and women   ladies and gentlemen   everyone   persons   population human beings   citizens

3 man   boy   gentleman   bloke   chap   fellow   person   guy   male

4 woman   lady   girl   person   female

5 food   nutrition   cuisine   cooking   feast   meal   banquet   something to eat

6 delicious   yummy   nice   tasty   appetising   quite nice   wonderful   superb

D 1 If you're meeting someone for the first time, which of these topics would you talk about – and which would you avoid?

sport   politics   your family   business   travel   hobbies   films   the weather   music
books   your education   your job   religion   TV   traffic   public transport   food

2 Imagine that you're sitting with an English-speaking stranger on a train, which has stopped for no apparent reason in the middle of nowhere. The stranger is considerably older than you. Decide who's going to play the role of the stranger. Then begin a conversation and continue with small talk.

3 This time you and an older stranger are sitting at adjacent tables in a café, where you've both been waiting a long time to be served. Begin a conversation and continue with small talk.

I wonder why we've stopped.
  – Yes, so do I. Perhaps . . .

I wonder where the waitress has got to.
  – Yes, so do I. Perhaps . . .

4.4 Simple + progressive aspect
Grammar

†† A **Discuss the difference in meaning between these sentences:**

1 *When we got to the station the train had just left.*
   When we got to the station the train was just leaving.

2 *He stood up when she entered the room.*
   He was standing up when she entered the room.

3 *He usually prepares the meal when his wife gets home.*
   He is usually preparing the meal when his wife gets home.
   He has usually prepared the meal when his wife gets home.

4 *I've been reading your book.*   *I've read your book.*

5 *I'm not having dinner until 8 o'clock.*   *I don't have dinner until 8 o'clock.*

6 *They always ask questions in class.*   *They're always asking questions in class.*

7 *We'll be having breakfast at 7.30.*   *We'll have breakfast at 7.30.*

8 *Will you join us for lunch?*   *Will you be joining us for lunch?*

9 *I think you're being silly.*   *I think you're silly.*

†† B **Look at these pairs of sentences, each of which illustrates how simple and progressive verb forms are used. Follow these steps for each numbered pair:**

1 First, look at the verbs in red and make sure you understand WHY that particular form is used.

2 Fill the gaps in the sentence that follows.

3 Write a similar example of your own for each rule illustrated.

(Number 1 has already been done to show you what to do.)

Present simple or present progressive: *does* or *is doing*

1 *Please don't phone me while I'm having dinner.*
   I usually read the newspaper while I'm having breakfast.
   He often listens to the radio while he's doing the washing-up. **(your own example)**

2 *Most days she has lunch at her desk but today she's eating out.*
   I usually ＿＿＿＿＿ *pancakes with honey, but today* ＿＿＿＿＿ *them with sugar, for a change.*

3 *When the sketch begins, a man arrives at a restaurant and starts eating.*
   In the end, the man ＿＿＿＿＿ *so much that he* ＿＿＿＿＿ .

4 *When are you having dinner this evening?*
   What time ＿＿＿＿＿ *your friends* ＿＿＿＿＿ *tomorrow?*

Past simple or past progressive: *did* or *was doing*

5 *I didn't want to phone her while she was having dinner.*
   She started to cough while she ＿＿＿＿＿ *and nearly*
   ＿＿＿＿＿ .

6 *I was wondering if you could tell me why you don't like her.*
   The meal isn't ready because I ＿＿＿＿＿ *you to arrive so early.*

7 *He didn't start preparing dinner until his wife got home.*
   They ＿＿＿＿＿ *the results of the exam until the end of the year.*

8 *Traffic was diverted because a new bridge was being built.*
   While the restaurant ＿＿＿＿＿ *redecorated, it* ＿＿＿＿＿
   closed to the public.

9 *He was just finishing dinner when his wife got home from work.*
   When the guests ＿＿＿＿＿ , *he* ＿＿＿＿＿ *still* ＿＿＿＿＿
   a bath.

Present perfect simple or progressive: *has done* or *has been doing*

10 I have been reading this book for a week but I've only read 23 pages so far.
   How long has she ▆▆▆▆▆▆ English and how many words has she ▆▆▆▆▆▆ ?

11 They have been living / they have lived in London for two years.
   My friend ▆▆▆▆▆▆ in London all her life / since she was a baby.

12 The restaurant is closed because the cook has been taken to hospital.
   Mmm! These carrots are delicious – have ▆▆▆▆▆▆ steamed or boiled?

Future: *will do* or *will be doing*

13 What will you be doing tomorrow evening? Will you be waiting for your guests to arrive?
   What will you do if they're late?
   This time tomorrow I ▆▆▆▆▆▆ and when I've done that I ▆▆▆▆▆▆ , I expect.

14 Will you be coming with us or are you busy tonight?
   Could you phone us later on to let us know what time you ▆▆▆▆▆▆ ?

15 Will you come with us? We'd love you to be there.
   ▆▆▆▆▆▆ you help me with the washing-up, please?

C **Find the errors in these sentences and correct them.**
One sentence has NO errors.

1 We are usually having lunch out on Sundays.

2 We can take a picnic but what will we be doing if it starts to rain?

3 She stayed at home because she was having a cold.

4 While I drove along I suddenly remembered that I had left the freezer door open.

5 The last time I saw him he was getting on a bus, eating an ice cream.

6 Breakfast is normally being served in the dining room but today it is served in the coffee shop.

7 Who is this recipe book that's lying on the table belonging to?

8 She was disliking vegetarian food at first but now she's enjoying it whenever she has been having it.

D **Find out about your partners' experiences of different kinds of food and drink, using the questions below.**

- Unusual foods they have eaten – vegetables, fruit, fish, sauces, salads, sweets, cakes, etc.
- Different cuisines – vegetarian, French, Italian, Chinese, Indian, Japanese, Greek, etc.
- Strange things they have eaten – for breakfast, lunch, dinner, supper, elevenses, tea, etc.
- Strange drinks they have drunk – hot/cold, alcoholic/soft
- Different kinds of meals – banquets, buffets, picnics, etc.

> Have you ever . . . ?
> When did you first . . . ?
> How many times have you . . . ?
> How often . . . ?

> Do you ever . . . ?
> How long have you . . . ?
> When do you . . . ?
> What was it like exactly?

Words easily confused
Word study

A Take it in turns to explain the differences in meaning between each of these pairs of words. Write sentences to help you to remember any tricky ones.

alternate = first one then the other – We eat out on alternate Saturdays.

alternative = different – He came up with an alternative menu.

anniversary · birthday
cancel · postpone
collaborate · cooperate
complement · compliment
cook · cooker
desert · dessert
economic · economical
experience · experiment
fantasy · imagination
historic · historical
homework · housework
immigration · emigration

memory · souvenir
menu · set meal
noise · sound
personal · personnel
principal · principle
receipt · recipe
rob · steal
satisfactory · satisfying
stationary · stationery
stranger · foreigner
sympathetic · likeable
tasteful · tasty

B Explain the difference in meaning between the words in each of these groups. Check any unfamiliar words in a dictionary.

actually · at present · presently · nowadays
alive · living · lively
author · editor · printer · publisher
broken · not working · out of order
destroy · ruin · spoil
discussion · argument · row · quarrel
elder · older · elderly
guard · guardian · attendant
husband · bridegroom · fiancé · boyfriend
leave · lie · let · lay
marriage · wedding · engagement

nervous · anxious · neurotic
notice · note · memo
outlook · view · scenery · landscape
possibility · chance · opportunity
print · publish · distribute · edit
professor · lecturer · teacher · tutor
propaganda · advertising · publicity
shadow · shade · shelter
thousand · million · billion
wife · bride · fiancée · girlfriend
wounded · injured · hurt

C **1** Write down some more words which YOU personally often confuse – maybe words that are 'false friends' with similar words in your language.

2 Pass your list to another group and ask them to explain the differences in meaning.

"Yes, thank you, everything's fine. Just to round off the evening,
could we have something to eat and drink?"

(4.6) *Bring, carry* and *take*
Verbs and idioms

> When a phrasal verb has a literal (as opposed to idiomatic) meaning, it's generally easy to work out what it means.

A Complete each sentence with a pronoun and a suitable particle from the list below.

1 I need my recipe book again, so could you bring   *it back*   to me, please?

2 While your friends are here, bring _____ to have a meal at my place.

3 There's a bottle of wine upstairs, could you please bring _____ to me?

4 When our glasses were empty we took _____ to the kitchen.

5 I'm upstairs and I'd like some tea – could you bring _____ to me, please?

6 We don't need these plates any more, you can take _____ .

7 It's not a good idea to take _____ if you don't know how to reassemble it.

8 There's a box of empty bottles by the back door, could you carry _____ , please?

9 The dog picked up the bone and carried _____ .

| apart   away   back ✓   back   down   off   out   round   up |

B Rewrite the sentences, replacing the phrases in red with a suitable phrasal verb or idiom from the list below.

BRING

1 He was very upset: I wonder what caused that to happen?   *brought (that) about*

2 She was cared for by her grandparents when her parents split up.

3 Burger Prince have introduced a new product: it's called a Lamburger!

4 After a long discussion I persuaded her to accept my point of view.

5 Why don't you raise the matter for discussion at the meeting tomorrow?

6 Her illness was caused by stress and overwork.

7 Can we arrange our dinner for an earlier time?

CARRY

8 Don't worry about me, just continue what you were doing as if I wasn't here.

9 I was very excited when I saw the buffet and took more than I could eat.

10 In the film the main character was having an affair with her brother-in-law.

11 The canteen will be closed until repairs to the kitchen have been done.

TAKE

12 There was so much information that we couldn't absorb it all.

13 Looking after five children occupies all their time.

14 This job carries a lot of responsibility – are you willing to undertake it?

15 Considering his inexperience it's amazing they gave him the job.

16 We assumed that you'd want to participate in the game.

17 She did a brilliant impression of the boss's voice over the phone but we weren't deceived when she said we could all have a day's holiday.

18 She gets very upset when people don't appreciate her.

19 As I'd never tried skiing before, I didn't think I'd develop a liking for it.

20 I'm sorry I was rude to you – I admit I was wrong in everything I said.

> Most phrasal verbs have idiomatic meanings. If you don't happen to know what one means, you may have to use a dictionary.

| bring about ✓   bring forward   bring on   bring out   bring round to   bring up   bring up get carried away   carry on with   carry on with   carry out   take back   take for granted   take for granted   take in   take in   take on   take on   take part   take a day off   take to   take up   take-off |

Five

Travellers or tourists?

(5.1) **Travelling abroad**
Vocabulary
and Listening

A 1 Look at the photos and write down ten words that come
into your mind when you think about travel and holidays.

2 Find out from your partners:

 • which foreign countries they would like to visit
 • which parts of their own country they would like to visit one day
 • what they enjoy and don't enjoy about travelling

B 1 Fill each gap in these paragraphs with a suitable word from the list below.

1 The first leg of our .... went smoothly and we arrived at the .... in good time to
catch the ferry. Unfortunately, the sea was very rough, so we had a terrible .... and we were
all seasick. We spent the first day .... in the city and then caught a bus to the seaside
.... where we were going to spend the rest of our ....

2 It's a very .... region where the only people you meet are the locals, who seem quite
.... at first, but when you get to know them they're very .... They still wear their
traditional .... and the old .... are still kept alive. Most of the villages are still
.... and not at all .... The few travellers who do visit the region are mostly
.... who are there to enjoy the magnificent ....

3 However much I travel I still get nervous when I cross a .... Why is it that ....
officers have guns and whenever they ask if I've got anything to .... , I feel .... ?
And the .... officer (also alarmingly armed) spends ages .... my ....
because the photo makes me look just like a .... !

> border   checking   commercialised   controlling   costumes   crossing   customs   customs
> declare   frontier   guilty   hikers   hospitable   immigration   isolated   journey   passport   port
> remote   reserved   resort   scenery   shy   sightseeing   smuggler   terrorist   traditions   travel
> trip   unspoilt   vacation   view   visa

2 Look at the words you DIDN'T choose from the list – where could they be used? What other words (not in the list) would fit equally well in the gaps?

C You'll hear an interview with Susan Davies, talking about her travels in Australia. Fill each gap in this summary with ONE word only.

For Susan, the advantages of travelling alone are:

— She likes the ₁ [____]

— She likes being able to do ₂ [____] what she wants

— It's easier to get ₃ [____] to people

But when something goes ₄ [____] it can be a ₅ [____] .

During her travels in Australia she worked on a ₆ [____] station (ranch) in Queensland.

She got the address from someone in a ₇ [____] bar in Sydney.

When the Greyhound bus driver ₈ [____] her off in the middle of ₉ [____] , she felt ₁₀ [____] .

After her first evening meal with the family she had to walk across the ₁₁ [____] , being careful not to tread on the ₁₂ [____] . She was also warned to shake her ₁₃ [____] . She shared her ₁₄ [____] with a flying ₁₅ [____] . And there was a ₁₆ [____] in the toilet.

Although she appreciates a hot ₁₇ [____] and a ₁₈ [____] bed, she could still wash in a ₁₉ [____] or sleep on a ₂₀ [____] if she had to.

Susan Davies

D Ask your partners these questions:

● How would you have reacted to Susan's experiences in Australia?
● What are some more disadvantages of travelling alone?
● Why do people travel? Why do YOU travel?
● What can you learn from travelling?
● What is the difference between a 'traveller' and a 'tourist'?

"Excuse me, those seats are taken."

ALL-INCLUSIVE RESORTS ▶▶▶

What could be more relaxing than not having to worry about money? Included in the price you pay before you go is your flight and accommodation as well as all your meals, drinks, entertainment and sports (often including expensive watersports such as waterskiing and sailing). All you need to take is spending money to pay for souvenirs and excursions.

1 Before you read the article, note down what you think might be some of the disadvantages of an all-inclusive holiday, and the problems that mass-market tourism causes.

2 Read the article and note down the answers to these questions:

Which island(s) has/have . . .

1 . . . few tourists?   *Dominica*

2 . . . depended mainly on agricultural exports?

3 . . . had a hit song criticising its tourism policy?

4 . . . hardly any resorts owned by local people?

5 . . . mostly all-inclusive hotels?

6 . . . not got an international airport?

7 . . . not got the kind of beaches that tourists prefer?

8 . . . not needed to import much agricultural produce from the USA?

9 . . . plenty of hotels owned by local people?

10 . . . prevented local people from getting onto the beaches?

11 . . . businesses that the tourists don't visit?

12 . . . tried to make tourism suit the needs of the local people?

Trouble in paradise   POLLY PATTULLO

1   It is said that the Prime Minister of Antigua, a man of enormous height and girth, was once banned from Club Antigua, one of the island's all-inclusive hotels, by a zealous security guard, who, not recognising him, refused him entry because he had no pass. The opposition newspaper, not usually a friend of the PM, commented dryly that once the people of Antigua had to have a pass "to be out of doors after the ringing of a church bell at night".

2   In St Lucia, where eight out of the 12 major hotels are all-inclusive, a calypso entitled *Alien*, with its chorus line "Like an alien in we own land," caught the public imagination. It began:

> *All-inclusives tax elusives,*
> *And truth is,*
> *They're sucking up we [our] juices,*
> *Buying up every strip of beach,*
> *Every treasured spot they reach.*

3   The calypso's sentiments were endorsed by St Lucians of all classes: by the fishermen whose access to beaches became barred, by entrepreneurs who discovered that all-inclusive tourists didn't patronise their restaurants or shops, and by the local élite who couldn't nip into an all-inclusive for a cocktail. Whatever their popularity with airlines and tour operators, all-inclusives somehow appeared less all-inclusive, more all-excluding.

4   While hotel ownership (in all shapes and sizes) in places such as Jamaica and Barbados has significantly passed into local hands, other islands, such as Antigua, have little control over their most crucial industry. As the leader of Antigua's opposition party says: "Most of the progress has come from tourism, but it is not in our hands. We can't lay a foundation on which we benefit." This may be sour grapes in not winning the election, but the facts suggest that he is right. There,

90 per cent of resorts are owned by foreigners and there are few locals in top hotel management.

5   What Antigua and other Caribbean islands with a mass-market tourism know now, the people of the nearby island of Dominica (no international airport, few white-sand beaches) have yet to find out. For example, the villagers of Vielle Case – an isolated settlement on the rugged north coast, surrounded by banana gardens, rainforest and the Atlantic below – rarely see a tourist. Even the adventurous ones do not penetrate that far along the pot-holed access road. So the people of Vielle Case are not, for the moment, waiters, hair-braiders or taxi-drivers; they do not sell duty-free Colombian emeralds or T-shirts printed with Vielle Case Jammin'; their young men do not sell drugs or go with young white women.

6   Yet even these farmers and fishermen are gearing themselves up for tourism. At one village council meeting, the ideas poured out as to what the village might offer tourists and how the locals could earn some dollars. For the Dominican government now sees tourism as one way out of a fragile dependency on bananas. Dominica is not alone: every government in the Caribbean has identified tourism as the region's "engine of growth".

7   So the numbers of tourists have rocketed: from 5.5 million stay-over visitors 20 years ago to 13.7 million now. From Cuba to Guyana, the Caribbean as a whole is more dependent on tourism (and increasingly so) than any other region in the world.

8   For it is both the Caribbean's fortune – and misfortune – to conjure up the image of paradise in the western imagination. To attract hotel investors, tour operators and airlines, Caribbean governments must provide a breeze-kissed environment swept clean of hurricane damage, unsightliness, poverty and crime. And, above all, its peoples must smile.

9   So, to a great extent, the region's tourist industry is forced to organise itself on other people's terms. And once the tourist enclaves form, the raw nerve endings of Caribbean societies are exposed. As the secretary-general of the Caribbean Tourism Organisation, Jean Holder, says: "There appears to be a deep-seated resentment of the industry at every level of society." Holder believes the root of this problem stems from race, colonialism and slavery. Disaffection among hotel staff is sometimes expressed in such terms. A hotel nurse, for example, told me how the staff had to eat their lunch under a tree, "like we were back in massa's [the slave master's] time".

10   The gulf between visitor and local becomes even more acute when hotels import supplies, ignoring the society outside the perimeter fence except as a source of labour. Too few farmers, for example, sell their produce to hotels and many tourists eat only American tomatoes and Hawaiian pineapples (two honourable exceptions are Jamaica and Nevis where schemes to link local farmers and hotels have been consciously developed). History is once again partly responsible. Agriculture is export-oriented and always has been.

11   Examples of an alternative, "new" tourism, in which the industry is integrated with other sectors of the economy and based on local need rather than external demand, were pioneered in the 1970s, first by Michael Manley, then Prime Minister of Jamaica, and later by Maurice Bishop in Grenada. Their attempts foundered, in part because antagonistic American governments, in the context of cold-war politics, encouraged tourists to stay away.

12   In a more conservative climate, the emphasis among Caribbean governments has been to develop mainstream tourism, to improve the arrival statistics (which inevitably has a social and environmental impact) with marketing campaigns and so fuel that "engine of growth".

13   Those who still urge an alternative way do so in the hope that the people of Vielle Case – and all those other communities newly drawn into the tourism web – will not one day have to compose their own versions of Alien.

B   **Highlight these words in the text and try to deduce their meanings without using a dictionary. Then choose a word or phrase from the list below that is closest in meaning.**

¶ 1 zealous   pass   ¶ 9 enclaves   disaffection

¶ 3 endorsed   entrepreneurs   élite   ¶ 10 gulf

¶ 5 settlement   rugged   ¶ 11 foundered   antagonistic

alienation   business people   division   enclosed grounds   failed   hostile   over-keen
permit   supported   top people   village   wild

C   **Discuss these questions:**

● **What surprised you in the article?**

● **Does the idea of an all-inclusive holiday (still) appeal to you? Why/Why not?**

● **How can travel broaden the mind?**

A 1 Look at these three different people's notes. Each example contains ONE extra idea, which isn't in the other two. What is the extra idea in each one?

2 What are the merits of each method? Which do you prefer?

1

> <u>Does travel broaden the mind?</u>
> YES
> 1 Learning about life in other countries makes you more tolerant
> 2 Even knowing a little about other places is better than being ignorant
> NO
> 1 Tourists see the tourist resorts: beaches, mountains, old cities – not rural areas, small country towns, poorer districts
> 2 The only local people most tourists meet are waiters and taxi-drivers
> 3 Local culture may be damaged by tourism – crime, begging, drugs
> 4 Prejudices and stereotypes can be confirmed by a short visit – need to live in a country for a long time to appreciate it properly
> <u>Conclusion</u>
> If you're open-minded, ready to learn, willing to talk to local people – then Yes.

2

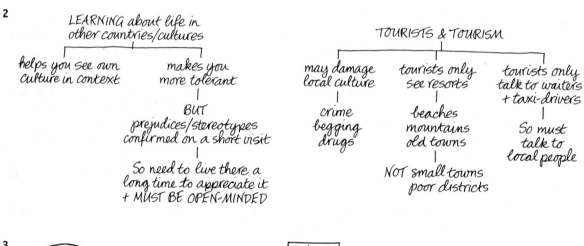

3

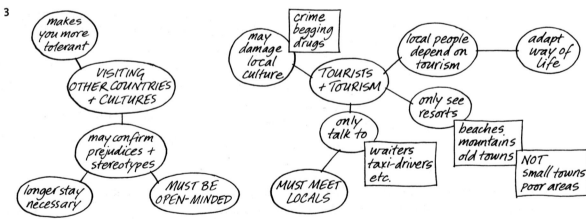

3 Add TWO more points to the notes you prefer above.

B   Use one of the methods above to make your own notes on ONE of these topics:

> **Is an active holiday preferable to a relaxing one?**
> **Is it best to get to know your own country before you travel to more exotic places?**
> **Which is better: a package holiday or a holiday you organise and book yourself?**

5.4 A letter of complaint
Creative writing

A 1 Read this letter to a travel agent. Decide how it can be improved.

> We've just returned from our visit to London, which you arranged for us. There were a number of problems that arose. Firstly, the tickets you sent us had been completed incorrectly and as a result we missed our flight and had to travel on a later plane, not arriving in London till midnight. When we arrived at the hotel you had booked for us, the rooms were no longer available, even though we'd paid you for the accommodation in advance. Fortunately, the hotel staff kindly found us a double room with shower in another hotel and paid for our taxi there. Unfortunately, although the other hotel (the Homeleigh Hotel in Hounslow) was surprisingly comfortable and friendly, it was way out in the suburbs and it took us an hour to get into the centre the next day, which involved a long train journey. Please send us a refund of the money we paid for the accommodation and also compensation for the inconvenience caused by your errors. Looking forward to hearing from you,
>
> Yours sincerely,

2 Delete the irrelevant information in the letter and then divide it into paragraphs.

B   You recommended the Hotel Fiasco to your friend and her family. Read the extract from a letter from your friend, and the brochure she's sent you with the notes she's made. Write a short note in reply to your friend (about 50 words) and a letter to the hotel (about 200 words).

> disappointed with the hotel you recommended. It certainly didn't live up to your description of it and we had a miserable time there. One of our rooms didn't have a toilet or shower and we had to use the bathroom down the corridor, which was very inconvenient. The food they served wasn't very good, either – maybe they've got a new chef since you stayed there two years ago.
>
> I spoke to the manager but he wasn't very sympathetic. Apparently the hotel has changed hands recently so that may explain why it's not as good as when you stayed there.
>
> Please don't think I'm blaming you for any of this, but I thought you'd want to know. It might be a good idea for you write to the hotel, perhaps?

▶▶▶

▶ **all rooms with en suite bathrooms**	*not in our room*
▶ **sea views from all rooms**	*only if you stood on a chair*
▶ **fine cuisine to suit all tastes**	*no vegetarian dishes*
▶ **a stone's throw from the beach**	*five minutes on foot*
▶ **large swimming pool**	*large yes, but too cold to swim in*

1 Plan your letter to the hotel. What important points must be included? What are you hoping to achieve by writing this letter?

2 Write the letter and the note to your friend.

3 Show your completed letter and note to another student and ask for feedback: does your partner feel you've achieved your aims?

> Including irrelevant information isn't just a waste of time, it detracts from the overall effect of your writing. Omitting important information may mean that your ideas aren't taken seriously.

Jonathan Raban

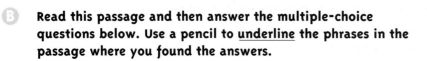

A **Find out from your partners if they:**

- use a guidebook when visiting an unknown place. Why/Why not?
- enjoy reading books about other people's travels. Why/Why not?

B **Read this passage and then answer the multiple-choice questions below. Use a pencil to <u>underline</u> the phrases in the passage where you found the answers.**

Yet actual journeys aren't like stories at all. At the time, they seem to be mere strings of haps and mishaps, without point or pattern. You get stuck. You meet someone you like. You get lost. You get lonely. You get interested in architecture. You get diarrhoea. You get invited to a party. You get frightened. A stretch of country takes you by surprise. You get homesick. You are, by rapid turns, engrossed, bored, alert, dull, happy, miserable, well and ill. Every day tends to seem out of connection with every other day, until living from moment to moment turns into a habit and travelling itself into a form of ordinary life. You can't remember when it wasn't like this. There is a great deal of liberating pleasure to be had from being abroad in the world, continuously on the move, like a lost balloon, but a journey, at least as long as it is actually taking place, is the exact opposite of a story. It is a shapeless, unsifted, endlessly shifting accumulation of experience.

For travelling is inherently a plotless, disordered, chaotic affair, where writing insists on connection, order, plot, signification. It may take a year or more to see that there was any point to the thing at all, and more years still to make it yield an articulate story. Memory, not the notebook, holds the key. I try to keep a notebook when I'm on the move (largely because writing in it makes one feel that one's at work, despite all appearances to the contrary) but hardly ever find anything in the notebook that's worth using later. Trifles are described at inordinate length. Events that now seem important aren't mentioned at all. The keeper of the notebook sounds stupid and confused. He grouses too much about tides and timetables, and all the forgettable mechanics of the journey; he fails to notice what I remember observing in near-photographic detail. When I'm writing the book, I get precious little help from him . . . the odd proper name, a date, an ascertainable fact here and there, but little or nothing in the way of intelligent comprehension of what he was doing at the time. Why was he so blind? Because he was travelling and I am writing, and the two activities are chalk and cheese.

Memory, though, is always telling stories to itself, filing experience in narrative form. It feeds irrelevancies to the shredder, enlarges on crucial details, makes links and patterns, finds symbols, constructs plots. In memory, the journey takes shape and grows; in the notebook it merely languishes, with the notes themselves like a pile of cigarette butts confronted the morning after a party.

In 1982, I took six months to sail slowly round the British Isles, stopping at every place I'd known as a child and adolescent. A year later, I was still trying to begin the book that was based on the journey. I had 30,000 words, but they seemed forced and wrong. There was writing, but as yet no story worth the telling. There was a title *Foreign Land*, but it didn't fit the writing.

5

10

15

20

25

30

from *For Love and Money* by Jonathan Raban

1 **How is a real journey different from a story?**
   A It has no order   **B** It is more frightening   **C** It is an interesting experience

2 **Why doesn't Jonathan Raban write his books straight after his return from a journey?**
   A He needs to read his notebook   **B** He never forgets the details   **C** His memory needs time

3 **How does he look upon the person who wrote the notebook?**
   A As a younger version of himself   **B** As an old friend   **C** As a stranger

4 **Why does he always make notes during a journey?**
   A To help him remember   **B** To make him feel he's working   **C** To fill the spare moments

5 **Why is memory more productive than the notes he made?**
   A Memory creates order   **B** Notes omit important details   **C** His notes aren't legible

6 **What useful information can he get from his notebook when he's writing the book?**
   A None at all   **B** A few names and dates   **C** The route he took

7 **How did the writer travel round Britain?**
   A On foot   **B** By car   **C** In a sailing boat   **D** By public transport

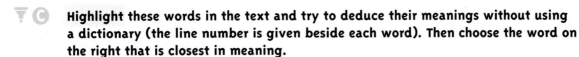

C **Highlight these words in the text and try to deduce their meanings without using a dictionary (the line number is given beside each word). Then choose the word on the right that is closest in meaning.**

haps	1	misfortunes pleasant happenings ✓ disasters
accumulation	10	collection lack selection
inherently	11	by the way by no means by nature
articulate	13	long amusing clear
trifles	16	meetings unimportant things exciting events
inordinate	16	fascinating excessive insufficient
grouses	18	writes celebrates grumbles
languishes	27	loses vitality becomes interesting improves

D **Ask your partners these questions:**

- How do your own experiences of travelling compare with Jonathan Raban's?
- Have you ever written a diary or used a notebook during a holiday?
- Do you take photos during a holiday? Why/Why not?
- Which travel book would you recommend to someone who is going to visit your own region for the first time?

5.6 *High, middle* and *low*
Idioms and collocations

Replace the words in red with expressions from the list below and make any other necessary changes.

1 I have searched everywhere for my keys.
2 Delays at the airport may be terrible in the main holiday period.
3 This CD contains the best parts of the show, not the whole thing.
4 Operas and chamber music are often considered to be intellectually superior, while shows like musicals are sometimes described as uncultured — or at least not so very artistic.
5 Good quality audio equipment is on sale in every main shopping street.
6 If you come across useful new words in a text, use a yellow pen to make them stand out.
7 Would you like to live in a tall multi-storey building — or do you think two to three storey buildings are more pleasant for people to live in?
8 Passengers and vehicles will be carried on ultra-modern shuttle trains.
9 Everyone was feeling elated before the weekend.

10 There's less room for holidaymakers on the beach when the sea comes up high than when it goes out.
11 I've got a bad cold and my work is getting me down — that's why I'm depressed.
12 Do you think a person is no longer young when they're 40, 50 or older?
13 In Britain, it's not only professional and business people who own their own homes.
14 Students who do well in their exams at secondary school can go on to university or college.
15 Don't put off doing this work any longer — you should do it now.

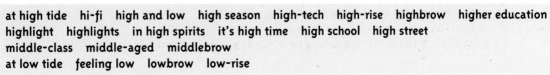

at high tide   hi-fi   high and low   high season   high-tech   high-rise   highbrow   higher education
highlight   highlights   in high spirits   it's high time   high school   high street
middle-class   middle-aged   middlebrow
at low tide   feeling low   lowbrow   low-rise

Six

It takes all sorts . . .

(6.1) What do they look like?
Listening and Vocabulary

A You'll hear seven of these people being described. Match the descriptions you hear to the photos below.

1	
2	
3	
4	
5	
6	
7	

B 1 Look at these ideas for describing a person's appearance and some expressions you might use if someone asked you:

What's special or remarkable about him or her? OR How would someone else recognise him or her?

Age
He or she is . . .
thirty-something   in her mid-twenties   middle-aged   in his teens
over sixty   in her early/late thirties   fortyish

Face, hair, eyes and complexion
He or she has . . .
an open face   curly/wavy/straight hair   a pale/dark complexion   bushy eyebrows
a good tan   wrinkles   a double chin   laughter lines

Height and build or figure
He or she is quite/very/fairly/rather . . .
athletic/well-built   slim/skinny   plump/chubby

Clothes and footwear
He or she usually wears . . .
casual/smart/conventional clothes   a formal suit   a sports jacket   running shoes
a sweater/jumper/pullover/cardigan

Family
He or she . . .
is an only child   is the eldest child   is single   is a single parent
has two kids

Job and interests
He or she . . .
is a lawyer/solicitor/attorney   works in the city
used to be an engineer
He or she . . .
enjoys sailing   spends a lot of time reading   is quite sporty   has a pilot's licence
once spent a year in the States

2 Add two more words or phrases to each set of examples above. Use a dictionary if necessary.

3 Compare the words or phrases you've added.

C Work in pairs Now take it in turns to describe the people on the previous page that the speakers *didn't* describe. Don't tell your partner who you're going to describe, but when you've finished, ask your partner to comment on the accuracy of your descriptions.

D 1 Take a good look at each other and then take it in turns to describe one of the members of the group — but do this WITH YOUR EYES CLOSED, so that you have to do it from memory.

Even if you can quickly guess who is being described, allow each speaker to continue. And, with their eyes still closed, ask them questions to test their memories and descriptive skills.

2 When everyone in the group has been described, describe some of the members of the other groups too.

E One of you should look at Activity 3, the other at 22. Describe the people in the photo to your partner.

(6.2) Politically correct?
Reading

A 1 What do you think follows in the rest of this story? What do you think the boy's parents said and what do you think his teachers said?

A kiss is not just a kiss if you are six

By David Sapsted in New York

A BOY of six has been punished by his school in America for sexual harassment after giving a girl classmate a kiss on the cheek.

2 One of you should look at Activity 12, the other at 32. You'll find out the rest of the story.

B Read this article and find the answers to these questions:

1 Where is naked dancing still allowed?
2 Where was it against the law to disarm a school pupil?
3 Who might go to court to be allowed drugs?
4 Who showed disrespect to a Native American?
5 Who successfully used a sexist image to attract customers?
6 Who thinks the Prevette case is ridiculous?

Stolen kiss puts PC on trial

A BACKLASH against years of political correctness is emerging in America, sparked by a case last month when a six-year-old boy was judged guilty of sexual harassment for stealing a kiss in the school corridor.

After more than two decades during which often well-intentioned efforts to eradicate discrimination in a host of fields — from sexism to racism, ageism to "homophobia" — have often ended up ensnaring the innocent in a legal morass, Americans are beginning to question the political correctness "industry".

Affirmative action programmes giving preference to people of Afro-Caribbean and Hispanic descent, sometimes over better-qualified whites and Asians, are being challenged in the courts.

So-called civil rights infringements which, for example, led to a court ruling making it illegal for a security guard in a New York school to remove a 15-year-old's loaded 9mm pistol from under his jacket, are generating public debate over whether the pendulum has swung too far.

Then there are the dafter lawsuits such as the $1 million claim by a retired 82-year-old doctor who says a health board denied her a job on the grounds of age.

Increasingly, TV programmes, including Seinfeld, the top-rated comedy, poke fun at the absurdities of PC. In one recent episode, Jerry Seinfeld, who is Jewish, offended an Apache girl he was trying to date by buying a wooden, cigar store Indian. He also unwittingly enraged a Chinese postman by asking him if he knew the whereabouts of a local Cantonese restaurant.

Meanwhile, advertisers are still being reminded that the lobbyists are alive, well and not about to disappear. When TWA advertised cheap flights to holiday destinations in Hawaii and Florida, it made the mistake of using a model holding down a billowing skirt à la Marilyn Monroe and suggested that people should fly to the sun to get rid of those "pasty white thighs".

The airline was bombarded with complaints that the ads were sexist, racist and morally offensive — but bookings went up by 50 per cent.

The case of Johnathan Prevette, whose stolen kiss led to his spending a day in isolation at his school in North Carolina caused many Americans to pause for thought.

Meg Greenfield, *Newsweek* columnist, said: "This creation of one-size-fits-all rulings and prohibitions not only creates preposterous incidents of this kind but also frees responsible authorities from dealing in the normal, human, community way, with the odd kid who is truly disturbed and needs to be singled out for attention."

Another problem of PC inveigling its way into law and the instruments of government is that it provides loopholes. Since the US Supreme Court upheld prison inmates' rights to practise their religious beliefs in a fitting way, jail governors have faced lawsuits from prisoners claiming they are being denied everything from cakes to drugs, all ostensibly essential for their religious observances.

Even apparently non-controversial attempts to curb indecency can hit problems. When a mayor in Vermont proposed banning nude dancing at two clubs, an organisation advocating breast-feeding said it would infringe a mother's right to suckle her baby.

C Discuss these questions:

● Have there been similar cases to the ones in the USA in your country?
● Political correctness has plenty of advantages — what are some of them?

(6.3) Modal verbs
Grammar

A 1 Discuss the difference in meaning between these sentences:

1 *They might tell me but . . .*   *They may have told me but . . .*
   They might have told me but . . .   *They may tell me but . . .*

2 *We could have tea early because . . .*   *We were able to have tea early because . . .*

3 *You mustn't tell her that . . .*   *You don't have to tell her that . . .*
   You needn't tell her that . . .   *You oughtn't to tell her that . . .*

4 *I should have trusted him but . . .*   *I had to trust him but . . .*
   I shouldn't have trusted him but . . .   *I didn't have to trust him but . . .*
   I needn't have trusted him but . . .

5 *She can't have lunch because . . .*   *She can't be having lunch because . . .*
   She couldn't have lunch because . . .   *She can't have had lunch because . . .*

6 *He may not have seen her, so . . .*   *He can't have seen her, so . . .*
   He may not be seeing her, so . . .   *He can't be seeing her, so . . .*
   He may not see her, so . . .   *He can't see her, so . . .*

2 Decide how each sentence might continue . . .

B Each of these groups contains pairs of sentences that share the same meaning. Match the sentences that mean the same as each other.

1 We'll probably have lunch soon.   We might as well have lunch soon.
   Maybe we'll have lunch soon.   We might well have lunch soon.
   We'll possibly have lunch soon.   We've got nothing better to do,
                                            so let's have lunch soon.

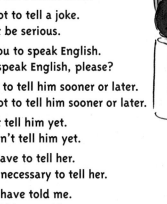

2 You must be joking.   You've got to tell a joke.
   You have to tell a joke.   You can't be serious.

3 Can you speak English?   I'd like you to speak English.
   Do you know how to speak English?   Can you speak English, please?

4 You'd better tell him sooner or later.   You have to tell him sooner or later.
   You ought to tell him sooner or later.   You've got to tell him sooner or later.

5 You needn't tell him yet.   You can't tell him yet.
   You don't have to tell him yet.   You mustn't tell him yet.

6 It wasn't a good idea to tell her.   I didn't have to tell her.
   I shouldn't have told her.   It wasn't necessary to tell her.

7 You might have *told* me.   You may have told me.
   I'm not sure whether you told me.   You should have told me.

8 You probably won't take too long.   I advise you not to take too long.
   You shouldn't take too long.   It shouldn't take you too long.

C **Find the 13 mistakes in this letter and correct them.**

Dear Jane,

As you can already know, we must start looking for a new receptionist in our office last month. Mr Brown our boss, can have chosen someone who already worked in another department but he didn't able to find anyone suitable so he got to advertise in the local paper. There ought have been a lot of applicants but surprisingly only a couple of replies came in and only one of those was suitable.

I told Mr Brown that he had better to get in touch with her at once. He decided we needn't to phone her as there was no hurry, and we must as well send her a card. Unfortunately we heard no more from her, so we've had to start advertising again – in vain so far.

For the moment, the job's being done by Mr Brown's son who hasn't to be working really because he's unhelpful and sometimes he should be quite rude to visitors. I haven't to tell you that we're all pretty fed up with the situation. Well, as I don't have to say any more, I'll stop there.

D **Use the modal verbs that have been revised in this section as you discuss what kinds of things are forbidden, allowed, obligatory and advisable in the following situations:**

in an office   in a cinema   in a restaurant   in a classroom   at a wedding   on a plane
driving in a built-up area   driving on a motorway   riding a bike   walking

> You have to dress smartly.   You don't have to . . .
> You can't . . .   You shouldn't . . .

6.4 Synonyms and opposites — 2
Word study

A **When describing someone we usually talk about their personality and behaviour. Some characteristics are more attractive or endearing than others . . .**

- Which of these characteristics do you and your partner consider to be more attractive and less attractive?
- Which unattractive characteristics can you tolerate in your friends and relations?

ambitious	enthusiastic	outspoken	self-confident
artistic	frivolous	passionate	sensitive
cautious	gregarious	reserved	serious
earnest	introverted	resourceful	shy
easy-going	out-going	ruthless	spontaneous

B **The adjectives in blue on the left are the OPPOSITES of the ones in red on the right. Match them up.**

clever	prejudiced	conceited	open-minded
generous	relaxed	cruel	self-confident
kind	sensible	mean/stingy	silly/foolish
modest	shy	naive	stupid
narrow-minded	sophisticated	nervous	tolerant

C **Decide which of the adjectives on the left have a SIMILAR MEANING to the ones on the right.**

clever	jolly
cunning	level-headed
excitable	reliable
fair	self-confident
forgetful	snobbish
frank	surly
glum	two-faced
good-natured	

absent-minded	insincere
bright	kind
cheerful	miserable
crafty	self-assured
direct	sensible
even-handed	stuck-up
grumpy	trustworthy
highly-strung	

D **Use a suitable prefix or suffix to form the OPPOSITE of each of the adjectives below. Here are some examples:**

un- *unhappy unpleasant* **in-** *insincere incredible*
dis- *dishonest dissatisfied* **im-** *impolite impossible*
-less *careless harmless* **il-** *illegible illegal*

agreeable	discreet	kind	predictable
approachable	efficient	likeable	reasonable
articulate	enthusiastic	logical	reliable
biased	flexible	loyal	respectful
competent	friendly	mature	sensitive
considerate	helpful	obedient	sociable
contented	hospitable	organised	tactful
decisive	imaginative	patient	thoughtful
dependable	intelligent	practical	tolerant

E 1 **Imagine that a good friend of yours has applied for this job and has asked you to write a character reference. What would you say about him or her in your letter, using the adjectives from A–D?**

Local resort representatives

As part of our ongoing expansion programme, we at Utopia Holidays are expanding our staff next season. As a leading tour operator, we are looking for first-class local representatives who are cheerful, imaginative and self-motivated. The representatives' duties will include:

- meeting clients at the airport and escorting them to their hotels
- organising and escorting coach excursions to local places of interest
- answering clients' questions and dealing with their problems
- liaising with our head office
- assisting clients who cannot speak the local language
- holding welcome parties for each group on the day after their arrival
- escorting clients from their hotels to the airport at the end of their holiday
- being on call 24 hours a day to deal with emergencies

Please apply in writing, enclosing your CV and a (character reference) to Alice Watson, Utopia Holidays, Utopia House, Skyway Drive, Crawley, RH12 4PJ

2 **Write a letter of reference for your friend (about 250 words), recommending him or her as suitable. If you mention one fault (but turn it into a virtue) this will make your reference seem more credible.**

Personalities
Reading

A **According to the horoscopes below, what star sign is someone who . . .**

1 . . . doesn't like people making adverse comments about them

2 . . . doesn't lose their temper easily

3 . . . is good at telling jokes or keeping people amused

4 . . . is not pessimistic

5 . . . is not very careful when organising things

6 . . . is soft-hearted

7 . . . likes other people to listen to them

8 . . . likes things to be different

9 . . . likes to keep old things

10 . . . likes working things out

11 . . . prefers traditional methods

12 . . . wants everything to be in its place

B **1** **Find out when each other's birthdays are. Then read the relevant personality descriptions here and on the next page. Find out to what extent the descriptions are true about each of you.**

2 **Try to guess what star signs your teacher(s) and the other members of the class might be. Later, find out what signs they really are.**

PISCES 20 February – 20 March

Pisceans are . . .
absent-minded adoring artistic careless compassionate emotional escapists imaginative loveable not competitive sensitive sympathetic temperamental unselfish

They . . .
can't bear to see suffering cry easily don't like hurting people get confused easily lack ambition put other people first

CAPRICORN 22 December – 20 January

Capricorns are . . .
ambitious hard-working demanding faithful good organisers patient persevering pessimistic resourceful serious severe shy suspicious of new ideas and inventions

They . . .
can put up with frustrations don't expect success to come quickly enjoy solitude like a fixed routine like to plan like to have money may worry unnecessarily need to organise, systematise and structure things

AQUARIUS 21 January – 19 February

Aquarians are . . .
broadminded dogmatic energetic fanatical friendly full of unusual ideas impractical inventive likeable rude tactless thinkers touchy unpredictable

They . . .
find it hard to get close to people need freedom and independence resent criticism think they are wonderful need to reform, create and understand

ARIES 21 March – 20 April

Arians are . . .
fearless impatient impulsive inconsiderate not philosophical not rational not very thorough perfect leaders pioneers punctual quick-witted ready to accept a challenge thoughtless

They . . .
can be bullies don't brood over their mistakes and failures don't foresee problems don't like being told what to do overlook details think quickly walk fast want quick results need to assert themselves and initiate events

TAURUS 21 April – 21 May

Taureans are . . .

good at gardening   methodical   musical   patient   practical
reliable   self-centred   slow to anger   stable   steadfast
stubborn

They . . .

hate changes   have great warmth   have strong feelings   love
good food   need security and possessions   only work hard
when they enjoy what they're doing   resent being contradicted
need to make things clear, be comfortable and to construct

VIRGO 24 August – 23 September

Virgos are . . .

calm   conscientious   critical   discriminating   fussy
good at remembering details   good learners   modest
perfectionists   practical

They . . .

can be hypocritical   don't suffer fools gladly   find it hard
to relax   hate untidiness   need to be of service   tend to
suppress their emotions

GEMINI 22 May – 21 June

Geminis are . . .

adaptable   always on the go   apparently two-faced
communicative   good at languages   inconsistent   light-hearted
versatile   witty

They . . .

can't stand waiting   don't like monotony   don't take things too
seriously   have sudden mood swings   like to find things out
love variety and change   need to communicate, make
connections and satisfy their curiosity

LIBRA   24 September – 23 October

Librans are . . .

ambitious   charming   considerate   diplomatic
good at persuading people   great entertainers
idealists   indecisive   over-sensitive   romantic
sociable   unselfish

They . . .

find friends everywhere   like to be liked   love nice
smells   smile a lot   need to find harmony,
balance and justice

CANCER 22 June – 23 July

Cancerians are . . .

artistic   good cooks   home-loving   imaginative
not keen travellers   sensitive   sentimental   untidy

They . . .

bring out the best in people   get upset easily   hate to throw
things away   hold grudges   like to stay in one place   may
seem aggressive   take things to heart   need to feel safe and
secure

SCORPIO 24 October – 22 November

Scorpios are . . .

attractive   courageous   good parents   jealous   loyal
secretive   strong, silent types   stubborn

They . . .

are difficult to live with   can be vindictive and cruel   don't trust
people   enjoy solving problems   have a magnetic quality   have
good self-control   need to change, investigate and reform

LEO 24 July – 23 August

Leos are . . .

creative   faithful   generous   good organisers   gregarious
loyal   playful   poor judges of character   self-confident
sometimes conceited   stylish

They . . .

like the sound of their own voices   like to be the centre of attraction
like to enjoy themselves   love power   make other people happy
need to shine as individuals and as leaders

SAGITTARIUS 23 November – 21 December

Sagittarians are . . .

boastful   clumsy   deep thinkers   extravagant
good-humoured   kind to others   open-minded
optimistic   outdoor types   outspoken   restless
travellers

They . . .

have a sense of adventure   have lots of interests
like exploring   look on the bright side   love sport
need challenges

Seven

Put it in writing

(7.1) Handwriting
Speaking

A 1 Look at these samples of handwriting. What sort of person do you think each writer is?

This is a sample of my handwriting. What sort of person do you think I am?

This is a sample of my handwriting. What sort of person do you think I am?

This is a sample of my handwriting. What sort of person do you think I am?

This is a sample of my handwriting. What sort of person do you think I am?

2 You'll hear an interview with a graphologist, explaining the personality of each of the writers. Note down the adjectives he uses to describe each person.

B 1 One of you should look at Activity 4, the other at 23. You'll each see some information about graphology.

2 When you've studied the information, collect some ANONYMOUS samples of handwriting from other members of the class and analyse them — what can you deduce about the personality of each writer?

(7.2) A professional writer
Listening

This is a sample of my handwriting. What sort of person do you think I am?

A You'll hear an interview with Isabelle Amyes, who writes television scripts. Each of these sentences contains ONE mistake — find the mistakes and correct them.

1 Unlike other writers she tries to put off the moment when she has to start work.
2 Self-discipline is not easier for her when she's working with a partner.
3 While she's working on a script she thinks about her characters some of the time.
4 Writing is an unsafe environment because you're working out your own fantasies.
5 The people who read her first script reacted in three different ways.
6 She thinks that rewriting a script is unnecessary.
7 She resents other people's criticisms and feels hurt by them for a long time.

Isabelle Amyes

8 Workshops for writers can help you to become a better writer.

9 When writing dialogue you don't have to be able to hear what the characters are saying.

10 She uses a word processor because she needs to see what she has crossed out.

11 She thinks that everyone needs food, and not everyone needs entertainment.

12 A television programme can't enlighten people.

⁞⁞⁞⁞ Ⓑ Discuss these questions:

● What are the similarities between Isabelle's experiences as a professional writer and your own experience in doing the Creative writing tasks in this book?

● What would you enjoy (and not enjoy) about her job?

● What are the pros and cons of using a word processor, rather than handwriting?

(7.3) Different styles
Reading

⁞⁞ Ⓐ 1 Here are ten extracts from various publications and documents. Decide together:

· what each extract is about and what topic it deals with

· what kind of publication or document each extract comes from

---

1 This book has been specially prepared to make it enjoyable reading for people to whom English is a second or foreign language. An English writer never thinks of avoiding unusual words, so that the learner, trying to read the book in its original form, has to turn frequently to the dictionary and so loses much of the pleasure that the book ought to give.

6 Dickie Kettleson is a ten-year-old boy growing up at a time when even the most ordinary life is a struggle. Dickie's world is his home and his neighbourhood – his family, his street, the threat of hunger and destruction that lurks just outside the door.

2 Most of the country will have another dry, warm day with long sunny spells, but there is the risk of one or two showers, perhaps heavy, later in the afternoon and evening.

7 Everyone must, in principle, have a visa to visit Japan. However, to help tourism, bilateral agreements with some countries mean you don't need a visa if you are from western Europe, the UK or most English-speaking countries, with the notable exceptions of the USA, Australia and South Africa.

AVOID LISTENING WITH YOUR HEADPHONES AT SO LOUD A VOLUME THAT EXTENDED PLAY MIGHT AFFECT YOUR HEARING. AS YOUR HEADPHONES ARE OF OPEN-AIR DESIGN, SOUNDS GO OUT THROUGH THE HEADPHONES. REMEMBER NOT TO DISTURB THOSE CLOSE TO YOU.

8 It's a dream come true when compared with making the journey by road. You don't have to contend with traffic jams, motorway hold-ups or the uncertainties of driving to the airport. You won't have to bother about parking either.

We found this really terrific place just a little way from the village and because the only way you could get there was on foot, it was completely unspoilt. We were practically the only people there.

9 One grey November morning I was running near the edge of a lake. On the path ahead of me an old man shuffled along slowly, using a cane. As I ran by I called out, 'Good morning!' He returned my greeting and then called after me rather unexpectedly, 'What do you gain by running?' I shouted back: 'It makes me feel good!'

5 The dose may be taken three or four times daily at intervals of not less than four hours. Do not exceed the stated dose. If symptoms persist, consult your doctor.

10 Claims under section 5 (Baggage) will not be considered unless substantiated by an original sales receipt or valuation for any item exceeding £50, or more.

▼ 2 Highlight the words or information that led you to your decision about each extract. Which was the main clue in each case?

⁞⁞ Ⓑ Find five more short quotes from different sources and write them out. Challenge another pair to tell you where they come from.

Long and short sentences
Effective writing

A 1 **Look at the headline of the article below — can you make sense of it? What information do you expect the article to give you?**

  2 **Find the answers to these questions in the article. To show your answers write** *HS* **(= Herbert Stein),** *AS* **(= Albert Sukoff) — or** *N* **(= neither of them).**

   1 Who copied a list of names from a phone book?

   2 Who had the more important job?

   3 Who quoted from the other writer's article?

   4 Who used a lot of dashes?

   5 Who wrote a sentence 1,286 words long?

   6 Whose sentence was 1,404 words long?

   7 Who wrote his article on a typewriter?

   8 Whose achievement was recorded in the *Guinness Book of World Records*?

   9 Whose article appeared in the New York Times?

   10 Whose article appeared in the San Francisco Chronicle?

   11 Whose article contained more serious information?

   12 Who wrote a sentence about 500 words long?

The unstoppable Albert Sukoff sets a wordy record

THE ODD BUT UNDENIABLE achievements of Herbert Stein and Albert Sukoff in writing sentences in newspapers of 1,286 words and 1,404 words respectively are only too likely to be emulated at even greater length as a result of that encyclopaedia of futile feats, the *Guinness Book of World Records*, which carried an entry alerting Mr Sukoff to the fact that on February 13, Mr Stein, an economist who served as chairman of the Council of Economic Advisers under presidents Nixon and Ford, wrote in the New York Times the 1,286-worder – his entire article – on his recollections of various personalities in previous administrations, doing so without the use of a single full stop (except at the end) but instead peppering it with dashes, a technique not employed by Mr Sukoff, a freelance writer and city planner in Berkeley, California, who found out about the Stein sentence when he saw it listed in a calendar detailing Guinness records on the date they were set, in this case on a Wednesday in February when it happened to be raining and Mr Sukoff had nothing much better to do than to sit down at his IBM personal computer (one wonders if he would have bothered as a two-fingered typist on a 1958 Underwood manual) and create a sentence deliberately longer than Mr Stein's though not, it must be said, of any profounder content, but indisputably passing time as he unabashedly went into laborious detail in his eventual 1,404 words published in the San Francisco Chronicle recently, about how he purchased the calendar, read the entry about Mr Stein, ruminated for a while, and then decided to out-ramble him, though not, Mr Sukoff goes on to explain, by the employment of dirty tricks such as stating that the longest sentence ever to pass an editor of an important newspaper was by Herbert Stein in the *New York Times*, and then merely to requote Mr Stein, or in another even more banal ploy, simply to say that, "the first 1,000 names in the Salt Lake City telephone directory are the following . . ." neither of which is a real challenge, although Mr Sukoff does become repetitive and, of course, constructed his sentence consciously as a record whereas one presumes that Mr Stein proceeded more spontaneously and therefore deserves more credit – if that is the word – for his achievement, now superseded by one that is certain to be challenged, especially when, as expected, it appears in the next *Guinness Book of World Records*, for it is a feat with particular appeal to newspaper writers who have always felt constrained by unwritten rules about sentence length and indeed the whole matter of limited space, in which there is never enough for the reporter, who however invariably delivers too much for the editor, a type likely to be strenuously opposed to 2,000- or even 1,500-word sentences landing on their desks, and might even be tempted to insert a full stop here and there, thus rendering the whole exercise pointless, if that is the word.

Christopher Reed

  3 **Approximately how many words are there in the article?**

  Look at one of your recent compositions. How many words are there per sentence, on average?

▼ B 1 Highlight these words in the article (the line number is given beside each word). Then match them with the definitions below.

> respectively ₃   emulated ₄   futile ₅   feats ₅   entry ₆   alerting ₆   freelance ₁₃   profounder ₂₂
> unabashedly ₂₃   ramble ₂₆   banal ₃₁   ploy ₃₁   superseded ₃₈   constrained ₄₁   invariably ₄₄

achievements   always   copied   limited   making aware of   more serious   self-employed
piece of information in a reference book   pointless   replaced   separately in the order mentioned
tactic   unoriginal   without shame   write/speak at great length

2 Fill the gaps in these sentences with the words you highlighted, changing them as necessary.

1 To some people it seems _____ to climb mountains, but others consider such _____ to be admirable.

2 The new edition of the dictionary has _____ the old one: the new and the old editions have 30,000 and 25,000 _____.

3 My attention kept wandering as he _____ on about his childhood experiences.

4 I _____ make notes before writing to prevent myself from _____ on.

5 I didn't find the novel _____ at all, I thought it was quite _____.

6 He said he was unwell, but it was just a _____ to gain our sympathy.

7 She knew his success would be _____ by the lack of money and staff, but she didn't _____ him to the problems till it was too late.

C 1 One technique of adding information to a sentence is to put extra information (such as a digression or a comment) in parenthesis by using brackets, commas or dashes – as in these examples:

> *He made a sandwich of jam and lettuce (together), saying it was delicious.*
> *Strawberries and cream, my favourite dessert, was on the menu.*

▼ Highlight all the brackets, commas and dashes used in the article opposite.

▼ 2 Another technique, frequently used in the article, is to use present or past participles. Look at these examples and then highlight FOUR more examples in the article.

> *. . . doing so without the use of a single full stop . . .*
> *. . . a technique not employed by Mr Sukoff . . .*

▼ D Over-long sentences are usually difficult to read and make sense of. Rewrite these single-sentence paragraphs in simpler, shorter, clearer sentences.

> The reason why language provides such a fascinating object of study is perhaps because of its unique role in capturing the breadth of human thought and endeavour: looking around us we are awed by the variety of several thousand languages and dialects, expressing a multiplicity of world views, literatures and ways of life; looking back at the thoughts of our predecessors we find we can see only as far as language lets us see, looking forward in time, we find we can plan only through language, and looking outward in space we send symbols of communication along with our spacecraft, to explain who we are, in case there is anyone there who wants to know.

> *The reason why this book has been specially prepared to make it enjoyable reading for people to whom English is a second or foreign language is that an English writer never thinks of avoiding unusual words, so that the learner, trying to read the book in its original form, has to turn frequently to the dictionary and so loses much of the pleasure that the book ought to give.*

In an essay or letter, shorter sentences tend to be easier to understand (and easier to write) than long ones. On the other hand, very short sentences may look rather childish. You have to strike a balance. This may be difficult. There are no fixed rules about this. The best ploy is to try to put yourself in your reader's position as you write. Ask yourself: 'How would I like to be reading this? Have I made my meaning clear?'

(7.5) Living with a computer
Reading

A 1 Find out from your partners:

- when they use a computer and what for
- how they think a computer can help you, entertain you, confuse you, etc.
- what they enjoy and hate about using a computer

2 Read this article and guess what the missing words are – fill each gap with one word.

Spammed

THE FIRST sign that something was _____ came Sunday afternoon, when I logged onto the Internet to check my weekend e-mail and found that someone had _____ me in a Barry Manilow fan club, a Mercedes owners discussion _____, a Fiji Islands appreciation society and 103 other Internet mailing lists I'd never heard of. I knew from _____ that any one of these lists can generate 50 messages a day. To avoid a _____ of junk e-mail I painstakingly unsubscribed from all 106 – even Barry Manilow's – only to log on Monday morning and _____ I'd been subscribed overnight to 1,700 more. My file of unread e-mail was growing by the _____.

I'd heard about "spam" – Internet jargon for machine-generated junk mail – and over the years I'd _____ my share of e-mail get-rich-quick pitches and cheesy magazine ads. But I had never experienced anything like this: a parade of mail that just got bigger and _____ . . . not only was I getting hundreds of subscription notices, but I was also receiving copies of every piece of mail posted to those lists. By Monday the e-mail was _____ in at the rate of four a minute, 240 an hour, 5,760 a day.

Philip Elmer-DeWitt

3 Compare your answers.

B 1 Where do you think these missing keys go on the English keyboard below:

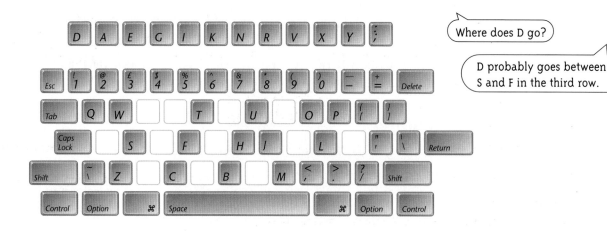

> Where does D go?

> D probably goes between S and F in the third row.

2 Discuss these questions:

- When you use a keyboard, which letters do you find the hardest to get right?
- Which are ~~hte~~ the English words that you mis-type ~~msot~~ most often?
- Different countries use different keyboards: how is your national keyboard different from the one above?
- If you're writing the following things do you prefer to use a computer or a pen? Why?
  **personal letters   homework assignments   business letters
  rough drafts   notes   essays   lists**

Seven   Put it in writing   60

C 1 Read this advertisement and fill each gap with one word:

Writing unlimited.

The freedom to write and think is for all of us. Now, there is a new word processor that's just _____ for us, too. It's called MacWrite® II, and it's made by Claris. MacWrite II makes it possible _____ share your ideas and thoughts with other computers and word processors. You'll be _____ to open documents from over 50 word processors, on all kinds of computers, with all kinds of _____, and work on them without reformatting.

But there's more you can do. (The feature is called XTND.) You can import graphics, not _____ from Macs, but many computers, guaranteed. And you can scale and crop them, _____ and all, in your MacWrite® II document. In short, MacWrite® II with XTND is a powerful word processor that lets you freely exchange text and graphics. You'll find also that your MacWrite® II _____ you change fonts, styles, sizes and colors, as well as _____ text with its find/change feature. And _____ can create custom styles and save them as stationery – with all formats preset. You'll _____ your reports and letters quickly.

But what good is freedom of expression if you find _____ editing to be a hassle? That's why the page layout and editing is fully WYSIWYG: the _____ you see are the thoughts you get. This WYSIWYG feature, by the way, is found only with MacWrite® II. It's another way Claris simplifies word processing for you, whether you're 52, 22, or 72.

Called upon daily MacWrite® II smooths your writing assignments and other chores. There's MacWrite II spell checking, for example, and foreign dictionary programs that are optional, _____ a host of other features that come standard. (Like a thesaurus, and a mail merge feature _____ discover saves lots of time.)

What it adds up to, you'll _____ is a simple and powerful tool designed for people. All the people. It is for writers, and _____ is for business people. And it is for those of us in between. The freedom to write is _____. Now technology is, too.

CLARIS™

2 Here is a list of the features of the application. Tick the ones that are mentioned.

MacWrite® II

1 makes it possible to share thoughts with computers ☐
2 can translate foreign language documents ☐
3 allows you to open documents from over 50 word processors ☐
4 produces drafts of letters for you ☐
5 writes speeches for you ☐
6 allows you to import graphics ☐
7 allows you to scale and crop graphics ☐
8 lets you freely exchange text and graphics ☐
9 What is the name of the feature that makes all these things possible? _____
10 WYSIWYG means _____ _____ _____ is _____ _____ _____

3 Highlight any useful vocabulary you'd like to remember in the advertisement.

Formal letters and personal letters
Reading and Effective writing

 A Find out from your partners:
- how they keep in touch with friends or relatives in another country
- why they enjoy/don't enjoy writing personal letters – and business letters

B 1 Read this advertisement.

THE SECRETS OF WRITING BUSINESS LETTERS

As far back as biblical times businessmen have used powerful communication to achieve wealth and position.

Even today the right message at the right time can lead to sweet success.

Want money? A promotion? To sell something? Explain something? Then write a good letter.

Letter writing is not a lost art just a forgotten one. The principles still exist. If you try them you'll see improvement in your very next letter.

TO BEGIN WITH

1. Start from the end. Decide what you'd like to happen as the result of your letter.

Make a list of all the things you'd like to say. Look them over. Find any that don't support your main cause, and cross them off without remorse.

Remember, the best letters have a strong sense of purpose.

2. Get to the point early. If your reader wanted a mystery, he'd be reading Raymond Chandler. A letter should tell whodunit in the first paragraph.

3. Put yourself in your reader's place. Think: if the same letter came to you, how would you respond?

Therefore, be friendly. Be nice. And find ways to turn negative statements into positive ones.

NO BUSINESS-ESE

4. Say it plainly. There is no such thing as a "business language". Phrases like "in compliance with your request and enclosed herewith" will only make you seem like a robot. Write the way you talk, naturally.

Keep your sentences short – one idea in each. Any sentence longer than two typed lines is automatically suspect.

5. Clear the deadwood. Chop out words, sentences, and even

whole paragraphs if they don't contribute. Work hard so your reader won't have to.

In particular, cast a questioning eye on adjectives. They can sap the strength from your words, or stretch your credibility. As Voltaire put it, "The adjective is the enemy of the noun."

6. Use active verbs. Face it, the passive voice is wimpy. "A decision has been reached by the committee" wouldn't last three rounds in the ring with "The committee has reached a decision."

Also, your reader will sniff a cover-up if you write: "Your order has been misplaced" instead of "I misplaced your order." Courage!

7. Be human. Your letter should read like a conversation, not a decree.

Address your reader by name: "Dear Ms Hartman." And if you can fit it in naturally, use Ms Hartman's name once or twice in the body. You want her to know you wrote the letter just for her.

Whenever you can, use pronouns like *I, we* and *you.* Especially *you* – it's an arrow straight to your reader's heart.

BE POSITIVE

8. Never write in anger. Your anger will evaporate; your letter won't. President Truman often vented his fury in letters. He also had the sense never to send them.

Devise a way to handle the problem in an upbeat manner. Your chances of success will multiply tenfold.

9. End it with an action step. The last sentence of your letter should suggest the reader's next move. Or your own next move.

Resist the hat-in-hand, shuffling type of exit: "Again, thank you for …" or "If you have any problems, please don't hesitate to call."

Instead, try closing with a plain and simple "Sincerely", and your signature. It may be the perfect ending.

10. Be professional. The strongest business letter in the world can't survive a bad presentation.

Set up a clean, logical format for your letter. A crowded or overdesigned page will distract from your message.

11. Develop a regimen. The keys to powerful correspondence are 1) writing often, and 2) responding quickly.

If it sounds like work, read on.

WRITE FOR POWER

The easiest way to more powerful correspondence is QuickLetter™ from Working Software.

Unlike heavy-duty word processors, QuickLetter is designed to do one thing and one thing only – write letters fast.

Here's how:

QuickLetter's built-in address book places your reader's name and address into your letter. Automatically.

QuickLetter's page preview displays your letter, vertically centred, in the format you've defined. Automatically.

QuickLetter addresses any size envelope. Automatically.

And the list of features goes on.

There you have it. All the secrets of brilliant business correspondence at your fingertips. Except one. And you can pick that up at your local software store.

▼ 2 Highlight the following words and phrases in the advertisement (the number shows which heading to look in). Try to work out their meanings from the context.

remorse ₁   whodunit ₂   suspect ₄   deadwood ₅   sap the strength ₅   credibility ₅   wimpy ₆
cover-up ₆   vented his fury ₈   upbeat ₈   tenfold ₈   hat-in-hand ₉   regimen ₁₁   heavy-duty

ᴉᴉ 3 Discuss these questions:

- Where was the ad originally published and who is it meant to be read by?
- Which of the 11 pieces of advice given do you agree with and which do you disagree with?
- Which of the advice also holds good for each of the following:

  personal letters   essays   reports   narratives   exam answers

ᴉᴉ Ⓒ 1 Decide which of these letterheads would be suitable for a personal letter, a business letter or neither:

```
99 Green Road
Cambridge CB2 2RU
UK

24 May 2000
```

```
99 Green Road
Cambridge CB2 2RU
Great Britain

24 May 2000
```

```
                    99 Green Road
                 Cambridge CB2 2RU
                            England
Ms Margaret B. Simpson
742 Evergreen Terrace
Springfield FX 09832
USA
                            24 May 2000
```

2 Decide which of these opening phrases would be suitable in:

a personal letter (P)   a formal business letter (B)   both (P+B) – or in neither (✗)

Dear Mrs Simpson,

Dear Ms Simpson,

Dear Margaret Simpson,

Darling Marge,

Dear Madam,

Marge!

Dear Marge,

Dear Friend,

Dear Mrs M B Simpson,

Hi Marge!

It's a very long time since I last wrote to you and I feel quite . . .

I'm pleased to inform you that . . .

I'm sorry not to have written earlier, but I've been very busy with . . .

I hope your new job is going well . . .

How are you? I'm fine.

Thank you for your enquiry about . . .

The reason I'm writing this letter is to let you know that . . .

I hope you enjoyed your visit to . . .

3 Decide which of these closing phrases would be suitable in:

a personal letter (P)   a formal business letter (B)   both (P+B) – or in neither (✗)

Good luck with your new job.

I'm off to lunch now, so I'll post this on the way.

I have to stop now because lunch is nearly ready.

I hope you enjoy your holiday.

I look forward to meeting you next month.

Well, I must stop now so as to catch the post.

Give my regards to your husband and the family.

Again, thank you for doing business with us.

Remember me to Homer and the kids.

Assuring you of our best attention at all times,

Yours,

Best,

All the best,

Kind regards,

Your loving friend,

Yours faithfully,

Yours sincerely,

Best wishes,

Sincerely,

4 Add one more opening phrase to C2 and two more closing phrases to C3.

(7.7) The differences between spoken and written English
Listening

A You'll hear the beginning of a lecture on spoken and written English. Read this summary of the lecture and fill the gaps as you listen.

> SPEECH: 'rapid conversational English'
> — happens face to face, it's ⬜⬜⬜⬜ , ⬜⬜⬜⬜
>
> WRITING: 'formal written English'
> — happens alone, it's ⬜⬜⬜⬜
>
> Main differences between speech and writing:
>
> 1 Hesitation
>   — in speech we hesitate to give us time to think while we're speaking
>   — in writing hesitation not apparent because the writer ⬜⬜⬜⬜ — but the ⬜⬜⬜⬜ doesn't notice the pause
>
> 2 Listener contact
>   — the people in a conversation are always ⬜⬜⬜⬜
>   — question tags (rather like a ⬜⬜⬜⬜ !)
>   — ⬜⬜⬜⬜ contact
>   — ⬜⬜⬜⬜ at end of lecture
>
> 3 'Silent language'
>   — body language e.g. ⬜⬜⬜⬜
>   — gestures e.g. ⬜⬜⬜⬜ , ⬜⬜⬜⬜
>   — invisible in a ⬜⬜⬜⬜ or on the ⬜⬜⬜⬜
>
> 4 Tone of voice

B 1 Discuss the lecture — what did you find most interesting (and least interesting) about it?

2 One of you should look at Activity 10, the other at 29. You'll each have some more examples of the differences between speech and writing. Use these ideas to continue your discussion.

(7.8) A tactful letter
Creative writing

A Choose ONE of these topics, make notes, and write a suitable letter (about 250 words).

> Write a letter to Mr and Mrs Brown, some English friends you stayed with for a few days last summer. You forgot to write them a thank-you letter after your stay. Now you're soon going to England again and you'd like to stay with them again.

OR

> Write a letter to your rich Uncle Peter in the USA, asking him to lend you some money for a round-the-world trip. You forgot to write him a thank-you letter when he sent you $50 for your birthday.

B 1 Show your completed letter to a partner. Would he or she let you stay/lend you money after reading the letter?

2 Write a postcard in reply to your partner's letter as if you were the Browns or Uncle Peter (about 50 words).

If you don't feel like writing a letter, or don't have the time, why not send a picture postcard? Although people like to receive personal letters, postcards can be more permanent — lots of people keep them and pin them up on their wall.

(7.9) *In . . .* and *out of . . .*
Idioms and collocations

A   **Fill the gaps with suitable expressions from the list below.**

1   'Poor Julie was ▒▒▒▒▒▒ when she read the letter,' he told me ▒▒▒▒▒▒ .

2   If you're ▒▒▒▒▒▒ about what to write, it's best to make notes beforehand.

3   ▒▒▒▒▒▒ business letters, personal letters are relatively easy to write.

4   I think he'll be upset and you shouldn't embarrass him ▒▒▒▒▒▒ , so ▒▒▒▒▒▒ it may be better to tell him off ▒▒▒▒▒▒ .

5   Writing an important letter is easier if you first write a rough copy ▒▒▒▒▒▒ before you write the final version ▒▒▒▒▒▒ or type it.

6   Orders may be placed by phone, by post or ▒▒▒▒▒▒ . You can pay by cheque, by credit card or ▒▒▒▒▒▒ .

7   ▒▒▒▒▒▒ the size of your order we are prepared to offer a special discount of 10% ▒▒▒▒▒▒ the usual trade discount.

8   We knew the firm was ▒▒▒▒▒▒ but not that they were ▒▒▒▒ such serious ▒▒▒▒▒▒ .

9   The book gave some information ▒▒▒▒ great ▒▒▒▒▒▒ but unfortunately the figures I needed were only given ▒▒▒▒▒▒ .

10   She did me a favour and then asked what I'd do for he ▒▒▒▒▒▒ . At first I thought she meant it ▒▒▒▒▒▒ but then I realised she was serious.

> **IN . . .**   addition to   brief   cash   the circumstances   comparison with   detail   difficulty   doubt
> **fun**   ink   pencil   person   private   public   return   tears   trouble   view of   a whisper

B   **Fill the gaps with suitable phrases from the list below.**

1   The passengers knew they were ▒▒▒▒ great ▒▒▒▒▒▒ when the pilot announced he was no longer ▒▒▒▒▒▒ of the aircraft.

2   Love letters will never be ▒▒▒▒▒▒ because people will go on falling ▒▒▒▒▒▒ .

3   We used to keep ▒▒▒▒▒▒ regularly but I've lost her address and so now we are ▒▒▒▒▒▒ .

4   Sorry, it's not a very good photo because it's ▒▒▒▒▒▒ – I used to do a lot of photography but now I'm ▒▒▒▒▒▒ .

5   Although she's still ▒▒▒▒ considerable ▒▒▒▒▒▒ , she's ▒▒▒▒▒▒ and back home.

6   Strawberries are ▒▒▒▒▒▒ this month but the shop hasn't got them ▒▒▒▒▒▒ .

7   He really is ▒▒▒▒▒▒ : he lost his job last year and he's been ▒▒▒▒▒▒ ever since. Now he's ▒▒▒▒▒▒ he can't afford to pay his mortgage – let's hope he doesn't end up ▒▒▒▒▒▒ !

8   The twins are learning the violin but as they always play ▒▒▒▒▒▒ , they aren't allowed to practise in the house and they have to play ▒▒▒▒▒▒ !

> **IN . . .** *or* **OUT OF . . .**   contact   control   danger   debt   doors   fashion   focus   hospital   love
> **luck**   pain   practice   prison   season   stock   touch   tune   work

"Write a letter to Santa? It's easier just to break into his computer distribution system."

Eight

Past times

8.1 The good old days?
Reading

A Look at each of the pictures and note down **FIVE** adjectives to describe each scene. Then decide:

* what century or period of history is shown
* what would have been pleasant about living at that time
* what would have been unpleasant about living then

B 1 This is the blurb from the dustjacket of *Chronicle of the 20th Century*. The paragraphs have been mixed up. Decide on a suitable sequence for the paragraphs.

A   Whether you turn to *Chronicle* for nostalgia, enlightenment, reference or simply for fun, this unique book will be a treasured and much-read possession in every home. For the youngest and oldest, it is the book of our lifetimes.

C   Follow the lives of legendary figures such as Winston Churchill, recapture the whiff of scandals such as King Edward's abdication, thrill to great sporting victories, be chilled by disasters such as Aberfan, marvel at scientific discoveries and cheer at artistic triumphs from Picasso's first exhibition to the Beatles' first record – it's all in *Chronicle*, as fresh and dramatic as today's news.

B   There has never been a century like it – and never a book like *Chronicle*. This lavishly-illustrated book gives you a front-row seat for all the dramas of the century – from world wars to the fashions of the day – as they happened, with all the immediacy and excitement of tonight's television news.

D   Now, at last, it is available in an edition specially prepared for Great Britain, almost entirely new and reflecting the distinctly British perspective on a century that began when Queen Victoria was monarch to much of the world. With thousands of illustrations, many in full colour, this book captures the changing social and cultural life of our turbulent times.

E

Chronicle of the 20th Century is more than a book; it's an experience, taking you back in time to relive history as it happens. No wonder it's been a best-seller wherever it has been published with more than two million copies sold in Germany, France and the United States.

F

Chronicle of the 20th Century puts you there when man first flies an aeroplane or invents the "talking pictures". Discover what happened at the great moments of history – the Russian Revolution, the rise of Hitler, the D-Day landings, the bombing of Hiroshima, the assassination of President Kennedy and the Moon landing.

2 Discuss these questions:

- What distinguishes *Chronicle* from other history books?
- What other editions of *Chronicle* have been published?
- How is the British edition different from other editions?

3 Write new versions of paragraphs B and D of the blurb to include the important events that happened in YOUR country in the 20th century.

C Read the blurb from the cover of *Dreams for Sale* below and then discuss these questions about it:

1 What is meant by 'popular culture'?
2 What kind of events and people do conventional history books describe?
3 Which parts of *Dreams for Sale* would you both find most interesting?
4 Which of the forthcoming titles would you like to read and why?
5 If you wanted just one 20th century history book, which would you buy: *Chronicle* or *Dreams for Sale*? Why?

Harrap's Illustrated History of the 20th Century

Dreams for Sale, the first in this new, six-volume history of the 20th century, offers both the general reader and student a fascinating insight into the development of popular culture since 1900. Drawing on a variety of images from the worlds of fashion, entertainment and sport, Dr Richard Maltby provides a highly-readable analysis of the way in which traditional cultural values have been replaced by a global industry which creates and markets cultural "products" for popular consumption.

- Coverage of all major fields of popular culture: film, music, fashion, design, sport, media
- Imaginatively illustrated with photographs and full-colour artwork
- Special features highlight events and personalities of particular interest
- Chronological tables and datafiles provide factual reference at a glance
- Text includes biographies of some 300 key figures of modern popular culture

Forthcoming titles in this series

Power: A Political History of the 20th Century
Wealth and Poverty: *An Economic History of the 20th Century*
The Family: *A Social History of the 20th Century*
The Arts: *A History of Expression in the 20th Century*
Science: *A History of Discovery in the 20th Century*

D Discuss these questions:

- What historical events happened in the year you were born?
- What are the most significant historical events that have occurred during your lifetime?
- History is a subject that's taught in every school: why is this?

A 1 Discuss the differences in meaning between these sentences.

1 *When I was younger we would spend our holidays at the coast and . . .*
When I was younger we spent our holidays at the coast and . . .
When I was younger we had to spend our holidays at the coast and . . .

2 *When I was a child I didn't use to stay in hotels so . . .*
When I was a child I wasn't used to staying in hotels so . . .
When I was a child I wouldn't stay in hotels so . . .

3 *I was going to tell him what had happened but . . .*
I was telling him what had happened but . . .
I told him what had happened but . . .
I had told him what had happened but . . .
I was about to tell him what had happened but . . .

4 *I could see that they had been doing some research because . . .*
I could see that they had done some research because . . .
I could see that they were doing some research because . . .
I could see that they were going to do some research because . . .

5 *I used to be interested in reading history books . . .*
I was interested in reading about history . . .
I was used to reading history books . . .

2 Decide how each sentence might continue . . .

B Correct the mistakes in these sentences – one contains NO mistakes.

1 I didn't knew that you came to stay with me next weekend.
2 In the 1970s people would be less well-off than they are now.
3 In the nineteenth century people weren't used to watching TV – they must make their own entertainment.
4 I just write a letter to her when she was phoning me.
5 I had been waiting so long in the cold that my feet were feeling numb.
6 He used to study history for three years.
7 It was the first time I went abroad and I was feeling very excited.
8 He arrived late because he had forgot what time the train will be leaving.

C Replace the words in red with a suitable form of the irregular verbs listed below. Be careful because some of them may be tricky!

1 She rested on her bed after the wasp had bitten her.
2 Have you made the tape go back?
3 The storm made her wake up in the middle of the night.
4 As he had never been in a plane before he held tightly to my arm.
5 He put all the clothes on the bed while he brushed the floor.
6 The problems happened because the firm selected the wrong software.
7 She cursed when someone stepped on her bad foot.
8 We knew in advance that the essay would have to be done again.
9 Napoleon sat on a white horse as he directed his troops in battle.
10 He cried when he saw that his new shirt had got smaller in the wash.

arise	awake	choose	cling	fly	foresee	lay	lead	lie	rewind	rewrite	ride	shrink
sting	swear	sweep	tread	weep								

D Fill the gaps in these two contrasting descriptions of Britain in the 19th century. Use the verbs below in their correct forms.

────── VICTORIAN BRITAIN ──────

When Queen Victoria _____ in 1901 she _____ for 63 years. During her reign many great scientific discoveries _____ and the population of Britain _____ from 18 million to 40 million. The British Empire _____ to become the largest empire the world _____ ever _____ and by then it _____ a quarter of the world's people. During her reign Britain _____ a time of peace and prosperity and _____ not _____ in any major war since the battle of Waterloo in 1815. No one _____ that the First World War, in which so many young men _____ , _____ some 13 years later.

break out   die   enjoy   fight   grow   include   kill   know   make   reign   rise   suspect

The Darker Side

During the reign of Queen Victoria (1837–1901) life for the middle classes and the aristocracy _____ never _____ better: the Industrial Revolution and the Empire _____ them with undreamed-of luxury, convenience and wealth – but at the expense of the lower classes. Although slavery _____ in the British Empire in 1834, the working classes in the slums of Britain's industrial cities _____ almost as badly as slaves, and even young children _____ to work long hours in factories and coal mines. During this period over 10 million people _____ from these appalling conditions and _____ to America and Australia. The magnificent Empire which _____ vast profits to Britain's manufacturers _____ the people of the colonies, who _____ cheap raw materials for British factories, and _____ nations of clients who _____ to depend on a supply of British products.

abolish   be   bring   come   create   emigrate   escape   exploit   force   produce   provide   treat

E Decide how to match the names in the first column with the places in the second and dates in the third. Then discuss the questions below.

Archduke Franz Ferdinand	Battle of Hastings	1963
Charles Lindbergh	Sarajevo	1914
Christopher Columbus	Dallas, Texas	1066
Ferdinand Magellan	Russia	1903
John F. Kennedy	Pacific Ocean	1917
Napoleon	Moon	1927
Neil Armstrong	Waterloo	1815
October Revolution	Atlantic Ocean	1969
Wilbur and Orville Wright	Atlantic Ocean	1521
William the Conqueror	Dayton, Ohio	1492

- What happened exactly? What were the long-term effects of each event?
- How would the world be different if these events hadn't happened?
- What are the three most significant historical events missing above?

A Imagine that the year is 1499! You'll hear two historical figures taking part in a radio broadcast. Fill each gap with a single word, date or number:

- **Vasco da Gama** left Lisbon on   July 1497 with   men and provisions for three years. Out of sight of land for   days between Cape Verde Islands and Cape of Good Hope (km). Finally arrived at Calicut in India on 22 May   after   -day voyage across   Sea.
- Left India in   1498 with cargo of spices,   , silk and precious   . Arrived back in September   with only   survivors — the rest died of scurvy (a disease caused by lack of vitamin C).

- **Christopher Columbus**'s first voyage was financed by King Ferdinand and Queen   of Spain. Left Spain on   August 1492 with   ships and   men to travel west via the   Islands. Out of sight of land for   days (km). Reached other side of Atlantic Ocean on   October 1492.
- Returned to Spain in   1493 with cargo of a small amount of   ,   'Indians' and some parrots.
- His second voyage began in   1493 with   men — set up first permanent European   on other side of Atlantic.
- His third voyage began on 30 May   : didn't find   route to the Indies.

B Discuss these questions with your partners:
- How would you describe the personalities of the men in the recording?
- Whose achievement was more significant at the time?
- Which historical figures would YOU like to be able to interview?

C Think of TWO historical figures from your country's history — one male and one female. Write two descriptions of their lives and achievements (each about 120 words) for a guidebook for foreign visitors to your country.

8.4 Forming adjectives
Word study

A Form adjectives from the nouns below and add them to the appropriate column. The first ones have been done as examples. The number of adjectives that should be added to each column is shown as + 5, + 15, etc.

-ous	-ic	-ical	-al
advantageous	historic	historical	continental
adventurous	apologetic		
+ 5	+ 15	+ 7	+ 11

advantage ✓   history ✓   history ✓   continent ✓   adventure ✓   apology ✓
ambition   art   catastrophe   commerce   courage   danger   drama   ecology   emotion   energy
finance   function   grammar   intention   Islam   logic   magnet   metal   mountain   nation
optimism   pessimism   philosophy   politics   profession   region   sarcasm   science   sensation
society   symbol   sympathy   synonym   system   theatre   theory   tradition   tragedy

B Form adjectives from the verbs and nouns below and add them to the appropriate column. The first ones have been done as examples. The number of adjectives that should be added to each column is shown.

-able	-ive	-y	-ly
acceptable	appreciative	bumpy	cowardly
believable		contradictory	
+ 9	+ 10	+ 16	+ 6

accept ✓   appreciate ✓   believe ✓   contradict ✓   communicate   compete   decorate   describe
destroy   enjoy   explode   forget   inform   jump   obtain   possess   prefer   produce   regret   rely
repeat   satisfy   shine   slip   supplement   sweat
bump ✓   coward ✓   day   dust   fortnight   gloom   guilt   haste   itch   knowledge   luck
memory   month   mood   neighbour   quarter   reason   sand   stripe   taste   year

C 1 Write a mini-exercise consisting of SIX sentences with gaps using the adjectives from A and B. Like this:

Because of turbulence we had a very . . . . . . flight.
He was very . . . . . . after dropping the vase.

2 Exchange exercises with another pair and do the exercise you've been given.

© 1994 LEO CULLUM

A We speak differently in different situations and to express different functions or intentions. You'll hear 15 clips. Which description matches each clip? Write the number in the box.

Anecdote	☐	Excuse	☐	Lecture	☐
Announcement	☐	Explanation	☐	Lie	☐ 1
Apology	☐	Friendly advice	☐	Rumour	☐
Complaint	☐	Interview	☐	Small talk	☐
Contradiction	☐	Joke	☐	Warning	☐

B The adjective nice is used a lot in spoken English, but less in formal writing. Look at these examples and find synonyms from the list below.

1 Did you have a nice time?
2 He said some nice things about you.
3 It was very nice of you to invite me.
4 You look very nice.
5 He's a very nice man.
6 It was nice and quiet there.
7 Please be nice to them.
8 It was nice of you to give me a present!

complimentary   enjoyable   friendly   generous   likeable   smart   thoughtful   pleasant

C Decide which of the following you'd be more likely to see in informal writing, such as a personal letter, fax or note (I) – or in a formal letter, article or essay (F):

1 Please ensure that sufficient photocopies are made.
2 Don't forget to make enough photocopies – we'll need about 100.
3 Our unexpected meeting developed into a very productive conversation.
4 I was most surprised to discover that he should suggest such an idea.
5 I was really surprised to hear your news. Congratulations!
6 Please let me know if there's anything I can do.
7 Please inform me if you have any special requests.
8 A suitable reference book should be used to check the information.
9 Why not look it up in a reference book or something?
10 Don't you think studying history is a bit of a waste of time?
11 Studying history can help us to understand the causes of current events.
12 Thank you for your invitation, which I am delighted to accept.
13 How are you? Got over your nasty cold, I hope. Isn't this winter weather awful!

D Imagine that two people came to talk to your class last week. One of them was a friend of yours, the other a distinguished professor. Here are two thank-you letters. Fill each gap with ONE word but use a DIFFERENT word from the one used in the first letter.

INFORMAL LETTER

Dear Sally,
Thanks a lot for coming to speak to us the other day. It was really nice of you to give up your time, I know how busy you are. I'd like you to know that everyone was really pleased with your session, and we were all still talking about it among ourselves the next day!
I'm sorry if we seemed a bit quiet during the talk. If so, this was because we were all listening carefully to what you had to say, not because any of us were bored – far from it!
Thanks again for coming – I hope you can come again soon.

FORMAL LETTER

Dear Professor Brown,

Thank you very much for the ₁_____ you gave to our class last Wednesday. It was very ₂_____ of you to ₃_____ the time to visit us. The session was much ₄_____ by us all. In fact, the topic was still being ₅_____ among the students the ₆_____ day.

In case you were ₇_____ by our response, I should like to ₈_____ you that every member of the class found your talk extremely interesting. The reason why the class may have seemed somewhat ₉_____ is that we were all ₁₀_____ hard on what you were saying, it was certainly not because you ₁₁_____ to capture our interest, quite the ₁₂_____!

Thank you once more. We look forward to ₁₃_____ you here again before ₁₄_____.

8.6 Get
Verbs and idioms

A **GET has got a lot of meanings! Match the synonyms below to these uses of GET:**

1 I must get my hair cut.
2 He got someone else to do the work.
3 We all get old eventually.
4 It's upstairs, can you get it for me?
5 How much does she get a week?
6 It may be hard to get to see him.
7 He didn't get the joke.
8 Did you get my letter?
9 Will you get the meal ready?
10 When did you get there?
11 I'm trying to get a new car.
12 Did she get an A in the exam?
13 It's time to get going.
14 His attitude really gets me.

Remember that there's rarely a one-to-one equivalence between 'synonyms'.

annoy   arrive   attain   become   earn   fetch   have   manage   obtain   persuade   prepare   receive   start   understand

B **Rewrite these sentences, replacing the phrases in red with the correct form of the expressions listed below which mean the same.**

1 She's a difficult person to have a friendly relationship with.   *get along/on with*
2 I tried phoning several times but I couldn't make contact.
3 It may be difficult to communicate these ideas to everyone.
4 I don't understand what you're implying.
5 Try not to let it depress you if someone criticises you.
6 The lecturer spoke so fast that we couldn't write everything he said.
7 I don't want to take part in the show, but how can I avoid it?
8 They were unable to recover from the setback.
9 I hoped we could meet but we never managed to find the time.
10 It may take you a while to become involved in the book.
11 I haven't got time for a holiday but I hope to escape for a long weekend.
12 The only way to succeed in politics is to have the right connections.
13 We'd better start moving – it's nearly lunchtime.
14 Leave a message and I'll return your call.
15 Look, it's clear we're having no success, let's try a different plan.
16 He got his revenge by letting her car tyres down.

SILENCE

Phrasal verbs tend to be used more in spoken English than in written English.

GET . . .   ahead   along/on with   at   at   away   back   going   into   down   me down   nowhere   on for   one's own back   out of   over   over/across   round to   through   together

Nine

You're as old as you feel

(9.1) **The Third Age**
Reading and
Listening

†† Ⓐ 1 Look at the photos and write down ten words that come into your mind when you think about growing older.

†††† 2 Imagine that you're due to retire next year — you're still fit and healthy but not very wealthy. Put these factors in order of importance:

☐ comfort and warmth in winter   ☐ privacy
☐ companionship   ☐ intellectual stimulation
☐ closeness to children/grandchildren ☐ financial independence
☐ a nice garden or nearby park   ☐ having a part to play in society
☐ peace and quiet   ☐ security from crime
☐ books and music   + *Any other factors:* ....

Ⓑ Read this article and find the answers to these questions:

1 How is the 'new' Cambridge University different from the old one?

2 Without U3As, how might old people feel in their retirement years?

3 What are the aims of the U3A movement in Britain?

Life begins at 50 for Third Age students

1 At first glance it's the usual Cambridge scene: the fight for places to park the bicycle, the hasty greetings called across the courtyard, the scramble for decent seats next to your friends, the silence before the lecture begins. The difference here is that the greetings are a little cheerier, the scramble a little more intense, the silence a little more avid, and, though you may not notice it, there are more grey hairs. The students at the new Cambridge University are all aged 50 or over.

The Wednesday afternoon lecture is the main event of the week for members of the University of the Third Age, or 'U3A' as they call it. But every day there are classes going on all over town ranging from Chinese to computers. The new university now has more than 700 members. It was the first of its kind in Britain, but the idea caught on quickly and Third Age universities have started up all over the country.

Although Shakespeare chronicled Seven Ages of Man, the new university makes do with four. The Third Age comes when the First Age of childhood and the Second Age of earning a living and bringing up a family are over. It may well last as long as 30 years, beginning in the fifties and going on into the sixties, seventies and eighties. The belief and the hope is that an active Third Age can postpone the Fourth Age of weakness and death, squeezing that into the shortest period possible.

Thirty years is a long time to feel bored, lonely and useless: it's not nearly long enough for the members of the University of the Third Age to do all the things they want to do. Barbara Taptiklis is a case in point. A widow and a grandmother, her life is still as busy and active as ever. 'We dash to classes and then we meet up for coffee. I'm learning French. I never had the time before. People say you can't learn a new language when you're old, but that's nonsense. It just depends on your drive and willingness to do it. The difference with U3A is that we feel we're using our brains.

We're not superior, not at all. We're just extending our knowledge, starting again really and it's fun.'

Students pay £10 for six months' membership of the university and for this they can go to as many or as few classes as they wish. There are also regular social and sporting events. One of the reasons why so much activity is possible and costs so little is that the teachers give their time free and seem to enjoy it just as much. Richard Bennett, a retired schoolteacher who takes one of the French classes, says the great joy is that everybody is motivated. There are none of those little boys in the back row trying to hide under their desks. 'Most of us who teach also learn. I'm doing cookery and music. We're doing areas of 20th-century music I'd never explored before and I'm finding out all sorts of things.'

Sonia Beesley

C Look at the first paragraph again and perhaps read it aloud. Notice the style of the writing and discuss these questions:

- How does the writer evoke the atmosphere of excitement?
- How does she make YOU feel that you're actually there?
- How does she emphasise the differences between the old and the new Cambridge University?

D You'll hear an interview with Geoffrey Smerden, a retired general practitioner (GP = family doctor), who founded the U3A in Colchester, Essex. Fill each gap in this summary with one word.

Geoffrey Smerden

1 Geoffrey teaches _____ and _____ at the U3A as well as doing _____ readings.

2 His wife, Mary, does _____ groups and a _____ group and embroidery.

3 People used to think 'I'm old therefore I'm _____' and 'This is for _____ people and not for the likes of me.'

4 Geoffrey is against preparing for exams because he and his group like _____ and they learn at different _____ and everyone is very _____ of each other.

5 He remembers that between the time when his mother was widowed at the age of _____ and died at the age of _____, she sat at home and did _____.

6 He finds that young people today are _____, _____ and _____. But sadly they don't have the _____ they should have.

7 He says that his parents tried to do their _____ for him, but they didn't _____ him.

8 Geoffrey's wife said to a depressed friend, 'You don't _____ an interesting life, you _____ an interesting life.'

E Discuss these questions:

- What educational facilities are provided for senior citizens in your country?
- What role do grandparents play in society in your country?
- What can we learn from other cultures about attitudes to older people?
- How much of a problem is ageism compared to sexism and racism in your country?
- How would you set about improving conditions for older people in your country and perhaps changing younger people's attitudes?

Paragraphs
Reading and Effective writing

Paragraphs break a text into easy-to-manage sections, making it easier for the reader to understand. Normally, related ideas and examples are grouped together in the same paragraph.

Each new idea requires a fresh paragraph.

A Here's the first part of a newspaper article. Decide WHY the writer has chosen to start each fresh paragraph in the places she has.

Greys set to shake up German political scene

1 Germany, which has Europe's youngest pensioners and oldest students, now has a rebellious Grey Party claiming that "old is beautiful" and calling for a greater say for the over 60s.

2 The leader of the new party, Mrs Trude Unruh, aged 64, says she has decided that remaining quiet is "no good." Clubs for old people should be turned into "centres for political education and agitation."

3 Mrs Unruh (her name in English means "restless") spent more than two years sitting as a Green in the Bundestag. But she says the Greens used her to attract pensioners' votes without rewarding the Greys with promised constituencies.

4 Equipped with a cloth cap and megaphone, she is ready to take on the established political parties in next year's general election. She will campaign for a guaranteed minimum state pension of up to DM1,500 a month (£600), and pledges to put an end to "old people being totally at the mercy of the system and the welfare mafia."

5 As far as possible, the Greys want to do without homes for the old, care institutions or psychiatric establishments. Old people should have a free choice of residence, where their freedom would be maintained and the necessary level of care provided.

6 "We want to lead autonomous lives, and move away from the concept that old people must be manageable," she said at the party's spacious headquarters in Wuppertal, which is also a "cultural centre" for pensioners.

B Here is the last part of the same article, printed here without paragraphs. Decide where to break it into paragraphs. (This part of the original text consisted of eight paragraphs.)

"We need cooperation and not polarisation," Professor Lehr said. Both the economy and society had to face the enormous challenge of adjusting to the demographic changes caused by a drastic fall in birth rates, she said. But she added that a minimum pension would not solve the problems linked to ageing. "The Greys have opted for the wrong path." At present, some 90 per cent of the two million Germans who need care are looked after by their families, and 600,000 people live in homes. But staffing problems in hospitals and in the care sector have reached alarming proportions, and reports of "scandalous conditions" in old people's homes make headlines almost every week. The anger of those involved in caring for the old has recently been fuelled by a decision of a Mannheim court which, in response to a complaint from residents in a small town in Baden-Württemberg, ruled that old people's homes should not be situated in "high-quality residential areas". The plaintiffs argued that they were "disturbed at night by the sound of ambulances and occasional screams from home inmates." It was high time, Mrs Unruh said, that those in power realised that Germany was fast becoming a society hostile not only to children, but also to the aged. She said her proposals for greater integration of the old and reduced dependence on the state welfare system had exposed the serious gap between private care provided by the family and the official welfare system in hospitals, homes and other institutions.

Anna Tomforde

C Look at two of your own recent pieces of written work. Are you happy about the way you've used paragraphs in them? Ask a partner for advice if necessary.

(9.3) Granny power
Listening and Speaking

A 1 Before you listen to the recording, look at the summary below — can you guess how to fill any of the gaps? How old will you be in the year 2025?

2 You'll hear part of a broadcast. Fill each gap below with one word or a number.

In 2025:

1 In Germany _____ % of the population will be over 50 (compared to _____ % now).

2 In Germany and Japan: _____ % will be over 75.

3 In most Western countries _____ % of people will be over 65.

4 _____ , _____ and _____ will be 'elderly countries'.

5 _____ , _____ and _____ will be 'young countries'.

6 Young workers are more _____ , _____ and _____ .

7 Older workers acquire _____ and _____ , but they lose _____ and _____ .

8 Younger workers are _____ to employ: they don't expect such high _____ .

In China:

9 In 2025 _____ % of the population will be over 60.

10 The retirement age is _____ for men and _____ for women, but retired workers often remain on the _____ .

11 Shanghai's textile mills employ _____ people, of whom _____ are retired people: they are paid _____ of an active worker's wages.

12 Before 1949 life expectancy was _____ . Traditionally, old people were looked after in extended families. Now, with the 'one-child' policy, couples face sole responsibility for all _____ parents.

13 The government encourages _____ and _____ to remarry, but some Chinese still believe that a widow who remarries is _____ .

The main problems facing the West are:

14 A relatively small working population will have to _____ a large number of _____ retired people.

15 Younger countries will be more _____ in the world market because young workers will be the _____ .

B 1 Consider these case studies — each one presents you with a different problem situation. Decide together how to solve them.

A   You have an elderly parent who can no longer look after him/herself. Should you persuade him or her to come and live with you, or should you find accommodation in a sheltered flat or a room in a rest home? Or should you persuade your brother or sister to look after him or her?

B   You are due to retire next year. Will you move to a more pleasant part of your country — or maybe to another country? What will you do with all your free time?

C   You are 70 years old and your estate is worth about £100,000. You have decided to make a will. You have three children (ages 39–45), seven grandchildren (ages 11–24) and one great-grandchild. How should the money be divided?

D   An elderly relative lives in an inexpensive flat in an inner city area, where there is a lot of crime. He or she can't afford to move to a safer, more expensive place. What should you do?

E   An old person, who you once helped with shopping and errands, leaves you £10,000 in his or her will, which must be spent for the benefit of local old people. What will you do with the money?

2 When you're ready, explain your solutions to the rest of the class.

Family life
Reading

A Decide where paragraphs **A** to **F** opposite fit in the gaps in this article shown with red arrows. There's one extra paragraph which doesn't fit anywhere.

1 IT'S SUNDAY teatime in the Turner household, and 14 people are about to sit down around the table. But this isn't a party or a special get-together. In fact, I am the only visitor. All the other 13 diners are Turners: Mike, Rowena, and their 11 children. Even around their big table it's a bit of a squeeze, but the Turners try to eat together most evenings. Even three-month-old Eleanor joins us, clamped to her mother's breast. For everyone else it's baked potatoes, a huge bowl of cheese, and a mountain of bread – one of the 10 loaves a week the family gets through.

2▶

3 Another time his classmates worked out that if the children continue to reproduce at the same rate as their parents, there will be billions of Turners in 10 generations' time. Everyone laughs but it could happen. Certainly the eldest of the clan, 20-year-old Sarah, a trainee accountant, thinks there's a lot to be said for big families. "There's always something going on, and people around to talk to. It's never lonely or boring." Eighteen-year-old David (who comes after Sarah), an apprentice mechanical engineer, weighs in: "Christmas is a real event when you've got this many people to enjoy the party with."

4▶

5 But what about the disadvantages? If you hate supermarkets, just imagine shopping for the Turners. The weekly shop involves at least two trolleys and a bill coming in at somewhere between £120 and £150. Often Rowena takes along one or two of the older children to help, but if she's alone she just fills one trolley and leaves it at the checkout before filling another. Not the customer to get stuck behind at the checkout.

6 "People think we're a couple with children from different marriages," says Mike, 45, an information systems manager. "But then you see them taking in the ages, and realising it's *just* possible they're all ours."

◀7

Holidays are one of the biggest expenses for a family of 13. Most summers see the Turners travelling in convoy, the bulk of them in their eight-seater people carrier, with Sarah and David following behind in their cars with the remainder. Until two years ago, the Turners and their then 10 children squeezed into a four-bedroom house (with one bathroom) in nearby Didcot. Today home is a bungalow which has two shower rooms as well as a bathroom. There are two bedrooms under the eaves – one for Sarah and Hannah, the other for David and Mark. Downstairs the three youngest boys – Colin, Neil and five-year-old Stephen – share one room, with two-year-old Elizabeth and baby Eleanor in another. Across the corridor is Mike and Rowena's room. John and Jacob share a room above the garage, reached via the garden and connected to the house by buzzer.

8

◀9

10

Four?!? It may sound mad to the rest of us, but there's every possibility they might. Rowena, after all, is only 44. Another child would, she says, be a blessing – the first four were hard work, but since then it's been plain sailing. "By the time I had Jacob, Sarah was old enough to help, and since then there's always been plenty of help on hand." But doesn't anyone ever feel the need for a bit of privacy? The chance to be alone without being surrounded by a dozen other people and their toys, clothes, belongings, needs and requests?

◀11

Joanna Moorhead

A · And then there's the expense. "It makes me laugh when someone at work who's probably earning more than I am says he and his wife have two children and would love another but they can't afford it. It's not a question of affording, it's how you choose to spend your money," he says.

D · Oddly neither of them is in any hurry to move out of the family home: both say they enjoy playing with the younger ones. And they don't even mind the chores. Tonight's supper has been prepared by Sarah and her 14-year-old sister Hannah, and nine-year-old Colin and Neil, seven, have set the table. When it's over David and his 13-year-old brother Jacob will tidy up and pile the plates into the dishwasher. So there are benefits to having a family the size of a baker's dozen.

B · Everyone looks a bit surprised at the question. Presumably they've had to live with each other for so long that they've either forgotten the joys of being alone – or have never known them.

C · Most parents are happy with two, maybe three, children in a lifetime. The more daring/foolhardy might venture to four or even five (to the probable amazement of the rest of the civilised world). The Turners of Harwell, near Didcot, Oxon, however see no such boundaries. Their 11 children range in age from 20 years to three months, and they don't appear to have any plans to stop there. John, who at 16 is the third eldest, is the most talkative. Yes, he agrees, when you see the family together it can be a bit daunting. At school he gets ribbed about it all the time. "When the pictures of the sixth form came out, someone said it was a snap of the Turner family," he says. "There are 300 people in my sixth form."

E · There's the usual family clutter of toys and clothes around. Six young friends have just stayed for the weekend, but you probably don't notice them when you've got 11 of your own. It's a tight squeeze, but Mike believes the bungalow could easily accommodate more if other children were to come along. MORE??? Surely not. Don't they like odd numbers or something? Well, Mike goes on, they could probably fit at least another four in.

F · The younger children look at me unhappily when I ask this question. "If only I could have more time on my own, life would be so much easier," says John. "Most of us can't wait to be old enough to leave home."

B 1 Choose a suitable headline for the article:

A large family   A visit to the Turners   Big is beautiful   The more the merrier

2 Which member(s) of the Turner family . . .

1 . . . cooked the meal?
2 . . . is the eldest child?
3 . . . is the most chatty person?
4 . . . is the youngest child?
5 . . . is 14?
6 . . . is 44?
7 . . . laid the table?
8 . . . sleep over the garage?

C Highlight the following words and phrases in the passage – ¶ shows the paragraph. Try to work out their meanings from the context. Match them to the definitions below.

¶ 3 reproduce   trainee   apprentice   ¶ C daring   foolhardy   boundaries   ribbed   snap
¶ 8 bulk   bungalow   ¶ D chores   a baker's dozen
                                            ¶ E clutter   odd

brave   have children   house with one storey   household jobs   learning a skilled trade   limits
majority   mess   not-yet-qualified   photo   reckless   strange   teased   13   1, 3, 5, 7, etc.

D Discuss these questions:

● Would you like to be a member of the Turner family? Why/Why not?
● Which would you prefer: a large nuclear family like the Turners, or a large extended family with different generations living together? Why?

(9.5) A letter to the editor
Creative writing

A This is the first part of an article that appeared in a magazine which is mainly read by 18- to 25-year-olds. After you've read it, discuss these questions:

- What are your reactions to the article?
- How relevant is it to the readers of the magazine?
- What kind of people and what age groups would be interested in this kind of article?

What will you live on when you retire?

Plan now to enjoy your retirement . . .

Properly planned, retirement should give you some of the best years of your life – with money to spend and the leisure to enjoy it. A personal pension plan will give you just that.

With your own personal pension plan you can retire with a pension for life, a substantial capital sum, and the opportunity to turn your dreams into reality!

It's your future. The sooner you start, the greater your pension. The later you leave it, the more you will have to pay for a similar benefit. It's never too early to start a personal pension plan and even small payments will grow over the years to give you a wonderful life when you retire.

B 1 Write a **letter** for the Letters page of the magazine (about 250 words). Explain your reactions to the article and your opinion about it being published in your favourite magazine.

2 Show your completed letter to a partner. Ask for feedback on your use of paragraphs, as well as on the ideas.

"There comes a day when you suddenly realise you don't mind being herded on a bus."

(9.6) Ages
Idioms and collocations

(A) **Fill the gaps in these sentences using the phrases below.**

1 If you are .... you're not allowed to buy drinks in a pub.

2 Columbus sailed from the .... to the ....

3 In an attempt to bring .... into the firm, they're only taking on people under 25.

4 She used go out with Terry — he's an .... of hers but she hasn't seen him ....

5 If you're a .... to the firm and you don't know the ropes, you can ask one of the .... for advice.

6 We are .... and whenever we meet we reminisce about ....

7 The Great Lakes in America are .... not saltwater lakes.

8 He didn't enjoy his work, so he decided to make a .... by applying for a new job.

9 I prefer paintings by the .... to modern paintings.

10 People in Britain .... at 18, when they are officially 'adults'.

11 You can't catch a cold from getting wet — that's an .... However, plenty of .... can keep you healthy.

12 Grandad's ideas are terribly out of date — he still seems to think he's living in the .... not the .... My grandma, I'm happy to say, is still .... and she always says 'You're only ....'

come of age	for ages	space age	Stone Age	under age
fresh air	fresh start	freshwater	new blood	New World	newcomer
old flame	old friend	old hand	old master	old times	old wives' tale	Old World
as old as you feel	young at heart		

(B) **Fill each gap with one word that collocates with the word before or after it:**

THE TOMB OF THE UNKNOWN FRIEND

I saw somebody on the street yesterday that I almost knew very well. It was a man with a kind and interesting ₁ .... Too bad we had never met ₂ .... We might have been very close ₃ .... if only we had met. When I saw him I almost ₄ .... like stopping and suggesting that we have a drink and talk about ₅ .... times, mutual friends and ₆ .... : Whatever happened to so and so? and do you ₇ .... the night when we . . . ?

The only thing missing was that we had shared no old ₈ .... together to talk about because you have to meet somebody before you can do that.

The man walked by me without any recognizing ₉ .... My face wore the same mask, but ₁₀ .... I felt as if I almost knew him. It was really a ₁₁ .... that the only thing that separated us from being good friends was the stupid fact that we had never met.

We both disappeared in ₁₂ .... directions that swallowed any possibility of friendship.

from The Tokyo-Montana Express by Richard Brautigan

Ten

Utopia?

(10.1) **An ideal home?**
Vocabulary and Listening

👥 Ⓐ 1 Look at the photos and discuss what it would be like to live in each of the places shown. Write down ten words that come into your mind when you think about apartments, houses, towns and cities.

👥👥 2 Find out where each of your partners lives. First ask them to describe their bedroom . . . then the rooms adjoining it . . . then the building . . . then the street . . . and finally the district they live in.

During your discussion **WRITE DOWN** any useful new words you come across and note down any questions about vocabulary that you want to ask your teacher later. If you have any difficulties with vocabulary, ask your partners or consult a dictionary.

📼 Ⓑ 1 You'll hear six people talking about their present homes (in Britain) and where they'd like to live. Match the name of the speakers to the points they make.

Catherine	American houses have screen doors to keep the flies out.
Melinda	American houses take up more land than British houses.
Blain	My home isn't in the country, but it seems like it.
Kate	My house is very isolated.
Richard	My ideal home would be an old house in the country.
Karen	My ideal home would have a large living room, with a bed.

👥👥 2 Find out how your partners reacted to what each speaker said and the ideas they expressed. Then find out:

- why your partners like their present home
- what the differences are between homes in their country and Britain
- what their ideal living room would contain
- about the advantages and drawbacks of living alone

(10.2) The perfect society?
Reading and Listening

(A) 1 Read this article and MAKE NOTES on what you think are the most desirable and least desirable features of Aldous Huxley's Pala (GOOD and BAD POINTS).

2 Compare your notes. Do you agree which features are good and bad? Which is the best feature? Which is the worst feature?

Island . . .

the book that spelled out the ingredients for Utopia

1 **LONG BEFORE JOGGING** in Central Park became the fashion, intellectuals on the tropical island of Pala used to put in a couple of hours hard digging every day. They weren't obliged to. But the Palanese were very advanced in matters of health: they didn't separate minds from bodies, venerating brains at the expense of the whole human organism.

2 In economic matters too, Palanese thinking was very advanced. Export crops were discouraged: the islanders were fed first. Money was wasted neither on status symbols nor on weapons. The government bought no armaments: there was no army.

3 Where was this utopia? Only, unfortunately, between the covers of *Island*, Aldous Huxley's final novel. In it he detailed his prescription for a sane society — especially for Third World countries short on money but rich in human resources.

4 Huxley showed how colonialism had carved out a false channel for most developing countries, draining them of their wealth and their culture. He advocated a siege economy, to stop the leakage. Pala was closed to the outside world, especially out of bounds to merchants, missionaries and media-men, the usual links between the developing world and the West.

5 Within the walls of the island fortress, radical changes were brought about. For example, wealth was shared more equally — the richest Palanese earning not more than four or five times as much as the poorest. And jobs didn't define personal worth, since the Palanese swapped jobs regularly. Being a doctor for six months and then a farmer for the rest of the year not only made a Palanese a more rounded person, but also made sure he didn't consider himself superior to people who got their hands dirty. The personal and social integration achieved were, for the Palanese, worth more than the time and money spent on making the changeover.

6 Huxley takes, one at a time, every important social ingredient that he can squeeze into a 300 page novel — schools, newspapers, politicians, religious and scientific beliefs, ideas about family life — and examines it to find its value. What, for example, is there worth saving in family life? And what is constraining about it? Huxley doesn't polarise the issue into pro-family or anti-family camps. He concocts his own variation of a family that accommodates both the closeness and security that come from a two-parent set-up as well as the variety and freedom that come from a child having several homes to choose from. Palanese society, therefore, is an amalgam of the best in every society that Huxley knows.

7 First published in 1962, *Island* had a powerful influence on the young idealists of the day. Many of the ideas were so advanced that they are only now being widely recognised — like Huxley's insistence that Western medicine and holistic health care techniques should be allies, not enemies.

8 But there is one huge snag. Pala is fiction. Huxley is the God of Pala. How are real people in real countries to shift to this paradisal willingness to live cooperatively? For instance, it might not help a real country to adopt a siege economy: who would stop the big bad unequal world outside the fortress walls from being reproduced within the walls as a small bad unequal world?

9 Huxley's answer leads him out of the political realm into the realm of spiritual values. His islanders have evolved inwardly. They have all experienced a transpersonal dimension where they are part of a universal oneness; when they return to the material world, they remain inspired by the glimpse of the ideal.

10 Dangerous waters. Perhaps to forestall critics tempted to dismiss Huxley as a dreamy 1960 mysticism-junkie, he included among his cast of characters a group of spiritual fakes, charismatic guru figures who use their followers' gullibility to gain political power and line their pockets. Huxley sets these vigorously apart from the genuinely spiritual, whose spirituality is infused matter-of-factly into their everyday lives, in everything they do — eating dinner, making love, coping with an injury. It is their constant awareness of the here and now — a phrase popularised more by *Island*, surely, than by any other book — that does the trick.

11 In Huxley's *Brave New World*, everything from muzak to mechanical sex was used to blot out consciousness and turn people into manipulable zombies. The result was a hell on earth. In *Island*, everything, including sex and drugs, is partaken of consciously to heighten individual consciousness still further. The result is Pala, Huxley's heaven on earth.

Anuradha Vittachi

B 1 You'll hear four short talks about these 'perfect societies':

Plato's *Republic* (360 BC) H.G. Wells's *A Modern Utopia* (1905)

Thomas More's *Utopia* (1516) James Hilton's *Shangri-La* (1933)

Match the features below to each 'perfect society' by writing P for Plato, M for Thomas More, W for H.G. Wells or H for James Hilton in the box beside each feature.

1 Politicians are not elected by the people.
2 There is no money.
3 Everyone lives for a long time.
4 Menial work is done by machines.
5 Menial work is done by slaves.
6 There is an army of well-educated men.
7 Nobody does any work.
8 The men can choose their occupation.
9 Only suitable people are allowed to have children.
10 Tests determine each person's future career.
11 The king is chosen by the people.
12 Children are not raised by their own parents.
13 Unsuitable babies are killed.

2 Listen to the recording again and MAKE NOTES of the Good points and Bad points of each one, in the same style you used in A.

When you attend a lecture, seminar, meeting or workshop you may need to make notes. This usually has to be done at the time, not afterwards, in case you forget the important points.

You may also need to make notes if you want to remember information that you read in a borrowed book or report. But if it's your own copy, you could use a highlighter instead.

(10.3) The best of all possible worlds
Reading and Speaking

Dear Friend,
Most of us have dreamed at one time or another of finding a place where we can be truly happy ... a Shangri-La with an ideal climate, remote from turmoil and confusion; where the air is fresh and free from pollution and the only noise we hear is that of the wind in the trees, the roar of the sea and the song of the birds — but still close enough to civilization to enjoy the benefits of a thriving, metropolitan city.

A 1 You'll hear the rest of the above letter being read aloud. Make notes on the main points and compare your notes with a partner.

2 Now read the leaflet on the next page and highlight what you consider to be the most interesting points.

3 Decide together what would be the main advantages and drawbacks of life in Nosara. What were the two most interesting points you highlighted?

"Costa Rica, sometimes called the Switzerland of Latin America, has been unscathed by the turmoil that typifies the rest of Central America. Its army was disbanded by constitutional decree in 1948, and most of the national budget goes into education and health care . . . There are four universities, and the nation boasts it has more schoolhouses than policemen. The literacy rate is above 90%, among the highest in the world, while the infant mortality rate is among the lowest . . . " The Los Angeles Times

Beach homesites for sale in beautiful Costa Rica ...

Now you can own property along the beaches of Nosara in peaceful Costa Rica for just $6,450 – only $150 down-payment, and $150 a month at absolutely no risk!

1 Imagine a home tucked away in a secluded cove or on a lush green hillside within a 10 minute walk of a broad, white sand beach caressed by gentle ocean breezes . . . a nearby river . . . year round temperature that seldom goes below 72 degrees or above 82 degrees . . . plenty of room for horses, a few cattle, ample gardens, and located in a country with one of the most stable democratic governments in the world, where the military establishment has been banned by constitutional decree, the literacy rate and health care systems are among the best in the world, and where foreigners are genuinely liked and appreciated and afforded all the legal protections of citizens.

2 Dreams don't come true by themselves. There comes a time to take action, and if you want to someday live in paradise, that time is now.

3 We have more than 3,000 acres subdivided into homesites and farms that range in size from 3 to more than 12 acres, with 25 miles of all-year roads, electricity and water systems already in operation, and an ecologically sound master plan that provides for parks and green areas.

4 Full title to the 3 acre homesites — all within a 10 minute walk of the beach — is being offered for only $150 down-payment and 42 payments of $150 a month, with NO INTEREST CHARGE! But we don't want anyone to risk buying something they're not completely sure of, so we also provide a unique guarantee: If you visit Nosara at any time within one year of signing the purchase agreement and decide for any reason that you don't want the property, WE WILL REFUND EVERY CENT YOU HAVE PAID, with no questions asked! Or if you find another site you would prefer to own, we will be pleased to work a trade and apply the money already paid toward the new site.

5 Nosara is on the beautiful Pacific West Coast just 100 miles from San José the capital city. There are already 65 homes built at the beaches of Nosara, and they range from comfortable $8,000 cabins to expansive villas of around $100,000 (construction cost averages only $25 per square foot). Hundreds of acres have been set aside for parks and wildlife refuges that abound with wild parrots and other birds, deer, pecary and other animal life. The beaches are without equal any place in the world, but remain tranquil and uncrowded.

6 Yes, you can find all the privacy you have ever dreamed of in Nosara, but there's no need to give up the amenities of the "good life". There are two luxurious hotels with a swimming pool and fine restaurants, tennis courts, horseback riding, some of the finest sportfishing in the world for marlin, sailfish, dolphin, wahoo, tuna, snapper and much more! If you crave the nightlife and shopping of a cosmopolitan city, drive to San José or fly by air service from the Nosara airport.

There's only so much time for dreaming . . .

SOL DE NOSARA
PO Box 1084 Centro Colon
San José 1007
Costa Rica

B 1 **Reread *The Castaways* on page 12.**

2 **Work as a team to design your own Utopia. Decide on these aspects:**

- the physical environment
- government
- possessions and wealth
- public and private transport
- education system
- food and drink
- work and employment
- science and technology
- family structures
- law and order

C **Write a description of your own idea of Utopia as an article for a student magazine (about 250 words).**

Articles
Grammar

A 1 Discuss the difference in meaning between these sentences:

1 *She has some grey hairs.*   *She has some grey hair.*
     She has grey hair.   *She has a grey hair.*

2 *There's a hair in my soup!*   *There's hair in my soup!*
     There's the hair – in my soup!   *There's some hair in my soup!*

3 *Ask a teacher if you have a question.*
     Ask any teacher if you have a question.
     Ask the teacher if you have a question.

4 *After leaving school he went to sea.*   *After leaving the school he went to the sea.*

5 *I'm going to buy a paper.*   *I'm going to buy some paper.*
     I'm going to buy the paper.   *I'm going to buy paper.*

B   Uncountable nouns (e.g. *furniture, money* and *advice*) can't be plural and can't be preceded by a or an. So we can say:

     I need some advice. ✓   *How much advice do you need?* ✓   *Advice is free.* ✓

But NOT:

     I need an advice. ✗   *How many advices do you need?* ✗   *Advices are free.* ✗

If we need to define an exact quantity, we have to refer to *two chairs* or *one table*, *five pounds* or *ten dollars*, or *both pieces of advice*.

Look at these pairs of words and decide which is countable (C) and which is uncountable (U). The first is done for you as an example.

advice ☑U   hint ☑C   — advices ✗   hints ✓

air ☐	breath ☐	gadget ☐	equipment ☐	poetry ☐	poem ☐
architecture ☐	plan ☐	harm ☐	injury ☐	progress ☐	exam ☐
behaviour ☐	reaction ☐	job ☐	work ☐	report ☐	news ☐
bridge ☐	engineering ☐	joke ☐	fun ☐	safety ☐	guard ☐
cash ☐	coin ☐	journey ☐	travel ☐	thunderstorm ☐	lightning ☐
clothing ☐	garment ☐	laughter ☐	smile ☐	traffic ☐	vehicle ☐
cooking ☐	kitchen ☐	luck ☐	accident ☐	tune ☐	music ☐
experiment ☐	research ☐	luggage ☐	suitcase ☐	university ☐	education ☐
fact ☐	information ☐	peace ☐	ceasefire ☐	water ☐	drop ☐
flu ☐	cough ☐	permit ☐	permission ☐	weather ☐	shower ☐

C   Some nouns may be either countable (C) or uncountable (U), depending on their meaning. Look at these examples and then write down your own examples for the nouns in the list below.

     U   *Our house is built of stone.*
        C *There's a stone in my shoe.*   *How many stones were thrown?*

     U   *She's away on business.*   *Business is improving.*
        C *The number of small businesses is increasing.*

     U   *How much fruit was sold?*
        C *An orange is a citrus fruit.*   *My favourite fruits are oranges and mangoes.*

     U   *Painting is not as easy as it looks.*
        C *What a beautiful painting!*   *I enjoy looking at paintings.*

> bone   brick   cake   cloth   crime   fish   glass   language   life
> light   metal   noise   pain   paper   plastic   pleasure   religion
> sound   space   wood

D **Find the mistakes in these sentences and correct them. One sentence contains NO errors.**

1 If there has been robbery you should call a police.
2 Her brothers were all in the bed asleep when she left the home in morning.
3 The most houses in South of England are built of the brick.
4 He's in the hospital having operation.
5 You need permission from the planning department before building a house.
6 What a wonderful news about the Henry's sister getting scholarship!
7 How many luggages are you going to take on plane?
8 I'd like some informations on holidays in USA. Can you give me an advice?
9 What magnificent view of mountains in distance!
10 He has some beautiful brown eyes and one moustache.

E **Write down what you would actually say if you were giving someone these pieces of information. The first is done for you as an example.**

1

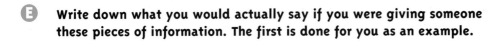

Earthquake victims still in tents one year after disaster

The victims of the earthquake are still living in tents one year after the disaster.

2

IMPORTANT
Make sure computer is disconnected from mains before lifting cover. To replace battery: use screwdriver to loosen screws A and B and lift cover. Remove old battery from socket Z and replace with fresh battery.

3

Is building like work of art or piece of engineering?
Designed for people in street and people inside?
Is building 'machine for living in' where every part has function?
Or can parts be for decoration: 'pleasure to eye'?

4

SHOPPING LIST
1 kilo potatoes
ketchup
bread
wine
food for cat –
   only eats sort
   with blue label

5

PLEASE SEND INSTRUCTION MANUAL FOR MACHINE WE ORDERED AT THE END OF THE MONTH. PRODUCTION MANAGER ALSO REQUIRES COPY OF SPECIFICATION SHEET.

F **Fill the gaps in this passage with *this*, *their*, *a*, *the*, or Ø (i.e. no article).**

60% of families in ____ UK own ____ own homes after borrowing money (known as ____ mortgage) from ____ building society or bank. They have to make ____ monthly repayments of ____ total sum (plus interest) for 20–25 years. People can usually borrow ____ sum equivalent to three times ____ annual salary, but need to put down ____ cash deposit of 10% of ____ purchase price. ____ people in Britain tend to move ____ house several times in ____ lives. ____ typical pattern is for ____ young couple to start as 'first-time buyers' in ____ small flat or house, then move to ____ larger house when they have ____ family and, when ____ children have left ____ home, to move into ____ smaller house or bungalow. Usually they move into ____ other people's houses or into ____ new home that has been built on ____ new estate by ____ builder. Families in ____ lower income groups are more likely to live in ____ rented accommodation, for example in ____ council house or flat.

Moving home can be ____ stressful experience, only slightly less traumatic than bereavement or divorce. Often ____ buyer and seller of ____ house are part of ____ 'chain', where ____ sale of one house depends on ____ whole series of strangers doing ____ same thing at ____ same time. If one deal falls through at ____ last moment, ____ whole chain breaks down and no one is able to move.

Describing a place
Speaking and Creative writing

A **You'll hear a description of these cities:**

Rome   New York   Amsterdam   Austin, Texas

1 Before you listen, find out what your partner already knows about each city.

2 Listen to the recording. MAKE NOTES on what each speaker likes about each place.

3 Compare your notes. Discuss which of the places sounded most attractive to you, and why.

B **Read this description of another city and fill each gap with one suitable ADJECTIVE:**

CAMBRIDGE – ACADEMIC TRANQUILLITY OR INDUSTRIAL PROGRESS?

Despite the phenomenal success of the IT industry in Cambridge, its many visitors regard the city as far from ₁ _____ . It is still best known as a historic town, home to one of Europe's ₂ _____ universities. Apart from the lively market square and one or two ₃ _____ avenues, the centre is a maze of narrow streets, contrasting with the ₄ _____ university buildings. Perhaps the most ₅ _____ view of Cambridge is the area called the 'backs'. In summer, the view there is of perfect tranquillity: the ancient buildings, sparkling river, cows grazing and students, preferring the grass of the ₆ _____ meadows to their studies.

But life wasn't always a rural idyll in Cambridge. Tourists today love the quaint cottages – they aren't looking for the ₇ _____ edifices of newer cities – but these tiny cottages once housed up to thirteen people. And the 'backs' did not not become Cambridge's ₈ _____ tourist attraction until the sanitation system arrived in the mid nineteenth century. Before that, the Cam was ₉ _____ , little more than an open sewer. Modern hygiene took even longer to penetrate the university: in the 1920s, baths were thought unnecessary, as students were only there for ten weeks at a time!

Today, pollution comes from different sources. New industry has brought more traffic, which has meant ₁₀ _____ multi-lane highways replacing the winding lanes to outlying villages. But because public transport from these villages is ₁₁ _____ , congestion is nevertheless a serious problem. (Ironically, the demise of the rural railway network has left the tracks of most village railway stations ₁₂ _____ . Trains to London are ₁₃ _____ , but this is no consolation to the local commuter.)

So Cambridge now faces a dilemma: can the city grow and still keep a hold on its charm? Cambridge is not a museum, and standing still is not an option. But has the 'city of knowledge' been too clever for its own good?

C 1 Discuss how you would answer these questions about YOUR OWN CITY, TOWN or VILLAGE (or the district you live in if you live in a very large city).

Try to imagine what it might seem like to a stranger. If you're very familiar with a place it's hard not to assume that 'it's obvious what it's like' — so you may have to try to distance yourself.

First impressions	Imagine you're returning there after being away — as you arrive there, what strikes you about the place? What kind of atmosphere is there? What is special about the place?
Basic facts	How big is it and where is it? (population of metropolitan area, distance from other cities, distance from coast, etc.)
Districts	What are the different areas and what are they like? (old town, commercial areas, industrial zones, shopping centre, residential districts, suburbs, slums and shanty towns, etc.)
Buildings	What is the style of the architecture? Where do people live? (public and commercial buildings, blocks of flats, etc.)
Open spaces	Where do people gather together out of doors? (squares, parks, open-air cafés, etc.) When is the weather suitable for this?
Roads and streets	What kinds of roads are characteristic of the place? (main thoroughfares, back streets, avenues, boulevards, alleyways, etc.)
Transport	How do people get about within the city and how do they travel in and out? (amount of traffic, public transport, commuter travel, rail connections, airport, etc.)
Entertainment	What do people do in their leisure time? (sports, cinemas, theatre, music, museums and galleries, nightclubs, restaurants, bars and cafés, etc.)
Employment	How do people earn their living? (manufacturing, commerce, public sector, etc.) What is the unemployment situation?
Education	What facilities are there for secondary and tertiary education? (schools, colleges, university, evening classes, etc.)
Visitors	What are the sights that tourists visit? What might a newcomer from abroad find strange or difficult about living there?
YOU	How do you fit into all this? What do you like about the place? What do you dislike about it?

2 Find someone from another group who does NOT know the place you've been discussing as well as you do. Find out about each other's town, city, village or district.

D Imagine that you've received this fax from a group of students at a high school in Austin, Texas. Write a letter in reply (about 250 words).

Our teacher has offered to arrange a two-week study visit for our class to your country — and your city is on our list of possible places to go to. We have read a brochure about the city and it sounds nice, but what is it _really_ like? What do you think we would enjoy there? Why would it be a good place for us to stay, bearing in mind that we are all 18-19 years old and none of us have traveled overseas before?

When you have a lot to say, and it all seems relevant, it's hard to decide what to omit. Thinking about your readers and what might interest them (rather than what interests you) can help you to decide what to write.

Synonyms and opposites – 3
Word study

(A) 1 Arrange the adjectives in green into one of these four categories:

VERY LARGE ← large   small → very small

colossal   big   little   miniature

big   colossal   little   miniature   extensive   gigantic
immense   insignificant   majestic   minuscule   minute
roomy   spacious   tiny   tremendous   vast   wide

2 Use a dictionary to check the pronunciation of any you're not sure about.

3 Decide which adjective you'd use to describe each of the following:

a city   a mountain   a lake   a fortune   a crowd   a hotel room   a ballroom   a palace
a luxury car   a car park   a toy gun   a mistake   an avenue   a city square

(B) Now do the same with the adjectives in green below:

1 very pleasant ← pleasant   unpleasant → very unpleasant

agreeable   annoying   appalling   atrocious   awful   charming   delicious   delightful   disgusting
dreadful   frightful   picturesque   spectacular   splendid   wonderful

a city   a person   a cocktail   a village   a beach   a flight   a holiday   a meal   a view

2 very beautiful ← beautiful   ugly → very ugly

attractive   enchanting   good-looking   glamorous
graceful   grotesque   handsome   hideous   lovely
plain   pretty   unpleasant

a city   James Dean   Marilyn Monroe   Frankenstein's monster
Sylvester Stallone   a cathedral   a young child   a palace
a friend's fiancée   a friend's husband

3 very old ← old   new → very new

all the rage   ancient   dilapidated   disused   fresh   historical   the latest   obsolete   run-down
traditional   ultra-modern   unfashionable   up-to-date   worn-out

a city   a game   a dress   a carpet   an airport   a hairstyle   a church   a flat   an idea

4 very safe ← safe   dangerous → very dangerous

deadly   guarded   fatal   harmful   harmless   hazardous   insecure   precarious   protected   reliable
risky   secure   unsafe   vulnerable

a city   a castle   a friend   a method   a pile of crockery   a job   a drug   an apartment block
a flight in an airliner   a flight in a hot-air balloon   New York   the district you live in

5 very far ← far   near → very near

accessible   a long way away   close   convenient   distant   faraway   handy   isolated   nearby
next door   opposite   out-of-the-way   remote

a city   a grocer's shop   a friend's flat   a village   Australia   your flat   a café

6 very quiet ← quiet   noisy → very noisy

calm   deafening   ear-splitting   loud   peaceful   restful   silent   sleepy   unobtrusive

a street   a park   a hotel room   wallpaper   a tie   an explosion   a party   the sea

(C) 1 Note down the POSITIVE and NEGATIVE aspects of the place you live in.

2 Write an article about the positive aspects and the negative aspects of your own town, city
or village (about 250 words).

10.7 *Hard, soft, difficult* and *easy*
Idioms and collocations

Fill the gaps in these sentences with hard, soft, difficult or easy.

1   A _____-hearted interviewer can give candidates a very _____ time and make life _____ for them.

2   Computer equipment is known as _____ware and the programs are known as _____ware.

3   A printout from a computer provides the user with a _____ copy.

4   A computer can save data on a floppy disk but much more can be stored on a _____ disk.

5   This new fabric is so _____-wearing that it will last a lifetime!

6   You can buy tools and screws and nails at a _____ware store.

7   I realise that he makes people feel un_____ when he's being _____, but deep down he's quite _____-hearted and _____-going — I must say I do have a _____ spot for him.

8   It's sometimes _____ to understand her because she's rather _____-spoken.

9   _____ drugs like heroin are more dangerous than so-called _____ drugs like marijuana.

10 We've been too _____ on customers who don't settle their accounts on time. We should start to take a _____ line.

11 These aren't guidelines, they are _____-and-fast rules.

12 A paperback is often half the price of a _____back.

13 Take it _____! There's no need to get so worried just because you're _____ up — it's payday tomorrow.

14 I'm very thirsty, so I'd prefer a _____ drink — is there any lemonade?

15 'When would you like to come?' 'I don't mind — I'm _____.'

16 Some salespeople favour aggressive _____ sell techniques, while others prefer gentle persuasion and go for the _____ sell.

17 Dollars and Swiss Francs (unlike the Zambian kwacha or the Albanian New Lek) are _____ currencies.

18 After a hard day at the office, I like to take it _____.

ON THE OTHER HAND IF THE WORLD WERE PERFECT WHERE WOULD I FIT IN?

© 1994 CHARLES BARSOTTI

Eleven

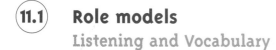

Fame and fortune

Role models

Listening and Vocabulary

A You'll hear three people talking about people they admire. Note down the names of the people and the MAIN reason they admire them.

Afterwards, compare your notes with a partner.

B Fill each gap in these paragraphs with a suitable word or phrase from the list below. In many cases there's more than one way to fill the gap.

1   Marie Sklodowska Curie was _____ two Nobel Prizes: she _____ the 1903 physics prize with her husband Pierre and won the 1911 chemistry prize in her own _____ . Her most _____ achievement was her work on radioactivity.

2   Andy Grove, who was born in Hungary, is the chief executive of Intel Corporation. He's one of the world's lesser-known _____ , even though his company is twice as big and twice as _____ as Microsoft. He tends to avoid _____ and keeps a fairly low _____ , though within the business community he is universally _____ .

3   The Sultan of Brunei is the world's richest man. He _____ Brunei, a tropical country the size of Belgium, on the coast of Borneo. His 300,000 _____ enjoy one of the world's highest _____ of living, thanks to Brunei's oil and gas _____ (enough for another 25 and 40 years, _____). The Sultan built the world's largest _____ at a cost of $450 million. He's a _____ , self-conscious man who avoids public _____ .

4   Richard Branson is a _____ British entrepreneur, who _____ Virgin Atlantic and Express airlines, Virgin Cinemas, Virgin Megastores and other businesses under the Virgin _____ name. He believes in a _____ on approach to managing his businesses. He _____ in his own TV commercials and is often in the _____ .

admired   appearances   appears   awarded   billionaires   brand   charismatic   executive
hands-on   headlines   outstanding   palace   profile   profitable   publicity   reserves
respected   respectfully   respectively   right   rules   runs   shared   shy   standards   subjects

C Ask your partners:

• which living woman and which living man they most admire
• which figure from the past (or historical figure) they most admire

Ask them to explain WHY the people are famous and WHY they admire them. Of all the people mentioned by your partners, which ONE do you admire most of all, and why?

(11.2) Emphasising the right syllable
Pronunciation

(A) 1 On which syllable is the main stress placed in each of these words?

síllable /ˈsɪləbl/   pronóunce /prəˈnaʊns/   pronunciátion /prənʌnsiˈeɪʃən/

quálified /ˈkwɒlɪfaɪd/   qualificátion /ˌkwɒlɪfɪˈkeɪʃən/

2 Take it in turns to say each of these words aloud and mark the main stress in each one.

acádemy academic   lecture lecturer
art artistic   literature literary
biology biological   maths mathematics mathematical
botany botanical   physics physical
chemist chemistry chemical   politics political
consult consultation   second secondary
economics economical economy secretary secretarial
educate educational   society sociology
examine examination   special specialise specialisation speciality
geography geographical   statistics statistical
grammar grammatical   zoology zoological
history historical

(B) Take it in turns to read each of these sentences aloud, paying attention to the word stresses.

1 She's stúdying pólitics at univérsity and hópes to becóme a politícian.
  /ʃiːz ˈstʌdijɪŋ ˈpɒlɪtɪks ət ˌjuːnɪˈvɜːsɪti ənd ˈhəʊps tə bɪˈkʌm ə ˈpɒlɪtˈɪʃən/

2 Maths is an interesting subject but I don't want to be subjected to a long lecture about it, thank you very much!

3 What a lovely present! I was present when they presented her with the award.

4 Wait a minute — I just need to make a minute adjustment to this machine.

5 When are you permitted to use the emergency exit?

6 You need a special permit to use this entrance.

7 I've read the contents of the book and now I feel quite content.

8 After our dessert, we watched a film about some soldiers who deserted and escaped into the desert and joined a group of rebels.

9 When a metal object cools down it contracts.

10 This contract is invalid because it hasn't been signed.

11 The people rebelled because they objected to the government's policies.

12 I don't normally mind being insulted — but I do when such dreadful insults are used.

(C) You'll hear 24 short clips. Choose the phrase below that shows the IMPLICATION of each statement. Write the number or numbers beside each phrase.

1 to 7: 'Terry had a stomach ache because the plums he ate were unripe.'
  not the *apples* ☐1 ☐3   not a *headache* ☐   not *overripe* ☐
  not *Sally* ☐2   it *is* really true ☐   not the ones *you* ate ☐

8 to 12: 'I need more time if I'm going to take up a new sport.'
  not *money* ☐ ☐   not *less* time ☐
  not a new *hobby* ☐   not if *you* are going to ☐

13 to 18: 'Most people like Helen because she has a friendly personality.'
  not an *unfriendly* one ☐ ☐   not *everyone* ☐
  they don't like *another* person ☐ ☐   not a friendly *smile* ☐

19 to 24: 'Ted has a cough because he smokes thirty cigarettes a day.'
  not a *sore throat* ☐ ☐   not *Helen* ☐   not *thirteen* ☐
  not *cigars* ☐   not per *week* ☐

Charlie Chaplin
Reading

A 1 Read the first paragraph of this magazine article. Then write down FOUR questions that you would like to find the answers to in the rest of the article.

Remarkable Charlie

ALEXANDER WALKER looks at his life and times

HE WAS BORN in the slums of south London. He wore his mother's old red tights cut down for ankle socks. He was sent to a workhouse when she was temporarily sent to the madhouse. Dickens might have created Charlie Chaplin's childhood. But only Charlie Chaplin could have created the great comic character of "The Tramp", whose ragged dignity, subversive mischievousness, hard-grained resilience and soft-hearted sentimentality gave his creator the dimensions of an immortal.

1 _____   3 _____

2 _____   4 _____

2 Read the continuation of the article and find out if your questions are answered.

2 Other countries – France, Italy, Spain, even Japan and Korea – show more surpassing love (and profit) where Chaplin is concerned than the land of his birth. It's not just that Chaplin quit Britain for good in 1913 when he journeyed to America with the Fred Karno vaudeville troupe to perform his mime, juggling and comedy acts on the stage where Mack Sennett's talent scouts recruited him for the Hollywood slapstick king.

3 Sad to say, many English filmgoers between the wars thought Chaplin's Tramp a bit, well, "vulgar". Certainly the middle-class filmgoers did: the working-class audiences were warmer towards a character who defied authority, using his wicked little cane to trip it up, or aiming a well-placed kick on its broad backside with the flat of his down-at-heel boot. All the same, Chaplin's comic persona didn't seem all that English or even working class. English tramps didn't sport tiny moustaches, baggy pants or tail coats: European dictators, Italian waiters and American *maître d*'s wore things like that. Then again, the Tramp's ever-roving eye for a pretty girl had a promiscuousness about it that was considered, well, not quite nice by English audiences – that's how foreigners behaved, wasn't it? And for over half of his screen career, Chaplin had no screen voice to confirm his British nationality.

4 Indeed, it was a headache for Chaplin when he could no longer resist the talkies and had to find "the right voice" for his Tramp. He postponed that day as long as possible: in *Modern Times* in 1936, the first film in which he was heard as a singing waiter, he made up a nonsense language which sounded like no known nationality. He later said he imagined the Tramp to be an Oxford-educated gent who'd come down in the world. But if he'd been able to speak with an Oxford accent in those early slapstick shorts, it's doubtful if he'd have achieved world fame – and the English would have been sure to find it "odd".

5 He was an immensely complex man, self-willed to a degree unusual even in the ranks of Hollywood egotists. The suddenness of his huge fame gave him the freedom – and, more importantly, the money – to be his own master. He already had the urge to explore and extend a talent he discovered in himself as he went along. "It can't be me. Is that possible? How extraordinary," is how he greeted the first sight of himself as the Tramp on the screen.

CHARLIE CHAPLIN
(*CHARLOT*)   125

But that shock set his imagination racing. Unlike Buster Keaton, Chaplin didn't work out his gags conceptually in advance. He was the kind of comic who used his physical senses to invent his art as he went along. Inanimate objects especially helped Chaplin make "contact" with himself as an artist. He turned them into other kinds of objects. Thus, a bust alarm clock in *The Pawnbroker* became a "sick" patient undergoing an appendectomy; boots were stewed in *The Gold Rush* and their soles eaten like prime plaice (the nails being removed like fish bones). This physical transformation, plus the adroitness with which he managed it again and again, are surely the secrets of Chaplin's great comedy. It may be a legacy from working alongside jugglers and acrobats on the English music-hall stage in his youth and developing something of their sensory proficiency. But Chaplin not only charged things with energy, he altered their personalities – and, in so doing, extended his knowledge of his own.

He also had a deep need to be loved – and a corresponding fear of being betrayed. The two were hard to reconcile and sometimes – as in his early marriages – the results were disastrous. Yet even this painfully-bought self-knowledge found its way into his comic creations. The Tramp never loses his faith in the flower girl who'll be waiting to walk into the sunset with him; while the other side of Chaplin, the man who's bought his cynicism dearly in the divorce courts, makes *Monsieur Verdoux*, the French wife killer, into a symbol of man's misogyny.

8   It's nice to know that life eventually gave Charlie Chaplin the stable happiness it had earlier denied him. In Oona O'Neill Chaplin, he found a partner whose stability and affection effaced the 37 years age difference between them that had seemed so ominous when the Santa Barbara registrar, who was marrying them in 1942, turned to the luminous girl of 17 who'd given notice of their wedding date and said, "And where is the young man?" – Chaplin, then 54, had prudently waited outside. As Oona herself was the child of a large family with its own turbulent centre, she was well-prepared for the battlefield that Chaplin's life became as unfounded charges of Communist sympathies engulfed them both – and, later on, she was the fulcrum of rest in the quarrels that Chaplin's act of stern fatherhood sometimes sparked off in their own large brood of talented children.

Chaplin died on Christmas Day 1977. A few months later, a couple of almost comic body-snatchers stole his coffin from the family vault and held it for ransom: the Swiss police recovered it with more efficiency than the Keystone Cops would have done. But one can't help feeling Chaplin would have regarded this macabre incident as his way of having the last laugh on a world to which he had bequeathed so many.

B   **Answer these multiple-choice questions about the article:**

1   Chaplin left Britain and went to the USA to
    A   act in movies.   C   direct movies.
    B   perform on the stage.   D   escape from his mother.

2   British audiences thought Chaplin's Tramp was
    A   heart-breaking.   C   unmistakably English in origin.
    B   very funny.   D   apparently foreign.

3   The Tramp
    A   never appeared in a talking picture.   C   appeared in one talking picture.
    B   appeared in several talking pictures. D   appeared in talking pictures but didn't speak.

4   Chaplin's comic scenes were
    A   carefully planned and scripted.   C   improvised.
    B   planned but not scripted.   D   improved.

5   When he married his last wife she was
    A   17.   C   37.
    B   42.   D   54.

6   After their wedding Chaplin's professional and family life was
    A   tranquil.   C   turbulent.
    B   uneventful.   D   disappointing.

C   **Highlight the following words and phrases in the passage. Try to work out their meanings from the context. Match them to the definitions below.**

¶ 1   subversive   resilience
¶ 4   headache   postponed
¶ 6   gags   inanimate   bust   adroitness   charged
¶ 7   corresponding   reconcile   cynicism   misogyny
¶ 8   stable   effaced   ominous   prudently   turbulent   unfounded charges
¶ 9   macabre   bequeathed

ability to recover from setbacks   allegations   broken   erased   filled   harmonise and resolve
hatred of women   horrifying   lack of trust   leave after one's death   matching   not living
problem   put off   secure   skill   threatening   undermining authority   violent   visual jokes   wisely

D Discuss these questions about the article:

- What were Chaplin's most admirable qualities — and what were his less admirable attributes?
- What were his greatest achievements?
- What brought him the greatest disappointment and greatest happiness?
- Why was he (and is he still) so famous and well-loved? How can you account for his success?
- What does the image of the Tramp signify for us today?

E 1 Select information from the article for your own 250-word article on 'The life and times of Charlie Chaplin' — and decide which you would omit. MAKE NOTES.

2 Compare your notes and justify your own decisions.

11.4 ## Style, tone and content
Effective writing

A Look at this chart of people who died before their time. Discuss:

- what each person achieved during their life
- if their personalities matched the supposed characteristics of their star signs (see pages 54–5)
- what they might have achieved if they'd lived longer

	born	star sign	died	age
Wolfgang Amadeus Mozart	1756	Aquarius	1791	35
Franz Schubert	1797	Aquarius	1828	31
Vincent Van Gogh	1853	Aries	1890	37
Rudolph Valentino	1895	Taurus	1926	31
John F. Kennedy	1917	Gemini	1963	46
Marilyn Monroe	1926	Gemini	1962	36
Martin Luther King Jr.	1929	Sagittarius	1968	39
James Dean	1931	Aquarius	1955	24
Elvis Presley	1935	Capricorn	1977	42
Buddy Holly	1936	Virgo	1959	22
John Lennon	1940	Libra	1980	40
Princess Diana	1961	Cancer	1997	36

B One of you should look at Activity 14, the other at 37, where you will find out about Marilyn Monroe and James Dean.

Share the information and ideas with each other, using some of these expressions:

> As you probably know . . .   One thing I didn't realise . . .
> Did you know that . . . ?   It's hard to believe that . . .
> If he/she were still alive . . .   It's tragic/amazing to think that . . .

C 1 Look at the opening paragraphs opposite from magazine articles, based on the information given in Activity 37. Discuss what features of each paragraph you prefer and why. Look at:

- the STYLE of writing and the REGISTER
- the writer's attitude as shown in the TONE of the article
- the CONTENT or information that is given

2 Highlight the phrases or pieces of information that you think are most effective in each paragraph.

James Dean was born on 8 February 1931 and died in a car crash on 30 September 1955 at the age of 24. For his generation he symbolised the torment and rebellion of the teenager. Even today his moody good looks, vulnerable eyes and that unmistakable glance from beneath his hair strike a chord with young people everywhere. His charismatic screen performances are all that we know of him. He died so young that he remains a mystery: the man, the actor and the characters he played are all the same to us.

James Dean was a young screen actor who was killed in a car crash at the age of 24. He made three films: *East of Eden, Rebel Without A Cause* and *Giant,* of which only the first had been released before his death. Young people of his generation admired his good looks and identified with his charismatic screen performances. The parts he played matched the image of the man: moody, rebellious and angry – yet vulnerable, arousing our protective instincts and perhaps making us want to defend him and comfort him.

Go into any poster shop in the world and there are two people whose images you will find there: one is Marilyn Monroe, the other is James Dean – a young man who had made only three films when he died at the age of 24 and who scarcely had time to make his mark on the world. So how can we explain the reasons for his continued appeal? Is it his moody good looks and his vulnerable eyes? Or is it that he symbolises for every generation the rebellious feelings and torment of being young, awakening a protective instinct in his fans? His screen performances were undoubtedly charismatic, but it is his image that lives on, not his acting.

What an amazing person James Dean was! Do you realise that he was only 24 when he died? And that was way back in 1955 – long, long before his present-day fans were born. And lots of them haven't even seen any of his films, believe it or not! I guess the impact he made (and, you know, he only appeared in three movies) was so great because he kind of epitomised the misunderstood teenager. It's no coincidence that *Rebel Without a Cause* is his best-known role because that's the image he's best remembered for today. But what if he'd lived longer.

1 Make notes for a similar opening paragraph for a magazine **article** (about 100 words) about Marilyn Monroe – decide what information from Activity 14 you will include.

2 Write a first draft, using the stylistic features that you thought were most effective in C.

3 Show your completed draft to your partners and ask for their comments and criticisms. Rewrite your paragraph, incorporating any improvements that have been suggested.

(11.5) Sharing opinions
Speaking, Listening and Reading

1 You'll hear some people giving their opinions. Imagine that they're friends of yours. How would you reply to each person, using the expressions below?

That's true, because . . . Sure, because . . . Right! Especially when . . . That's right! For example when . . .	**I agree + reason**
I'm not sure that I agree, because . . . With all due respect, I'd say that . . . I see what you mean, but . . . I see what you're getting at, but . . . There's a lot in what you say, but . . . I think it all depends on . . .	**I don't agree** or **I partly agree** + reason
Why? What makes you say that? Why do you think that? Do you really think so? Are you quite sure about that?	**Encouraging someone to justify their views**

2 Listen to the recording again and note down the phrase that each person used to INTRODUCE his or her opinion – none of them said simply: *'I think that . . .'*

B You'll hear ten short conversations, in which the second speaker reacts to the first one's opinion. Listen carefully to the tone of voice used. Decide whether the second person agrees with the first one or not – if he or she agrees put a tick ✓, if he or she disagrees put a cross ✕.

1		3		5		7		9	
2		4		6		8		10	

C Find out your partner's views on SOME of these topics – make sure he or she justifies their views and then give your own opinion (and justify it).

- Is it better to save money for a rainy day or spend it all?
- Should millionaires keep their money or donate it to charity?
- Should family sizes be restricted, or should everyone have as many children as they want?
- Should murderers and terrorists be put in prison for life or executed?
- Should cars be banned from driving in city centres or should there be no restrictions?
- Should shops be open 24-hours a day 7 days a week?
- Should every home have a computer?
- Are people less polite and considerate than they used to be?
- Were the good old days better than the present day?
- What is the best way to prevent crime?
- Is money the root of all evil, or is it a blessing?

D 1 Find out your partner's views on lotteries and gambling.

2 Decide where paragraphs **A** to **F** opposite fit in the gaps in this article shown with red arrows. There's one extra paragraph which doesn't fit anywhere.

Record-breaking lottery winner faces onslaught from estranged wife and family

1 THE unveiling of the National Lottery's biggest ever winners descended to farce yesterday amid personal acrimony and widespread uneasiness over the size of the £22.5 million jackpot.

2 ➧

3 Kim Gardiner, who married the lottery's latest multi-millionaire in November 1991, said: "I'm after half his cash."

4 ➧

5 Flanked by National Lottery public relations staff, Mr Gardiner, aged 33, said he was "very sad" at the remarks made by his adoptive mother. He added: "If you went to Hastings and spoke to my real friends you would get a completely different story."

6 ➧

7 He has since changed his name and now lives in the south of England.

8 ➧

9 But the news prompted renewed calls for limits on lottery prizes.

Labour urged the Government to consider capping payouts at £5 million, arguing that the £22.5 million was unlikely to deliver an "extra slice of happiness" for the winner.

"It would be better if there is a very large jackpot to spread the benefits among the runners-up," Chris Smith, the shadow heritage spokesman, said.

The Methodist Church said huge jackpots fuelled "negative feelings about one person receiving such a large sum."

A spokesman for Oflot, which regulates the lottery, said capping jackpots would make the game less popular.

Mr Gardiner's third wife, from whom he is estranged, could well profit from the windfall – but not to the tune she is demanding. Lawyers last night said that a more realistic target would be about £1 million.

Lawrence Donegan and Andrew Culf

A
Double-glazing salesman Mark Gardiner, of Hastings, East Sussex, who shares the jackpot with his business partner Paul Maddison, had hardly finished a glass of celebratory champagne when he was confronted with reports that his estranged wife planned to sue.

B
The previous biggest winner, a Blackburn factory worker, also suffered from a series of personal problems and unwanted media coverage. .

C
The winner's woes were compounded by remarks by his adoptive mother, 63-year-old Irene Cressweil, who said: "I hope he drinks himself to death with his money."

D
Camelot is the company that operates the National Lottery in Britain.

E
But Camelot ruled out revising its prize structure, saying that weeks where prize money rolled over as a result of no one winning generated additional ticket sales and more cash for the lottery's good causes.

F
The publicity is embarrassing for lottery operators Camelot, who wanted to avoid a repeat of last year's event and might have hoped to capitalise on such a huge jackpot.

1 Imagine that a friend of yours has won the lottery — not the jackpot, but £50,000. Write a letter congratulating your friend, giving him or her some advice on what to do with the money (about 250 words).

2 Look at your partner's letter. What would your reactions be if you, as the lottery winner, received this letter?

(11.6) Household names
Listening and Creative writing

Anita Roddick

1 Before you listen to the interview, discuss these questions:
- What do you already know about The Body Shop? Does it have shops in your country?
- What kind of products does it sell? What kind of image does it have?

2 You'll hear an interview with Anita Roddick, who founded and runs The Body Shop. Tick (✓) the points that she makes, and put a cross (✗) beside the things that are not mentioned or which are untrue.

1 Before founding The Body Shop, she . . .
   a taught French and history
   b travelled around the world
   c worked for the United Nations
   d lived with people in the Third World

2 The Body Shop and its products have been successful because . . .
   a women feel at home in the shops
   b customers aren't pressurised to buy
   c they don't celebrate youth and passivity
   d they celebrate women and social justice
   e political and social issues are publicised
   f they help women to look younger
   g of the thoughtfulness behind the scenes
   h the products are good value

3 She enjoys . . .
   a the wide variety of things she does
   b staying in the best hotels
   c learning as she travels around the world
   d being in uncomfortable situations

4 She doesn't enjoy . . .
   a being responsible for so many people
   b not having enough time for herself
   c dealing with hierarchy
   d talking about emotions and feelings at work

5 She relaxes by . . .
   a spending time with her granddaughter
   b going to the cinema and the theatre
   c going for long walks
   d eating out with people she loves

6 She is proud of . . .
   a challenging the beauty industry
   b redefining the idea of beauty
   c helping people in the Third World
   d making business kinder and gentler

B 1 Make a list of people who are 'household names' in YOUR COUNTRY – famous (living) people that most people in your country have heard of.
Try to include a woman and a man in each category. How would you explain to a foreign visitor WHY each person is famous?

1 sportsman

1 sportswoman

2 singers or entertainers

2 business people

2 politicians

2 actors or film stars

2 writers

2 Take it in turns to role-play a conversation between a local person and a foreign visitor who wants to know about the people in your list.

C 1 Make notes on THREE of the people you discussed in **B** in preparation for writing about their lives and achievements. (You may need to gather more information before you begin writing.)

Look at this example first:

> Anita Roddick, the woman who founded The Body shop and built it up into one of Britain's best-known chains, was born in 1942. The shops sell shampoos, skin cream, perfumes and other beauty products, all of which are made from natural ingredients such as plants and natural oils. Anita Roddick spends much of the year travelling round the world searching for new products to sell. Her first shop, which opened in 1976, was a great success and since then 1,500 more branches of The Body shop have opened in 46 countries, with one in most High Streets in Britain.

2 Write three paragraphs (about 80 words each) for a guidebook for foreign visitors to your country. Your target readers know nothing about the people, but they want to know who each person is when they hear them mentioned on TV, or read about them in the press.

3 Show your completed work to a partner and ask for feedback.

If you're writing about your country, it may be best to assume that foreigners know very little – but hopefully that they are keen to learn more about your people and their way of life. This may involve stating the obvious and giving information that your fellow citizens know.

11.7 *For* and *on*
Idioms and collocations

A **Fill the gaps with the phrases below.**

1 There are some lovely desserts _____ but I won't have anything because I'm _____ .

2 He claimed it wasn't his fault and that he hadn't done it _____ .

3 I should like to thank you _____ the whole department.

4 She promised to help me _____ I returned the favour another time.

5 We haven't been out together _____ . Would you like to come _____ with us on Sunday?

6 It was long drive so we stopped _____ to have a meal.

7 How much does a worker earn _____ in your country?

8 Did you see the news _____ last night?

9 Trains leave every hour _____ .

10 It takes much longer to get there _____ than by bus.

11 No, I don't dislike Chaplin at all: _____ , I admire him greatly.

12 We've done a lot of this recently, so let's do something different _____ .

> on a diet   on average   on behalf of   on condition that   on foot   on purpose
> on television   on the contrary   on the hour   on the menu   on the way
> for a change   for a long time   for a walk

B **Rewrite each sentence, replacing the words in red with a suitable form of the word in green on the right and adding FOR or ON.**

1 She's well-known because she broke the world record.   famous

   She's famous for breaking the world record.

2 We admire her because of her intelligence.   account

3 Are you trying to find your hat? When did you wear it last?   search   have

4 I am sorry that I was rude to you.   apologise

5 I don't want you to sympathise with me.   feel sorry

6 The price they charge varies according to the quantity you order.   depend

7 He stopped to look in a shop window and then continued walking.   walk

8 She knows all about cars.   an expert

9 I told the visitor you'd be late but she was determined to wait.   insist

10 To hear the next track you should make the tape go forward.   wind

11 It was a tall story but he was so gullible that he believed it.   fall

12 I used to hate that song but then it became more pleasant to me.   grow

13 You can't trust him, but you can trust me.   rely   count

14 Would you like to give me your opinion of my work?   comment

Twelve

Education and science

(12.1) Science and technology
Listening and Vocabulary

A 1 You'll hear an interview with Wendy Fielder, a research scientist who works in the field of microbiology. Listen to what she says and complete each sentence below with an appropriate word or short phrase.

Wendy Fielder

Scientists in different places have to ₁ _____ .

Computers have ₂ _____ science.

She gets excited when she looks down a microscope and sees ₃ _____ .

A bacteria is only visible through a microscope if it is ₄ _____ .

She doesn't get lonely because she works in a(n) ₅ _____ and her job includes ₆ _____ .

Research is funded less by governments because of ₇ _____ .

In the future, thanks to microbiology, everyone will be ₈ _____ .

Pupils at school would learn more if they did more ₉ _____ .

She would love to work on a project which aims to use tissue culture to replace ₁₀ _____ .

2 Find out from your partners:

- which were/are their favourite science subjects at school
- if both girls and boys are encouraged to become scientists or engineers in their country
- what technical subjects are taught at schools in their country

B   Work out the answers to these questions:

1   Look at these things which are used for fixing things together – what are they called?

2   What are these controls called?

3   What are these tools called?

4   Can you think of four more tools? Write down their names.

C **Take it in turns to say what these pieces of equipment or products are used for:**

a pencil sharpener *a pencil sharpener is a device/gadget/thing you use for sharpening pencils*

a zip *a zip is a thing that's used for closing openings in clothes or bags*

a ruler a spirit level a bicycle pump a torch/flashlight a safety pin a rubber band a stapler
a corkscrew a penknife a test tube a tin opener a fuse a plug a padlock a telescope
a microscope a pair of binoculars an air conditioner hair conditioner a rubber stamp
a postage stamp a toolbox a chest of drawers a drawing pin/thumbtack a drawing board

D **You'll hear ten short spoken extracts. As you listen, note down:**

- the SUBJECT the speaker is talking about
- the TONE OF VOICE he or she is using (patronising, bored, enthusiastic, etc.)
- WHO he or she seems to be talking to (a group of students, a child, etc.)

subject	tone of voice	talking to
1 *bicycles*	*friendly, unpatronising*	*a group of adults or young people*
2		

(12.2) First day at school
Listening and Speaking

A **You'll hear two accounts of a first day at school – one from a new pupil's point of view, the other from a new teacher's point of view.**

1 **Read this extract from *Cider with Rosie* by Laurie Lee (1959) before you listen to the recording. What do you think happened on Laurie's first day?**

> The village school at that time provided all the instruction we were likely to ask for. It was a small stone barn divided by a wooden partition into two rooms – The Infants and The Big Ones. There was one teacher, and perhaps a young girl assistant. Every child in the valley crowding there remained till he was fourteen years old, then was presented to the working field or factory with nothing in his head more burdensome than a few mnemonics, a jumbled list of wars, and a dreamy image of the world's geography. It seemed enough to get by with, in any case; and it was one up on our poor old grandparents.

2 Listen to the recording. You'll hear more about Laurie's first day at the local village school. Find out if you guessed correctly.

3 Before you listen to the extract from *Decline and Fall* by Evelyn Waugh (1928), discuss what you think happened in Paul's first lesson:

> Paul Pennyfeather is an inexperienced new teacher at a private school in Wales. The bell for the first lesson has just rung. Paul and two other masters are on their way to their classes . . .

4 Listen to find out if you guessed correctly.

B 1 Discuss how your OWN experiences of your first day at a new school compare with Laurie's and Paul's.

2 Imagine that a good friend has moved to a new city and is worried about starting at a new school or college. To reassure him or her, write a letter (about 250 words) giving an account of your own first day at a new school or in a new class. (Perhaps write about your first day in THIS class.)

Education systems
Reading

A **Fill the gaps in this text with suitable words from the list below. Use a dictionary if necessary.**

A British university year is divided into three _____ . Students are known as _____ .
At the end of a university course, graduates are awarded a _____ – probably a BA
(_____), BSc (_____) or BEd (_____). After graduating, if they wish to continue at
university, _____ can take a further course or do _____ and write a _____ in the
hope of becoming an MA (_____) or a PhD (_____).
In America, first-year students are known as _____ and second-year students are called
_____ . Their year is divided into two _____ . A university is often called a _____ .

> Bachelor of Arts   Bachelor of Education   Bachelor of Science   college   degree   dissertation
> Doctor of Philosophy   freshmen   Master of Arts   postgraduates   research   semesters
> sophomores   terms   thesis   undergraduates

B **Look at this article. In which paragraphs (A–N) are the following questions answered? Scan the text to find the answers and then write the paragraph letter beside the question.**

1 What does the acronym 'Cat' stand for? ☐ L
2 What does the acronym 'Sat' stand for? ☐
3 At what ages is the Cat taken? ☐
4 At what age do students take the Sat? ☐
5 Do all American students take the same school-leaving exam? ☐
6 How are pupils in the USA evaluated by their teachers? ☐
7 How are Scan-Tron tests completed and marked? ☐
8 How can American parents influence the school system? ☐
9 How many students take the Sat? ☐
10 What are the three national tests that American pupils take? ☐
11 What is the attitude of American people to education? ☐

12 What is the attitude of people in Britain to multiple-choice questions? ☐
13 What proportion of American students go to college? ☐
14 What skills does the Cat cover? ☐
15 Which answers in a multiple-choice test should you pick if you don't know the answer? ☐
16 Which pupils do less well in national tests? ☐
17 Who controls and pays for education in the USA? ☐
18 What is the main underlying principle of American education? ☐
19 Why is the relationship between pupils and teachers different in the UK and USA? ☐
20 Why is there a discrepancy between the attitude of different colleges to Sat scores? ☐

The Cat Sat on the test

School testing, like baseball, is crucial to the American way of life. Michael White in Washington offers a parent's view of the results

A NOT MANY days pass without one or other of my kids getting out a number 2 pencil in their American suburban classroom and shading in the dots of a Scan-Tron paper in the correct number 2 lead so that the computer can read it.

B And what is this Brave New World all about, you may be wondering? The answer is standardised testing, a national passion in this vast country of endless diversity.

C So a Scan-Tron paper is what you use to answer the multiple-choice questions you get in maths, science, world studies (history and geography) or whatever it happens to be. Why did denim trousers become popular in the 1850s? Because they were (a) blue; (b) durable; (c) attractive; (d) inexpensive? Shade in the correct letter (incidentally it is (b)) in this 13-year-old's comprehension test and the computer will machine-read it.

D British parents, teachers and pupils may already be fuming – or jeering – at the mention of pernicious multiple-choice techniques, let alone no. 2 pencils. But American education has its own ends: a system democratically designed to educate the many rather than nurture the brightest few. Even though its public (i.e. state) as well as private schools actually do nurture an elitist core, an astonishing near-50 per cent of

E   Americans go on to some form of higher education. And there are 240 million of them.

Tests are part of the means to that end. Education is primarily a state and local function.

F   So there has to be some way of objectively evaluating Boston and Biloxi's idea of an A-student in the name of both progress and value for money. Americans are practically-minded. Education is utilitarian. The consumer's parent is king – and can vote out the school board. Quantification is a national instinct which finds expression in both IQ and baseball scores.

G   There is another reason why routine testing and published results matter so much. The US boasts no national exam system, no Himalayan range of GCSEs, A levels or Baccalaureates to scale. Pupils are evaluated in two ways; in a process of continuous assessment by their teachers, via class work, homework, occasional essays and Scan-Tron exercises which produce term grades; and by national tests conducted at the ages of 8, 10, 13 and 17 – at least in our state, though practice varies.

H   For college aspirants there is the Scholastic Aptitude Test (Sat) taken by about one million 17-year-olds a year, plus anyone younger who wants a practice run. Even at graduate level a host of tests exist.

I   Susan Sullivan, who teaches at one of Washington's best schools, regrets this emphasis. "In the British system the teacher is a coach. You work towards the same goal and the enemy to be overcome is the A level. In our system the end of year assessment is so important, the teacher can be the enemy." And the multiple-choice test can be the enemy of real learning, the crucial technique being how to spot the "right" answer.

J   My 13-year-old at the local Junior High School offers a few basic tips on multiple-choice technique, "Statements are more usually 'true' than 'false' in these tests. If in doubt pick (c) or the longest answer." He does not have to write many essays and idiosyncrasy/creativity sits uneasily in the system. On the other hand, he is in the fast stream, laden with homework and kept busy.

K   That too is a function of early diagnostic and formative testing, bolstered by teacher evaluation. In the restless, anxious debate about the quality and direction of US education ("Why are the Japanese winning?") one familiar complaint is that the strongest and the weakest are identified and helped: but it is the 80 per cent in the middle whose fate is vital to the nation's social and economic health.

L   We happen to live in Maryland suburbs but the standardised national test our kids take at 8, 10, 13 and 17 is the California Achievement Test (Cat) widely used, as are the comparable Iowa and Stanford tests in some states. Covering such basics as reading, vocabulary, spelling, language expression and math computation, they produce results expressed in stanine bands (1–9) and national percentiles. If you are bright, white and middle class your scores will probably be in the 90 per cent band: 60 per cent is the high school failure rate. If you are a poor black or Puerto Rican your scores may lag horribly.

M   Contemplating the jungle of American testing systems Britons might usefully note that anxiety about the efficacy of testing has produced more and more tests and refinements of tests. In college selection it has also produced greater reliance on teacher assessment.

N   The much-vaunted Sat scores may be helpful to the top 50 colleges in weeding out lesser applicants for entry. Most US colleges don't suffer heavy over-subscription and some publish misleading Sat scores, gleaned from their freshman intake, to boost their image in the marketplace. Good for business, say the critics, bad for education. "The tyranny of the Sats" frightens away promising students.

C **Highlight the following words and phrases in the article and try to work out their meanings from the context. Match their meanings to the synonyms below.**

¶D fuming   pernicious   nurture   ¶H aspirants   ¶N much-vaunted
¶F A-student   utilitarian   quantification ¶J idiosyncrasy   fast stream
¶G continuous assessment   grades   ¶M efficacy

bright pupil   cultivate   effectiveness   evaluation throughout the course   harmful
hoping to be admitted   marks   measurement   over-praised   practical   top class
unconventional behaviour   very angry

D 1 **Make a list of the school subjects which are/were YOUR favourites – and the ones you dislike(d). Explain to your partners why you enjoy(ed) or don't/didn't enjoy them.**

2 **Find out your partners' opinions on the following topics. Encourage them to talk about their personal experiences.**

national school and college exams   international exams
regular performance tests   continuous assessment by teachers/lecturers
the use of computers to assess learning   the use of computers to assist learning

3 **If the members of your group come from the same country, discuss what improvements should be made to your country's education system. If you're from DIFFERENT countries, find out about the education systems in each country represented.**

The sixth form
Reading and Creative writing

A Eight phrases have been removed from this newspaper article. Read it through and then decide where the phrases below (A–H) fit into the gaps (1–8).

That sixth sense of plus and minus

My last exam was history and finishing it signalled the completion of 12 years that I once thought would never end.

For over a decade I have had to trudge off to school five times a week, 39 weeks a year. As the day I had looked forward to for years approached I expected a feeling of elation, of breaking free – just think: old So-and-so cannot criticise my homework ever again. Yet in the event it ₁ _____ . I am going into the sixth form for A levels, but so many of my friends have left, and the sixth form, while being a whole lot groovier, ₂ _____ without my old mates.

It has taken until now for me to understand how important these friendships are. Some have taken years to build up, and it was a jolt to realise that some people whom I ₃ _____ had decided to leave, and it is possible that our paths will not cross again. Just two months ago they were lending me their calculators or sharing a bag of crisps and the latest joke. Now they ₄ _____ in banks, garages, farms and shops.

The comradeship was built not just on similar interests and common attitudes: we ₅ _____ , lumped together because of where our parents chose to live. In such an environment there are bound to be disagreements and fights – adolescence is nothing if not volatile, and those who tell us to grow up fail to understand that that is exactly what we are doing, learning by our mistakes and experiences. By sharing the things that naturally befall you, companionships ₆ _____ , quietly b_____s of black and white, male and female.

Luckily, there are also some who are staying on for the sixth form, so why should I feel saddened at leaving Year 11 when a lot of my friends will stay on? Well, I ₇ _____ in that I have friends in every year of the school, but sixth-formers rarely seem to socialise with any year below 11.

It is one of those peculiar conventions, caused, I suspect, by the sixth form's wish to seem aloof from the rest. It is a custom that next year, like the insensitive tourist, I shall have great fun disregarding entirely.

So now I return to school to begin the A-level trail. There will be some new faces – my school has the sixth form for a wide area – and the teachers are said to regard you as halfway human, so it should be an enjoyable two years. And once they are over it ₈ _____ whether I sink or swim. There is no one to copy homework from in big business.

Tom Smithies

A spring up   B knew and liked   C will be up to me   D were all victims of circumstance
E consider myself lucky   F was rather sad   G will go off to work   H won't be the same

B 1 Discuss how your own experiences are similar to or different from the writer's. What advice would you give him?

2 Imagine that the writer of the article is a friend of yours. Write him a **letter** (about 250 words), giving him your reactions to what he wrote and comparing your own experiences.
OR
Write an **account** of your own feelings at finishing a course/year and moving to another course/year/school, in the same style as Tom Smithies' article (about 250 words).

"So what if my grades are lousy? You always said it's not what you know, it's who you know."

(12.5) Comparing and contrasting
Grammar

THE SOLAR SYSTEM	Distance from Sun (million km)	Length of one year*	Diameter at equator (km)	Length of one day+	Number of moons
THE SUN	–	–	1,322,900	–	–
Mercury	58	88 days	4,880	59 days	0
Venus	108	225 days	12,104	243 days	0
Earth	150	365¼ days	12,756	24 hours	1**
Mars	229	687 days	6,787	24½ hours	2
Jupiter	780	12 years	142,800	9¾ hours	16
Saturn	1,427	29½ years	120,000	10¼ hours	18
Uranus	2,871	84 years	51,800	11 hours	15
Neptune	4,496	165 years	49,500	16 hours	8
Pluto	5,913	248 years	6,000	6⅕ days	1

* A 'year' is one revolution of the planet around the Sun. The length is given in Earth days or years.

+ A 'day' is one rotation of the planet. The length is given in Earth hours or days.

** Our Moon is about ⅕ million km from the Earth and 3,473 km in diameter.

A 1 Fill the gaps in these sentences with suitable words, using information from the table.

1 Earth is _closer_ to the Sun _than_ Mars.

2 Venus is .... from the Sun .... Mercury.

3 Pluto is the most .... planet from the Sun.

4 Mercury is .... the Sun.

5 Venus is .... closer to the Sun than Saturn.

6 Jupiter is not as close to the Sun .... Mars.

7 Jupiter is .... from the Sun than Mars.

8 Neptune .... Earth.

9 Pluto's year is nothing like .... short .... Mercury's.

10 Pluto is the .... planet that's also a Walt Disney cartoon character.

11 A Martian year is about .... as long as an Earth year.

12 A year on Jupiter is about .... the length of a year on Saturn.

13 A day on Uranus is .... Earth.

14 A year on Venus .... a year on Mercury.

15 A day on Venus is about the .... length as a year on Pluto.

16 A day on Mars is slightly .... than a day on Earth.

17 A day on Jupiter is .... Saturn.

18 A day on Neptune is 8 hours .... than a day on Earth.

19 A day on Venus is .... a year!

20 There's no .... planet that's also a chocolate bar .... Mars.

2 Write nine more sentences, comparing the planets – each sentence about a different planet.

B 1 Imagine that a group of aliens from another planet has come to visit your country. What might they find strange about life there? Make notes of your best ideas.

2 Compare your ideas.

C Complete each gap in this text with one suitable word.

In England and Wales, ₁_____ children attend primary school from the ages of 5 to 11, then they attend a secondary school from the age of 11 to 16. About 50% stay two years ₂_____ to study three subjects in depth, and around half of these continue their education at a college or university.

In the USA students can leave school at the ₃_____ age ₄_____ in England, but ₅_____ all students go to senior high school after graduating from junior high school at the age of 16. They continue studying a broad range of subjects at high school. Twice as ₆_____ students go to college ₇_____ their English contemporaries. They might do a two-year course at a junior college or go to a university where the course is twice ₈_____ long ₉_____ that.

In Australia many pupils attend primary school for two years ₁₀_____ ₁₁_____ in England, starting high school at the age of 12 or 13. The ₁₂_____ school-leaving age is ₁₃_____ the ₁₄_____ as in England and the USA, but ₁₅_____ students continue at school to take their university entrance exams.

D 1 Look at these phrases which can be used when comparing things. Decide which you'd find more useful in formal writing than in conversation.

Describing similarities

| The Australian education system . . . | is rather like · is similar to · is much the same as · is comparable to · is equivalent to · reminds me of · resembles · seems like · has a lot in common with | . . . the American system |

Similarly, . . .   In the same way, . . .   Moreover, . . .

Describing differences

| The American education system . . . | is very unlike · is quite different from · isn't the same as · differs from · bears no resemblance to · is nothing like · has very little in common with | . . . the English system |

On the other hand, . . .   In contrast, . . .   Conversely, . . .   However, . . .

2 Discuss the SIMILARITIES and DIFFERENCES between SOME of the following – as well as the pros and cons. Use the phrases above.

> learning languages – learning science subjects
> learning English – learning your language
> the English school system – the school system in your country
> private schools – state schools
> boarding schools – day schools
> co-educational schools – single sex schools
> school uniforms – wearing whatever you like at school
> specialising in 3 subjects in the sixth form – studying a broad range of subjects
> pupil power and student councils – teacher power
> starting primary school at age 4 – starting at age 7
> staying at school till age 18 or 19 – leaving earlier
> operating a VCR – operating a TV
> driving a car – riding a bike

12.6 How does it work?

Reading, Listening and Creative writing

A Read this article and decide where paragraphs **A** to **E** below fit in the gaps shown with red arrows. There's one extra paragraph which doesn't fit anywhere.

Clock of ages   Toby Young

1 WHY is it that no one over 30 can operate a video recorder? My mother can manage the household budget, file a tax return and negotiate the pitfalls of French property law, but she is totally baffled by the VCR. She even has a first class degree in English from Cambridge but, as far as she's concerned, the manual may as well be in Japanese.

2 Whenever I go round to my parents' house, the time display on the video is always flashing 12.00. This must be one of the most depressing sights in the modern world – a constant reminder of our defeat by ever more sophisticated forms of technology. Even my father has grown impatient with this incessant blinking, claiming it distracts him from watching the news. Yet rather than try and set the clock, he simply drapes a cloth over it.

3 ➤

4 The answer is that my mother switches off the video along with the television whenever she goes to bed. This is another thing about your parents: no matter how much you remonstrate with them to the contrary, they are convinced that if you leave any electrical appliance plugged in overnight it is guaranteed to catch fire.

5 ➤

6 Evidently it was. The next time I went round I found the whole family trying to watch a film on a television which, effectively, had no aerial. They had managed to switch off the video without switching off the television – some feat, I can tell you – but they had left the TV aerial plugged into the video instead of plugging it straight into the TV. Consequently, there was virtually no picture on the screen.

➤ **7**

8 So I bought my mother one for Christmas. At first, she didn't seem too impressed. She made all the right noises but I could tell from the look on her face she was thinking: "Not another bit of technology." But after I'd set it up and showed her how to work it she perked up a bit. She even managed to record a programme unaided – a procedure about as complicated as making a telephone call.

➤ **9**

10 I ran through the checklist – "Are you sure the television's switched on?" – and everything seemed to be OK. But somehow I doubt Dixons will give her a refund. VideoPlus may be "idiot-proof" but that's no guarantee your parents will be able to use it. Next time my father complains about the "three-minute culture" I shall point out that, while he may be able to read a philosophy book at one sitting, at least I can work the video.

A Recognising that it was too much to hope for them to leave the video plugged in, I suggested to my parents that they leave it unplugged and only plug it in when they want to watch a video. That way, at least my father wouldn't have to play around with dishcloths before he could watch television. Was that too much to ask?

B A few days later she called wanting to know where I'd bought it. For a moment I thought she might be about to recommend it to all her friends. But no. It was broken and she wanted to take it back to the shop.

C One of the most mysterious things about this is that whenever I leave the house I always set the clock to the correct time. Indeed, this is something of an occasion, the entire family standing round as if I've just disarmed a nuclear warhead. So how come the next time I'm round it is flashing "12:00"?

D Shortly after this she phoned me. She'd lost the remote control and she couldn't make the television work. Where could she buy a replacement remote control, she wanted to know.

E I had more or less given up hope when along came VideoPlus. This is a remote-control device which enables you to record programmes in advance by punching in the numbers corresponding to them, which are printed in the Radio Times. It even works if the time display is flashing "12:00". Provided I could persuade my parents not to switch the video off at night they would be home and dry.

B Find out from your partners:
- if they empathise more with the writer of the article or his parents
- how good they are at operating electrical appliances
- what is the most complicated gadget or piece of equipment they use

C 1 Before you listen to the recording, check how much your partner already knows about how a VCR works.
Which of the missing information in the diagrams below can you fill in?

2 Listen to the recording and fill each gap in the captions with one word or number.

VHS VIDEO RECORDER

A TV screen is scanned at $_1$ ▓▓▓▓▓ frames per second.
A one-hour recording consists of $_2$ ▓▓▓▓▓ separate pictures.

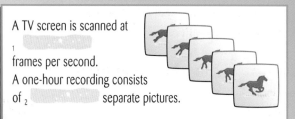

The magnetic tape in a video cassette first passes an erase $_3$ ▓▓▓▓▓, which erases previous signals.

Then the tape travels round a fast-spinning drum. There are two video recording heads on opposite sides of the drum. The drum is $_4$ ▓▓▓▓▓ slightly – as the tape goes past the drum the recording heads pass the tape repeatedly many times, leaving a message in $_5$ ▓▓▓▓▓ 'stripes'.

$_6$ ▓▓▓▓▓ stripes contain the information for just one picture – a three-hour video cassette has $_7$ ▓▓▓▓▓ stripes recorded on it.

Then the tape passes the audio head – this records the $_8$ ▓▓▓▓▓ along the top edge.

As a video tape moves quite slowly, the sound $_9$ ▓▓▓▓▓ is not as good as on an audio cassette. Hi-fi stereo videos have $_{10}$ ▓▓▓▓▓ extra tracks which are recorded in the stripes with the video signals.

PLAYBACK: The recording heads work as playback heads $_{11}$ ▓▓▓▓▓ the information instead of $_{12}$ ▓▓▓▓▓ it. A video recorder contains over $_{13}$ ▓▓▓▓▓ components (a TV only has $_{14}$ ▓▓▓▓▓ components).

D 1 Half the pairs should look at Activity 6 (how a MOVIE SOUNDTRACK works), the other half at 25 (how a MOVIE PROJECTOR works).

2 Work with a pair who were studying different information and share your knowledge.

E Imagine that a friend is coming to stay in your home while you and your family are away for a week. Your friend will need to know how to operate everything. Write instructions for your friend explaining how to operate TWO pieces of equipment in the kitchen and/or the living room (about 250 words).

If instructions are numbered or laid out clearly they're easier to understand. Using headings can help your reader to see at a glance what you're referring to.

(12.7) *Look* and *see*
Verbs and idioms

A **Fill the gaps in these sentences with a suitable particle or preposition:**

1 I'm looking ▓▓▓ my keys.

2 He came to see me ▓▓▓ at the station.

3 Look ▓▓▓! There's a car coming.

4 We all saw ▓▓▓ his lies.

5 She looked the word ▓▓▓ in a dictionary.

6 The pupils look ▓▓▓ ▓▓▓ their teacher.

7 The police are looking ▓▓▓ the crime.

8 If you're leaving I'll see you ▓▓▓.

B **Rewrite the sentences, replacing the phrases in red with the expressions below.**

1 If you're travelling in the rush hour, beware of pickpockets.

2 If you're ever in London, don't forget to call in to see me.

3 If we're both at the show, let's watch for each other in the interval.

4 They have a lovely room, it has a view of the sea.

5 He regards people who are less intelligent than himself as inferior.

6 When I said that I looked up to him, he glanced at me strangely.

7 Even the best of friends don't always agree on everything.

8 'Listen to me, if you don't give me back my money I'll call the police,'
I shouted. Soon a crowd of curious people had gathered around us.

9 Can I see the photos? Oh, you and your brother do have a similar appearance, don't you?

10 She wants to complete her current project before she retires.

11 You have such a good excuse that I won't take account of what you've done wrong.

12 A group of tourists were waiting outside the palace, hoping to catch a glimpse of the Queen.

13 Leave all the arrangements to me: I'll attend to everything.

14 His story turned out to be a pack of lies but none of us disbelieved it at first.

15 When she called him stupid he became angry.

16 Old people like to remember their younger days with nostalgia.

---

onlookers   overlook   overlook   give someone a funny look   have a look at   look alike
look back on   look here   look down on   look out for   look out for   look someone up
see eye to eye   see red   see something through   see through something   see to something   sightseers

---

C **Match these beginnings to the endings. There are several possible endings to each beginning.**

1 He glanced at . . .

2 She stared at . . .

3 He gazed at . . .

4 She peered at . . .

5 He noticed . . .

6 She watched . . .

7 He glared at . . .

. . . television all evening.

. . . the painting for a long time.

. . . her with admiration.

. . . the person sitting opposite on the bus.

. . . the small print in the brochure.

. . . the view of the mountains.

. . . the people who were making a noise.

. . . the football match until the end.

Thirteen

Communication

(13.1) The art of conversation
Listening and Vocabulary

The ART of CONVERSATION
Er... Er...

i – What a conversation is:
I speak first...
Then I speak...
Then I speak again.

Then is it my turn once more?
Yes, then me again, and so on.

What if I change the subject?
But you haven't.

ii – Introducing a third person:
Are you having a conversation?
Yes, but it's private.
Splendid! My favourite kind!

iii – A common conclusion:
Goodnight. Thank you for the nice conversation.
Oh – we never finished it!
Another time

iv – Sometimes everyone has the same conversation at the same time:
What are they saying?
What are they saying?
Sssh – let's listen...
Sssh – let's listen...

v – A familiar interruption:
MUM! Where's Death Valley? How big is a Tyranosaurus? I want a biscuit...
Darling – can't you see mummy and Steven are having a conversation!
Yeah, small-fry.

A **1** **Before you listen to the recording, look at the flowchart below. Can you think of any examples to fill some of the gaps? Look at the cartoon for clues!**

2 **Listen to the recording and fill each gap with ONE of the examples given by the speaker.**

A typical one-to-one conversation begins with this Opening Phase:

Participants make eye contact
⬇
They assume conventional facial expresssions: e.g. 1 _____
⬇
They reach a position of comfortable proximity: i.e. 2 _____
⬇
They adopt an appropriate posture: e.g. 3 _____
⬇
They exchange ritual gestures: e.g. 4 _____
and greetings: e.g. 5 _____
⬇
They exchange channel-opening remarks: e.g. 6 _____
⬇
The main business phase can begin . . .

. . . the conversation ends with this Parting Phase:

One or both of the participants decides it's time to stop.
⬇
They exchange appropriate cordial facial expressions: e.g. 7 ▬▬▬▬▬
⬇
They exchange ritual gestures: e.g. 8 ▬▬▬▬
and phrases to signal parting: e.g. 9 ▬▬▬▬
⬇
They increase the distance between them: e.g. 10 ▬▬▬▬
⬇
Eye contact is broken, the participants turn away and the conversation has ended.

B Discuss these questions and adapt the flowchart accordingly:

- How does a 'typical conversation' begin and end differently if the participants are, for example:
complete strangers   very close friends or relations   boss and employee
- How is a 'typical conversation' different in your country?
- How is a phone conversation different from a face-to-face conversation?
- How does a 'typical English lesson' begin and how does it end?

C Fill the gaps in these paragraphs with suitable words from the list below:

1 Words like 'the telly', 'the tube' or 'the box' are ▬▬▬▬ words which are more common in ▬▬▬▬ conversation than in ▬▬▬▬ writing. Learners are often advised to avoid using ▬▬▬▬ words in a foreign language, in case they sound out-of-date or aren't used ▬▬▬▬. And they should certainly avoid using ▬▬▬▬. Every profession has its own ▬▬▬▬ that is only used within that trade.

2 We can often find out about people's feelings by listening to their ▬▬▬▬ and watching their ▬▬▬▬ and ▬▬▬▬. A person's ▬▬▬▬ may convey their real feelings better than the words they speak. If someone says your work is 'brilliant' they may be sincere or they may be being ▬▬▬▬.

3 'It's a small world' is a(n) ▬▬▬▬ we use when we meet someone in an unexpected place. 'Many hands make light work' and 'Too many cooks spoil the broth' are contradictory ▬▬▬▬.

> appropriately bad language bilingual body language colloquial expression expression
> formal gestures informal intonation jargon proverbs regional sarcastic saying slang
> stress swear words tone of voice

(13.2) Joining sentences – 2
Effective writing

A 1 One way of putting extra information into a single sentence is to use RELATIVE CLAUSES. Decide which of the relative pronouns in red can be replaced with a different one (which instead of that, that instead of who, etc.).

1 A dialect is a variety of a language that uses non-standard grammar and vocabulary.

2 Everyone speaks English with an accent, which is the way they pronounce the language.

3 Tracy, who used to go out with David, has just got engaged to Paul, who is his best friend.

4 The office in which he works has fluorescent lighting, which gives him headaches.

5 Paul has just got engaged to Tracy, who is the daughter of Claire and Frank, who are the owners of Acme Bookshops Ltd, which has just opened a branch in the new shopping centre, which we went to last weekend with David, who used to go out with Tracy and whose best friend is Paul — which goes to show that it's a small world!

2 Too many relative clauses in a single long sentence can be confusing for the reader. Rewrite the last example above in shorter sentences.

B Another technique for adding extra information is to use PRESENT or PAST PARTICIPLES — look again at 7.4. Rewrite these sentences using *-ing* forms or past participles.

1 Albert Sukoff wrote a long article, which he did without the use of a single full stop.
2 The first island which was discovered by Columbus was one of the Bahamas.
3 As soon as she realised what had happened she called the police.
4 You might rotate your forefinger against your temple, which indicates 'a screw loose'.
5 You might rotate your finger close to your temple, which signals that the brain is going round and round.

C Find the errors in these sentences and correct them:

1 The person, which phone number you gave me, was not very helpful.
2 The most important point what he made was that we should approach each culture with an open mind.
3 The person, whom I spoke to, was rather rude that upset me.
4 Thanks to Pat without who help the work would have been impossible.
5 Considered that you're so clever and you're the one, that know all the answers I'm surprised you got it wrong.

D Expand each line of notes into one sentence to make a complete story, using *-ing* forms, past participles or relative clauses. All these events happened in the PAST.

1 David stays with us — finds out Paul and Tracy's plans
   While staying with us, David found out about Paul and Tracy's plans.
2 Hears about plans — upset and angry
3 Feels absolutely furious — pushes over table — knocks best glasses to floor
4 While picks up broken glass — cuts finger — starts bleeding
5 Handkerchief from pocket — wraps round cut
6 After gathers up broken pieces — pieces on floor — apologises
7 Realises how stupid — offers to replace broken glasses
8 Intends buy us new set — knows they are good quality ones — goes to store in town — store has good stock of glassware
9 Looks round store — discovers glasses very expensive — gives him quite a shock
10 Since breaking glasses — careful to keep temper!

(13.3) Gestures
Reading

A Read these two extracts from *Manwatching* by Desmond Morris. Then note down your answers to questions 1 to 7 opposite.

GESTURES

A gesture is any action that sends a visual signal to an onlooker. To become a gesture, an act has to be seen by someone else and has to communicate some piece of information to them. It can do this either because the gesturer deliberately sets out to send a signal – as when he waves his hand – or it can do it only incidentally – as when he sneezes. The hand-wave is a Primary Gesture, because it has no other existence or function. It is a piece of communication from start to finish. The sneeze, by contrast, is a secondary, or Incidental Gesture. Its primary function is mechanical and is concerned with the sneezer's personal breathing problem. In its secondary role, however, it cannot help but transmit a message to his companions, warning them that he may have caught a cold.

Most people tend to limit their use of the term 'gesture' to the primary form – the hand-wave type – but this misses an important point. What matters with gesturing is not what signals we think we are sending out, but what signals are being received. The observers of our acts will make no distinction between our intentional Primary Gestures and our unintentional, incidental ones. In some ways, our Incidental Gestures are the more illuminating of the two, if only for the very fact that we do not think of them as gestures, and therefore do not censor and manipulate them so strictly. This is why it is preferable to use the term 'gesture' in its wider meaning as an 'observed action'.

A convenient way to distinguish between Incidental and Primary Gestures is to ask the question: Would I do it if I were completely alone? If the answer is No, then it is a Primary Gesture. We do not wave, wink or point when we are by ourselves; not, that is, unless we have reached the unusual condition of talking animatedly to ourselves.

SYMBOLIC GESTURES

A Symbolic Gesture indicates an abstract quality that has no simple equivalent in the world of objects and movements.

How, for instance, would you make a silent sign for stupidity? You might launch into a full-blooded Theatrical Mime of a drooling village idiot. But total idiocy is not a precise way of indicating the momentary stupidity of a healthy adult. Instead, you might tap your forefinger against your temple, but this also lacks accuracy, since you might do precisely the same thing when indicating that someone is brainy. All the tap does is to point to the brain. To make the meaning more clear, you might instead twist your forefinger against your temple, indicating 'a screw loose'. Alternatively, you might rotate your forefinger close to your temple, signalling that the brain is going round and round and is not stable.

Many people would understand these temple-forefinger actions, but others would not. They would have their own local stupidity gestures, which we in our turn would find confusing, such as tapping the elbow of the raised forearm, flapping the hand up and down in front of half-closed eyes, rotating a raised hand, or laying one forefinger flat across the forehead.

The situation is further complicated by the fact that some stupidity signals mean totally different things in different countries. To take one example, in Saudi Arabia stupidity can be signalled by touching the lower eyelid with the tip of the forefinger. But this same action, in various other countries, can mean disbelief, approval, agreement, mistrust, scepticism, alertness, secrecy, craftiness, danger or criminality. The reason for this apparent chaos of meanings is simple enough. By pointing to the eye, the gesturer is doing no more than stress the symbolic importance of the eye as a seeing organ. Beyond that, the action says nothing, so that the message can become either: 'Yes, I see', or 'I can't believe my eyes', or 'Keep a sharp look-out', or 'I like what I see', or almost any other seeing signal you care to imagine. In such a case it is essential to know the precise 'seeing' property being represented by the symbolism of the gesture in any particular culture.

So we are faced with two basic problems where Symbolic Gestures are concerned: either one meaning may be signalled by different actions, or several meanings may be signalled by the same action, as we move from culture to culture. The only solution is to approach each culture with an open mind and learn their Symbolic Gestures as one would their vocabulary.

from *Manwatching* by Desmond Morris

1 What do a sneeze and a wave of the hand have in common?

2 What kind of gesture is a yawn?

3 What kind of gesture is a raised fist?

4 Why is the phrase *unusual condition* used at the end of the first section?

5 How many different signs does the writer describe for stupidity?

6 How many different meanings does the writer describe for the gesture of touching the lower eyelid with the tip of the forefinger?

7 How does the writer suggest one should learn the gestures of different cultures?

B Discuss these questions:

● Can you think of three more examples of incidental gestures – and three primary gestures?

● According to the writer, a sneeze and a yawn are involuntary, incidental gestures. What do these gestures mean when they are done deliberately:

blinking   clearing your throat   clenching your fist   folding your arms   grabbing someone's wrist
licking your lips   scratching your head   sighing   sniffing   tapping your fingers on a table

C Look at these pictures and decide (or guess) what each of the gestures might mean to a British person AND to someone from your own country.

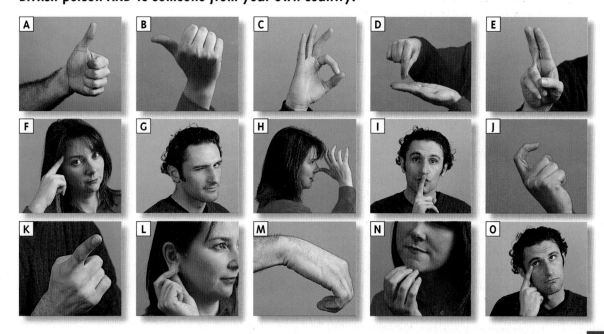

You just don't understand!
Reading

A Read the two extracts and decide which writer makes the following points: John Gray JG, Deborah Tannen DT – or neither of them N.

1 Don't tell someone their motives are bad if they're doing their best.
2 Long ago men and women lived in harmony.
3 Men and women are never in full agreement.
4 Men and women will still have arguments.
5 Communication can improve if you take the blame but not if you blame your partner.
6 People don't like to be told they are behaving in the wrong way.
7 The cause of disharmony between men and women is the way they speak.
8 The cause of disharmony is forgetting women and men are different.
9 Women and men are constantly disappointed in each other.
10 Women and men come from different planets.
11 Women and men do speak the same language.
12 Women and men should respect their differences.
13 Women expect men to become more like women, and vice versa.

1 Imagine that men are from Mars and women are from Venus. One day long ago the Martians, looking through their telescopes, discovered the Venusians. Just glimpsing the Venusians awakened feelings they had never known. They fell in love and quickly invented space travel and flew to Venus.

2 The Venusians welcomed the Martians with open arms. They had intuitively known that this day would come. Their hearts opened wide to a love they had never felt before.

3 The love between the Venusians and Martians was magical. They delighted in being together, doing things together, and sharing together. Though from different worlds, they reveled in their differences. They spent months learning about each other, exploring and appreciating their different needs, preferences, and behavior patterns. For years they lived together in love and harmony.

4 Then they decided to fly to Earth. In the beginning everything was wonderful and beautiful. But the effects of Earth's atmosphere took hold, and one morning everyone woke up with a peculiar kind of amnesia – *selective amnesia!*

5 Both the Martians and Venusians forgot that they were from different planets and were supposed to be different. In one morning everything they had learned about their differences was erased from their memory. And since that day men and women have been in conflict.

6 Without the awareness that we are supposed to be different, men and women are at odds with each other. We usually become angry or frustrated with the opposite sex because we have forgotten this important truth. We expect the opposite sex to be more like ourselves. We desire them to "want what we want" and "feel the way we feel".

7 We mistakenly assume that if our partners love us they will react and behave in certain ways – the ways we react and behave when we love someone. This attitude sets us up to be disappointed again and again and prevents us from taking the necessary time to communicate lovingly about our differences.

8 Men mistakenly expect women to think, communicate, and react the way men do; women mistakenly expect men to feel, communicate, and respond the way women do. We have forgotten that men and women are supposed to be different. As a result our relationships are filled with unnecessary friction and conflict.

9 Clearly recognizing and respecting these differences dramatically reduces confusion when dealing with the opposite sex. When you remember that men are from Mars and women are from Venus, everything can be explained.

from *Men Are from Mars Women Are from Venus* by John Gray

1 Many experts tell us we are doing things wrong and should change our behavior – which usually sounds easier than it turns out to be. Sensitivity training judges men by women's standards, trying to get them to talk more like women. Assertiveness training judges women by men's standards and tries to get them to talk more like men. No doubt, many people can be helped by learning to be more sensitive or more assertive. But few people are helped by being told they are doing everything all wrong. And there may be little wrong with what people are doing, even if they are winding up in arguments. The problem may be that each partner is operating within a different system, speaking a different genderlect [i.e. a male 'dialect' and a female 'dialect'].

2 An obvious question is, Can genderlect be taught? Can people change their conversational styles? If they want to, yes, they can – to an extent. But those who ask this question rarely want to change their own styles. Usually, what they have in mind is sending their partners for repair: They'd like to get him or her to change. Changing one's own style is far less appealing, because it is not just how you act but who you feel yourself to be. Therefore a more realistic approach is to learn how to interpret each other's

messages and explain your own in a way your partner can understand and accept.

3   Understanding genderlects makes it possible to change – to try speaking differently – when you want to. But even if no one changes, understanding genderlect improves relationships. Once people realize that their partners have different conversational styles, they are inclined to accept differences without blaming themselves, their partners, or their relationships. The biggest mistake is believing there is one right way to listen, to talk, to have a conversation – or a relationship. Nothing hurts more than being told your intentions are bad when you know they are good, or being told you are doing something wrong when you know you're just doing it your way.

4   Not seeing style differences for what they are, people draw conclusions about personality ("you're illogical", "you're insecure", "you're self-centered") or intentions ("you don't listen", "you put me down"). Understanding style

differences for what they are takes the sting out of them. Believing that "you're not interested in me", "you don't care about me as much as I care about you", or "you want to take away my freedom" feels awful. Believing that "you have a different way of showing you're listening" or "showing you care" allows for no-fault negotiation: you can ask for or make adjustments without casting or taking blame.

     If you understand gender differences in what I call conversational style, you may not be able to prevent disagreements from arising, but you stand a better chance of preventing them from spiraling out of control. When sincere attempts to communicate end in stalemate, and a beloved partner seems irrational and obstinate, the different languages men and women speak can shake the foundation of our lives. Understanding the other's ways of talking is a giant leap across the communication gap between women and men, and a giant step toward opening lines of communication.

5

from *You Just Don't Understand* by Deborah Tannen

 B   **Discuss these questions:**

- To what extent do your own experiences mirror the views of the writers?
- Do you believe that males and females are different? Give your reasons.
- How important do you think communication is in a relationship?
- Is it easier for a man to communicate with men, and a woman with women? Why (not)?

(13.5) Advertising

Listening and Creative writing

Bob Stanners

 A   **You'll hear an interview with Bob Stanners, who works for Leo Burnett — one of the world's leading advertising agencies. Complete each sentence with a word or short phrase.**

An art director is responsible for 1 _____ . A copywriter is responsible for 2 _____ .

The two people function as a 3 _____ .

It's easier to write 15 minutes of dialogue than 4 _____ .

Every advertisement has to appeal to 5 _____ .

Clients often want to aim too 6 _____ .

One shouldn't underestimate the consumer's 7 _____ .

Twenty years ago, in Britain, bottled mineral water was an 8 _____ .

He got the idea for a McDonald's commercial from his son, who is a 9 _____ .

10 All these qualities are important for a copywriter — but tick only the things Bob mentions:

adaptability	communication	childlike faith	listening to others	resilience
ambition	common touch	a sense of proportion	optimism	sense of humour
analytical brain	enjoy selling	honesty	realism	working in a team

B Discuss these questions:

- How much attention do you pay to . . .
  TV commercials? radio commercials? posters? ads in magazines?
- Think of a particular advertisement you like – what do you like about it?
- Think of one you hate – why don't you like it?
- What do you think are the differences between British advertisements and advertisements in your country?

C 1 Look at this advertisement from a magazine for computer buffs and discuss these questions:

- Does it make you see red? Why/Why not?
- What are your reactions to political advertising (propaganda) like this?
- Is it suitable for the readers of such a magazine?

JUST SAY NO.

America is hooked on foreign oil. Today we import almost 40 per cent of the oil we use – even more than in 1973, when the Arab embargo plunged us into gas lines, rationing, and recession.

The more we can use nuclear energy, instead of imported oil, to generate electricity, the less we have to depend on foreign nations.

The 110 nuclear plants in the US have cut our foreign oil dependence by over three billion barrels since 1973. And they have cut foreign oil payments by over one hundred billion dollars.

But 110 nuclear plants will not be enough to meet our growing electricity demand. More plants are needed.

To help kick the foreign oil habit, we need to rely more on our own energy sources, like nuclear energy.

For a free booklet on nuclear energy write to the US Council for Energy Awareness, P.O. Box 66103, Dept. SN01, Washington, D.C. 20035.

US COUNCIL FOR ENERGY AWARENESS

Nuclear energy means more energy independence.

2 Find a copy of a magazine that you enjoy reading. Imagine that the editor has asked you for a report on how suitable the advertisements are for a typical reader, like yourself.

✒ Write a **report** describing the ads in the magazine. Recommend what kinds of ads the editor should encourage – and what kinds of ads he or she should try to discourage.

Before you start writing, make notes and decide:
- how you will begin (your opening paragraph)
- what your main points will be
- how you will end (your conclusions or recommendations)

3 Show your work to a partner and ask for feedback.

> A report is usually a fairly objective account plus your personal recommendations or conclusions. The purpose of a report is to give your readers information as well as giving them your views. A report can end with a paragraph headed 'Conclusions' or 'Recommendations'.

13.6 COLOURS
Idioms and collocations

A **Each of these sentences contains a colourful expression. What do they mean? Don't use a dictionary – the context will help you to guess.**

1 Everyone in the class passed the exam with flying colours.
2 She didn't go to work because she was feeling a little off colour.
3 The detailed descriptions in the story gave local colour to the book.
4 Far more men are colour-blind than women.
5 All the documents in this office are colour-coded.
6 What do you think of the colour scheme in this room?
7 Don't allow your personal interest to colour your judgement.
8 It was only when he had won the match and started jeering at his opponent that we saw him in his true colours.

B **Replace each word or phrase in grey with one of the idioms below:**

1 Most manual workers receive wages and are paid weekly.
2 He phoned me completely unexpectedly to tell me he was back in town.
3 She's very famous so we must give her VIP treatment.
4 How environmentally friendly are you?
5 They were very jealous when they saw my new Porsche.
6 He became very angry when I told him he had made a mistake.
7 Dealings with government offices usually involve bureaucratic delays.
8 I'm ready to start when you tell me to go ahead.
9 Our new clerk makes a lot of mistakes because he's still inexperienced.
10 A lucky coincidence like this happens very rarely.
11 I can't afford to buy anything because I'm still in debt after my holiday.
12 The police caught him in the act of committing the crime.

in the red   red-handed   see red   red carpet   red tape
once in a blue moon   out of the blue   blue-collar
green   green   green with envy   give the green light

C **Fill the gaps in these sentences with one of the idioms below:**

1 He showed his disapproval by giving me a ______ .
2 Send me a letter about this – I need to have all the details ______ .
3 During the war, some things could only be bought on the ______ .
4 It's a hilarious ______ about an unsuccessful murderer.
5 He must have been in a fight – he's got a ______ .
6 They're not getting married in a registry office: they're having a ______ .
7 I told a ______ because I didn't want her to get into trouble.
8 Most ______ workers receive a salary and are paid monthly.
9 She had a ______ and didn't regain consciousness for several minutes.
10 No one will visit the new museum – it'll be a ______ .

black comedy   **black eye**   **black look**   **black market**   **blackout**   **in black and white**
white-collar   **white elephant**   **white lie**   **white wedding**

Fourteen

ways in which these parts can be combin... ...ce messages that have meaning • *Human lang*... ...on...ts of ...ords that are usually spoken or written. ...speak *any foreign languages?" "Well, I learnt* ...gu...ges *at school, but I don't speak any of them fluen*... ... ...w old is the English language? [C] • I found ...re quite difficult to follow because she used a ...hnical lang...e. [... • COBOL, C and BASIC are thr... ...mputer programming langu... ...ng instructions). [C] • We come ... gro...nds, so we speak/talk the s...

The English-speaking world

(14.1) English in the world
Reading

(A) 1 Name six countries where English is the first language or main language.

2 Read this passage and find the answers to these questions.

How many . . .

1 people speak English as a first language?

2 people speak English as their second language?

3 children study English in schools?

4 students does the British Council teach annually?

5 countries have English as an official language?

6 countries receive broadcasts in English?

7 English speakers are there altogether?

8 scientists write in English?

In the minds of many people there is no longer an issue. They argue that English has already become a world language, by virtue of the political and economic progress made by English-speaking nations in the past 200 years, and is likely to remain so, gradually consolidating its position.

An impressive variety of facts about usage support this view. According to conservative estimates, mother-tongue speakers have now reached around 300 million; a further 300 million use English as a second language; and a further 100 million use it fluently as a foreign language. This is an increase of around 40% since the 1950s. More radical estimates, which include speakers with a lower level of language fluency and awareness, have suggested that the overall total is these days well in excess of 1,000 million. The variation results largely from a lack of precise data about English language use in such areas as the Indian sub-continent, where the historical impact of the language exercises a continuing influence on many of its 900 million people, and China where there has been a burst of enthusiasm for English language studies in recent years, with over 100 million people watching the BBC television English series *Follow Me*. Even if only 10% of these learners become fluent, the effect on totals is dramatic: the number of foreign learners is immediately doubled.

Surveys of range of use carried out by UNESCO and other world organizations reinforce the general statistical impression. English is used as an official or semi-official language in over 60 countries, and has a prominent place in a further 20. It is either dominant or well established in all six continents. It is the main language of books, newspapers, airports and air-traffic control, international business and academic conferences, science, technology, medicine, diplomacy, sports, international competitions, pop music, and advertising. Over two-thirds of the world's scientists write in English. Three-quarters of the world's mail is written in English. Of all the information in the world's electronic retrieval systems, 80% is stored in English. English radio programmes are received by over 50 million in 120 countries. Over 50 million children study English as an additional language at primary level; over 80 million study it at secondary level (these figures exclude China). In any one year, the British Council helps a quarter of a million foreign students to learn English, in various parts of the world.

from *The Cambridge Encyclopedia of Language* by David Crystal

(B) 1 Discuss these questions:

● Which countries can you name where English is used as a second language or *lingua franca* between people who speak different local languages?

● How many different non-English-speaking nationalities have you communicated with in English yourself?

2 Look at this map. Can you work out where the local people:

- pronounce the letter **r** in arm, farm, horse and flower
- don't pronounce the letter **h** in house, happy and hurry
- pronounce last, fast and castle with the same vowel sound as fat, cat and hat: /æ/

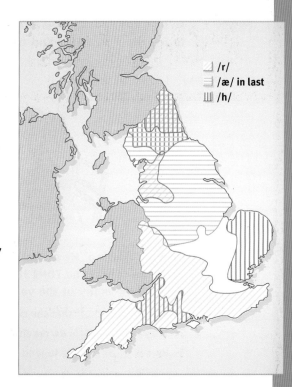

◢ /r/
▤ /æ/ in last
▥ /h/

C Discuss these questions:

- How many different national or regional accents of English can you recognise?
- How many different national or regional accents of your own language can you recognise?
- What are some of the differences in the spelling, vocabulary or grammar of different varieties of your own language?

(14.2) Indirect speech
Grammar

Although direct speech is often used like this in novels and stories:

> "Shh! Be quiet!" she whispered urgently, "My husband's in the other room and he mustn't know you're here . . . "

— it's not used so much like this in everyday conversation or writing. It's generally easier to remember the GIST of a conversation than to remember the exact words. Moreover, the actual words may not always be terribly interesting:

> "Hello," he said. "Hello," I said. "How are you?" I asked. "I'm fine...fine," he said. "Good," I said, "and...er...how's your wife?" I asked. "Oh, you know, same as ever," he said . . .

A Discuss the differences in meaning between these sentences:

1 *He told us that he had visited Australia in the summer.*
   He told us that he visited Australia in the summer.
   He told us that he would be visiting Australia in the summer.

2 *She asked me if I had been to New Zealand.*
   She asked me when I had been to New Zealand.
   She asked me whether I had been to New Zealand.

3 *David says he wants to visit his relations in Canada.*
   David said he wanted to visit his relations in Canada.
   David said he wants to visit his relations in Canada.
   David said, 'He wanted to visit his relations in Canada.'

4 *Ruth phoned to say that she would be flying to India the next day.*
   Ruth phoned to say that she would be flying to India tomorrow.
   Ruth phoned to say that she was flying to India the next day.

5 *I didn't find out when the show starts.*
   I didn't find out when the show started.
   I didn't find out when the show will start.
   I didn't find out when the show would start.

B Two of you should look at Activity 7, the others at 26. You'll each have two short passages to rewrite into direct and reported speech.

> I don't like this book I'm reading now.

> He told me he didn't like that book he was reading then.

C 1 Instead of using 'He said that . . .' or 'She asked if . . .' in reported speech, an appropriate verb can reflect the TONE that was used in direct speech and the FUNCTION of the sentence. Decide how many of the verbs below can be used to fill each of the gaps in these sentences:

1 She ⬚⬚⬚⬚ that she came from Australia.

2 They ⬚⬚⬚⬚ us/me that they were feeling tired.

3 He ⬚⬚⬚⬚ me to lend him some money.

> admit allow announce ask assure beg call out claim convince deny encourage
> explain inform insist instruct invite mention mumble notify order permit persuade
> repeat reply scream shout suggest tell urge warn whisper

2 Highlight the ten most useful verbs in C1 that you don't already use. Then compose five sentences, each including one of the verbs you have chosen.

3 Compare your sentences.

D Each of these sentences gives a report of what various people said. Rewrite each report, using direct speech, giving the exact words you think each person might have used.

1 I tried to find out what part of America Kate came from.

   "Could you tell me what part of America you come from, Kate?"

2 Kate wanted me to guess, but in the end she revealed that she was from Toronto — in Canada!

3 Jane complimented me on my handwriting.

4 Jerry suggested that I should enrol for a course in Japanese.

5 Pippa insisted on paying for the whole meal, including the drinks.

6 Stephen encouraged me to go in for the exam and reassured me that I had a good chance of passing.

7 I warned Stephen not to be too confident as it was a long time since I'd last taken an exam.

8 Although they were strangers I asked the people in the corridor to stop talking so loudly as it was after midnight.

E 1 You'll hear seven people talking about the places where they were brought up. Make notes as you listen. The speakers are:

   1 Blain   5 Nick
   2 Rupert   6 Ken
   3 Gay   7 Karen
   4 Enzo

2 Write a short summary (two sentences only) giving the GIST of what each person said:

   Blain said he was brought up in Northern Canada, where his family lived in very tiny isolated settlements. The summers were very hot and the winters extremely cold with a great deal of snow.

(14.3) Spelling and pronunciation 1 — Consonants
Pronunciation and Word study

A Decide whether the consonants in green in the words below are pronounced:

/tʃ/ as in cheer   /ʃ/ as in fish   /ʒ/ as in usual   or   /dʒ/ as in jump

average badge beige cabbage courage damage decision future injury insurance
literature machine march vision moustache opposition partial picture prestige question

B Arrange the words below into four groups, according to the pronunciation of the letters gh or g (shown in green), as in these examples:

/g/ ghost /f/ enough /dʒ/ giant [silent] high

enough high giant ghost nought gesture sign signature margarine guilty draught
gypsy thorough sigh naughty borough gymnasium gherkin generation
laughter ginger George giggle genuine drought engineer genius

C Here are some groups of words, each containing the letter on the left. Underline the words in which the letters in green *are* pronounced (i.e. *not* silent).

k knowledge <u>acknowledge</u> knot kneel knife <u>nickname</u>

b climbing subtle symbol numb dumb debt bribed

g campaign hungry champagne ignorance foreign

h honour exhibition rehearsal behalf exhausted vehicle honorary inherit

l behalf salmon chalk yolk yield failure palm

p psychology psychiatry couple cupboard receipt raspberry hypnotise pseudonym

t castle attitude Christmas whistle postpone soften bright

d sandwich sadness Wednesday handkerchief second-hand

In most regional and national accents of English, it's the vowel sounds that tend to be pronounced differently, rather than the consonants — apart from these sounds:
  r at the end and in the middle of words:
  far farmer harder charge
and **t** in the middle of words:
  forgotten butter better

D 1 Everyone has difficulties with English spelling — even educated native speakers sometimes have to think twice about some words. Correct the spelling mistakes in these words — but be careful because three of them are *correctly* spelt.

adress *address* acomodation advertisement arguement comittee developping embarassed
four o'clock independant medecine pronounciation recieve reliable replaceing responsability
sieze skillfull therefor untill

2 To remind yourself of the words *you* spell wrongly, look at your own previous written work and highlight the spelling mistakes that were corrected.

E 1 In British English and American English some words may be spelt (British)/spelled (American) differently.

The following words are printed in the usual American English way. Decide how they would usually be written in British English.

catalog *catalogue* center *centre* color *colour* defense *defence*
draft beer favor honor humor jewelry labor pajamas quarreling skillful
specialty theater traveler's check traveling TV program woolen

2 Can you think of any more words that are spelt differently in British and in American English?

Words like these can be spelt either **-ize** or **-ise** in British English:
  realize/realise modernize/modernise apologize/apologise etc.
  — but normally with **-ize** in American English (except *advertise*)

Although you may see spellings like *gotta* (got to) and *wanna* (want to) in the lyrics of songs, for example, they aren't used in normal American English writing.

Fourteen The English-speaking world

123

14.4 | **I ♥ signs**
Speaking and Writing

A Here are some well-known slogans. What does each one signify and what ideas do you associate with it? Can you think of any more slogans?

I ♥ New York	Feed the world	Small is beautiful
Power to the people	Make love not war	Nuclear power – no thanks
Survival of the fittest	All you need is love	The world's favourite airline
Unity is strength	Liberty, fraternity, equality	One man, one vote
The customer is always right	Workers of the world unite	

B What do these symbols signify for you? Can you think of some more?

C Can you explain what these traffic signs mean?

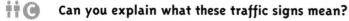

D English is used in many countries as an international language to communicate with people who don't speak or can't read your own language. But not everyone writes very good English.

1 What do you think each of these signs is supposed to mean?

2 Rewrite each one in better English.

1

JEUX D'ENFANTS
NON SURVEILLES
NOT LOOKING AFTER
THE CHILDREN'S GAME

2

We take your bags and send them in *all directions*.

3
Ladies, leave your clothes here and spend the afternoon having a good time.

4

Our wines leave you nothing to hope for

5

Special Today
No ice cream

6
Colds and Heats
– If you want just condition of warm in your room, please control yourself.

7
LADIES ARE REQUESTED NOT TO HAVE CHILDREN IN THE BAR.

8
THE FLATTENING OF UNDERWEAR WITH PLEASURE IS THE JOB OF THE CHAMBERMAID.

9
Visitors are expected to complain at the office between the hours of 9 and 11 am daily.

10
Please leave your values at the front desk.

11
You are invited to take advantage of the chambermaid.

12
Please do not feed the animals. If you have any suitable food, give it to the guard on duty.

E Look at these (authentic) safety instructions. Although you can probably work out what they mean, you'll agree that there's room for improvement.

1 Use a pencil to <u>underline</u> or correct the most glaring mistakes.

2 Two of you should rewrite the odd-numbered instructions together, the others should rewrite the even-numbered ones. When you're ready, look at the other pair's work.

FIRE PROOFER INSTRUCTIONS FOR THE TENANTS

1) Advice the plan which is in front of you in board where are marked the exits, the corridors, the place of the portable fire engines, etc.

2) Ask what the signs mean, where are located at the corridors on each exit, elevators, etc.

3) When the alarm system rings for fire don't be in panic, keep calm and follow the instructions.

4) When you realise that there is fire inform the staff of the hotel with the best possible way and if you are capable act for extinction with fire engine.

5) Follow the instructions which you are listening from microphones.

6) Don't use the elevators in case of fire explotion, but the steps.

7) We inform you that it is not allowed to use spirit lamp stoves in the room, or other heat appartus of open (unprotected) flame.

8) When you leave your room check if there are lighted cigaretts left or any other electric apparatus on.

F Imagine that a group of English-speaking students are coming to study at your school or college. Write the instructions on what to do in case of fire, which will be put on the notice-board in their classroom (about 250 words).

(14.5) **British and American English**
Word study

Most of the vocabulary used in the UK and USA is identical, so British and American people do understand each other perfectly well most of the time!

A Look at the words in the first list, which are often used in American English. Match them to the common British English terms below. The words with an asterisk (*) can be used in both varieties, with similar meanings.

 apartment* attorney to call someone* checkmark closet couch* downtown
drugstore/pharmacy* the fall faucet garbage/trash movie theater potato chips
schedule* sidewalk zero* zipper

autumn* chemist's cinema city/town centre* cupboard/wardrobe* flat*
rubbish* nought pavement potato crisps to ring someone up sofa
solicitor/barrister tap* tick (✓) timetable* zip

B **1** Fill the gaps in these sentences with suitable words from the lists below – one of you using the British English words, the other the American ones.

1 Turn left at the next *crossroads* (BrE) / *intersection* (AmE).
2 When you arrive, report to the reception desk on the .... floor and then take the
.... or walk up the stairs to the .... floor.
3 Every man was wearing a three-piece suit: jacket, ... and ....
4 Does the .... go all the way to the airport or do I have to take a bus?
5 We had to .... for tickets at the .... station.
6 We had to drive off the .... to fill up with ....
7 If there's a power cut you may need to use a .... to see in the dark.
8 If I'm not in the office you can call me on my ....
9 If you're applying for a job you should send your ....
10 Do you need to go to the .... before we leave?

 crossroads CV first ground lift mobile phone motorway petrol queue
railway toilet torch trousers underground waistcoat

 bathroom cellphone/cellular phone first elevator flashlight freeway/highway
gas intersection pants railroad resumé second stand on line subway vest

2 Can you think of any more words with different meanings in British and American English?

"I was driving along, talking on my cellular phone, when suddenly my other cellular phone rang."

In different regions of Britain there are also some variations in vocabulary.
In Scotland, for example, these words are sometimes used:

wee (= small) *aye* (= yes)
infirmary (= hospital) *bairn* (= child)
pinkie (= little finger)
forenoon (= morning) *bonny* (= pretty)
burn (= stream) *loch* (= lake)

14.6 *Speaking* and *thinking*
Verbs and idioms

A **Fill the gaps in the sentences with suitable forms of the verbs below, adding pronouns if necessary.**

1 Can you ▨▨▨▨ the difference between a Yorkshire and a Lancashire accent?
2 I can't ▨▨▨▨ you the exact time but at a guess I'd ▨▨▨▨ it was ten o'clock.
3 What did Sharon ▨▨▨▨ when you ▨▨▨▨ her she had to work harder?
4 I'll have the answer for you tomorrow, can you ▨▨▨▨ then?
5 I can't make up my mind right away, I'll need more time to ▨▨▨▨ . In fact, I'll ▨▨▨▨ the problem with my family this evening.
6 I know Bob doesn't want to do it, but I'll try to ▨▨▨▨ helping us.
7 Children hate it when adults ▨▨▨▨ them — it seems arrogant.
8 I'm afraid I can't hear you very well, could you ▨▨▨▨ , please?
9 We'll have to ▨▨▨▨ the lecture because the speaker is ill.
10 He was afraid to ▨▨▨▨ at the meeting in case he made a fool of himself.
11 The children were ▨▨▨▨ by their teacher for their bad behaviour.
12 The twins look alike — it's impossible to ▨▨▨▨ .

say say	speak up speak out
tell tell tell tell off tell apart	talk down to talk someone into talk something over
call off call back	think something over/through

B **Replace each phrase in red with a suitable form of the expressions below.**

1 I'll start pouring out your wine — please tell me when to stop pouring.
2 When two business people meet, they often discuss work or business.
3 They had an argument and now they are not on friendly terms.
4 It's obvious that it takes time to get used to an unfamiliar accent.
5 'It's terribly hot, isn't it?' 'It certainly is!'
6 'Can you turn on the air conditioning?' 'That's more difficult than you might expect because the switch is broken.'
7 'Could you open the window, please.' 'Yes, that can be done quickly.'
8 She always expresses her views frankly.
9 I knew it was an empty threat, so I challenged him to carry it out.
10 The voters have a low opinion of the present government's record.
11 I haven't made up my mind yet, I was just saying my thoughts out loud.
12 We were going to go by car, but then we decided it wasn't a good idea.
13 The influence of the USA in the world is a favourite discussion topic.
14 It sounded a good idea, but I believe you should reconsider.

call someone's bluff   say when   easier said than done   it goes without saying
no sooner said than done   You can say that again!   not on speaking terms   speak one's mind
talk shop   talking point   think again   think aloud   think better of it   don't think much of

Fifteen

How strange!

(15.1) **Truth or fiction**
Speaking and Reading

The Lovers, 1928, by René Magritte

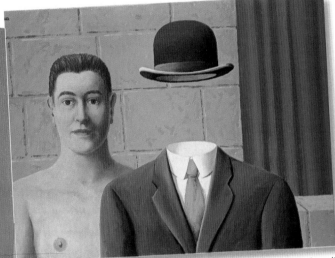

The Road to Damascus, 1966, by René Magritte

A 1 How would you describe the two pictures? How do they make you feel? Note down ten words that come into your mind in connection with them.

2 You'll hear the first part of a story. What do you think happened next?

3 Listen to the end of the story. Find out if you guessed right and then discuss your reactions to it with a partner.

B Discuss these questions – and encourage your partners to expand on their answers:

- Do you believe in ghosts?
- What was the last coincidence that happened to you?
- Do you know anyone who seems to be accident-prone?
- If the only vacant rooms in a hotel were 7 and 13, which would you choose and why?
- Are any of the following believed to be lucky or unlucky in your country?

C Read the passage opposite and find the following information in the text:

1 What do modern legends reflect?
2 Apart from being retold by people, how are modern legends and tales disseminated widely?
3 Find an example of one ancient legend and one modern legend.

New Legends for Old

We are not aware of our own folklore any more than we are of the grammatical rules of our language. When we follow the ancient practice of informally transmitting "lore" – wisdom, knowledge, or accepted modes of behavior – by word of mouth and customary example from person to person, we do not concentrate on the form or content of our folklore; instead, we simply listen to information that others tell us and then pass it on – more or less accurately – to other listeners. In this stream of unselfconscious oral tradition the information that acquires a clear story line is called narrative folklore, and those stories alleged to be true are legends. This, in broad summary, is the typical process of legend formation and transmission as it has existed from time immemorial and continues to operate today. It works about the same way whether the legendary plot concerns a dragon in a cave or a mouse in a Coke bottle.

It might seem unlikely that legends – urban legends at that – would continue to be created in an age of widespread literacy, rapid mass communications, and restless travel. While our pioneer ancestors may have had to rely heavily on oral traditions to pass the news along about changing events and frontier dangers, surely we no longer need mere "folk" reports of what's happening, with all their tendencies to distort the facts. A moment's reflection, however, reminds us of the many weird, fascinating, but unverified rumors and tales that so frequently come to our ears – killers and madmen on the loose, shocking or funny personal experiences, unsafe manufactured products, and many other unexplained mysteries of daily life. Sometimes we encounter different oral versions of such stories, and on occasion we may read about similar events in newspapers or magazines; but seldom do we find, if even seek after, reliable documentation. The lack of verification in no way diminishes the appeal urban legends have for us. We enjoy them merely as stories, and we tend at least to half-believe them as possibly accurate reports. And the legends we tell, as with any folklore, reflect many of the hopes, fears, and anxieties of our time. In short, legends are definitely part of our modern folklore – legends which are as traditional, variable, and functional as those of time past.

Whatever the origins of urban legends, their dissemination is no mystery. The tales have traveled far and wide, and have been told and retold from person to person in the same manner that myths, fairy tales, or ballads spread in earlier cultures, with the important difference that today's legends are also disseminated by the mass media. Groups of age-mates, especially adolescents, are one important American legend channel, but other paths of transmission are among office workers and club members, as well as among religious, recreational, and regional groups. Some individuals make a point of learning every recent rumor or talk, and they can enliven any coffee break, party, or trip with the latest supposed "news". The telling of one story inspires other people to share what they have read or heard, and in a short time a lively exchange of details occurs and perhaps new variants are created.

from *The Vanishing Hitchhiker* by Jan Harold Brunvand

D **Now referring back to the text, match these questions to the answers below – one of the answers is wrong and some of the questions have two answers.**

According to the writer,

1 why are we not aware of our own folklore?
2 how do legends acquire a clear story line?
3 why do legends still play an important part in our lives today?
4 why are urban legends never documented?
5 why do we accept such stories even though they cannot be verified?
6 where in the USA are you most likely to hear a modern legend?
7 what generally happens when people in a group have heard a legend?

A We half-believe them.	F They are part of our modern folklore.
B In groups of contemporaries.	G They are passed from person to person.
C An expert storyteller makes them his or her own.	H We don't pay enough attention to the form.
D Other people are inspired to tell similar stories.	I We don't pay enough attention to the content.
E They are not accounts of events that really happened.	J We enjoy them as stories.

E 1 **One of you should look at Activity 8, the other at 27. You'll each have another urban legend to retell to your partner.**

2 **Have you recently heard any stories that may be urban legends?**

A good introduction and conclusion

Reading and Effective writing

A Each of these sentences about the article below contains ONE mistake. Find the mistakes and correct them:

1 When René Magritte was a baby his mother fell into a river and drowned.

2 All of Magritte's paintings are like myths.

3 Magritte made up the titles for his paintings.

4 He wanted his viewers not to notice how reality and painting are different.

5 The pictures he painted in the war were drab.

6 Magritte's images have had a slight influence on advertising.

Odd, odder, **oddest**

ON THE evidence of one or two favourite images – perhaps of bowler-hatted gents raining down from the sky or of a steam engine emerging from a domestic fireplace – many people regard René Magritte merely as a witty punster; a coiner of memorable "stills" who anticipated the most slick of modern advertisements. That he was considerably, and chillingly, more than that is revealed by the Magritte retrospective exhibition at London's Hayward Gallery, which will later move to New York, Houston and Chicago.

"I detest my past and everyone else's," Magritte wrote, and he had reason to. His mother drowned in 1912, when he was 13. He claimed that some hours later he saw her body fished from the river, her nightdress covering her face. Investigation has since shown this was not so, as the body was recovered 17 days later. Magritte made a myth out of an unbearable reality, and this mythic quality pervades many of his works. Faceless or impassive figures are often depicted on the seashore; living bodies are seen decomposing (or metamorphosing, for example, into wood). In "The Lovers", painted in 1928, a man and woman embrace in quasi-cinematic close-up, their heads bizarrely shrouded by white sheets.

An encounter in 1923 with the mysterious art of Giorgio de Chirico, an Italian Surrealist, moved Magritte to tears. Chirico's work made such a deep impression on him that his own pictures contain many of the standard ingredients of early Surrealism (airless streets, mannequin heads, theatrical curtains), but invested with his own disquieting, morose humour.

Magritte courted bowler-hatted anonymity. His colours are usually darkly subdued. His portrayal of familiar images, eerily juxtaposed, is at once workmanlike and intense, in some ways reminiscent of the old Flemish Masters. He painted in a business suit in his cramped flat and, following financial success in the 1950s, in a bourgeois salon of his Brussels house. On Saturday nights he invariably entertained fellow Belgian Surrealists. The parlour game for the guests was to invent metaphysical titles for their host's paintings.

Unlike mainstream European Surrealism, Magritte's imagery is usually mundane, but his treatment of it could be out of Alice in Wonderland. A metal tuba is seen in flames. A giant green apple fills a room. A bird cage contains only a huge egg. He used optical illusion to jolt the viewer into questioning the nature of artifice and reality. A favourite device was to depict a canvas of a landscape almost exactly over that part shown from the original scene. One such painting he called "The Human Condition".

One of the surprises of the exhibition is Magritte's garish wartime "Impressionist" paintings, in which he decided to cheer everybody up. Instead he disgusted his most loyal supporters. Some of his last works, before his death in 1967, are his most universal and serene. These include one of a giant bird in flight, its silhouette figure composed of white cloud and blue sky.

Magritte's images have, unusually, proved immensely popular with art critics and the general public as well as Madison Avenue. They have changed the face of advertising, where they have been used to sell everything from books and insurance to cars, calculators and clothes.

B 1 Look at the OPENING PARAGRAPH of each reading passage in Units 11 to 15, including the one above. Discuss these questions with your partner:

● What effect does each opening paragraph have on you as a reader?

● Which of the paragraphs encourage you to read on and find out more?

● Does the very first SENTENCE of each passage catch your attention?

2 Now look at the CONCLUDING PARAGRAPH of the same reading passages, including the one above. Discuss what the effect is of each one on the reader. Which of them leave you feeling better informed and satisfied?

Relativity, 1953, by M. C. Escher

👥 **C** **Here are four alternative opening paragraphs for an article about the picture above in a book about the artist. Discuss these questions:**

- Which of them do you prefer?
- What features of style and content make your favourite paragraph effective?
- Which paragraph do you like least – and why?

We can look at this enigmatic picture from three sides but not from above. The artist is playing with our sense of direction and creating illusions: as we turn the page different people come into view with the staircases apparently connecting each scene. In all, there are sixteen people, with featureless heads like mannequins, going about their business in or near the same house.

The picture is an enigma, playing with our sense of direction and creating illusions. We can see sixteen people in the picture, but as we look at it from the left, from the right or from below (but not from above), different ones come into view on or near each interconnected staircase. The heads of the people going about their business are like mannequins: their heads and clothes have no features.

The artist is forcing us to question what is 'true', creating the illusion that the staircases are interconnected. We can look at the picture from three sides but not from above. As we turn it round sixteen different people come into view, going about their business in or near a house. But they aren't really people: they are just mannequins with featureless heads.

What a strange picture! When you look at it you get a different view, depending which way round you hold it. I've counted the number of people and there are 16 altogether, but they aren't really people, they look more like crash test dummies – you know, the ones in TV commercials that tell you how safe a car is. I'm not quite sure what the point of it all is – just who are these people/dummies? Am I supposed to follow their routes as each one goes up and down the stairs, or what?

👥 Ⓓ 1 **The class is divided into an even number of pairs. Half the pairs should look at Activity 18, the others at 34. Each pair has a different picture to describe.**

✎ 2 **Write a short description of your picture (about 100 words). Try to cover these aspects:**

- What has happened? Who are the people? What are they doing?
- What's happening now? What's going to happen next?

👥→👥 3 **Show your paragraphs to another pair and ask for comments. They should compare your paragraph with the picture you were looking at in Activity 18 or 34.**

(15.3) ## A sense of humour
Listening and Reading

> Sarcasm can be a dangerous weapon: you can easily upset or annoy people. Your attempt to be humorous may be misunderstood and people may think you're being nasty. But you do need to be aware if someone is being sarcastic to you.

📼 Ⓐ **You'll hear 12 short clips from conversations – decide in each case whether the second speaker is being SINCERE or SARCASTIC and tick the appropriate box.**

> What did you think of my work – was it good?
> – Yes, it was really good. I liked it a lot.   ← sincere
> – Oh yes, it was brilliant, I really enjoyed reading it!   ← sarcastic

	sarcastic	sincere
1		✓
2	✓	
3		
4		
5		
6		

	sarcastic	sincere
7		
8		
9		
10		
11		
12		

👥 Ⓑ **Read the text opposite and then discuss your answers to these questions:**

- Which of the writer's examples sound familiar to you?
- Which of her examples don't make you smile at all?
- What is her nationality? How do you know? Highlight the words that tell you this.

🔻 Ⓒ **Highlight these words and phrases in the text. Then match them to the definitions below.**

> letting myself down   victories   keep me going
> 1 standing on line   gloat   2 peek   rationalize
> 4 gives me the giggles   bandage   blender   7 constant   9 glee

> be happy at someone else's misfortune   disappointing myself   enable me to continue living
> examples of success   happiness and pleasure   have a quick, secret look   unchanging
> kitchen appliance for mixing liquids   make me laugh uncontrollably   queue up
> provide a (reassuring) explanation   piece of cloth tied around an injury

👥👥 Ⓓ **Discuss these questions:**

- What do you think are some of the other things the writer might be ashamed of?
- What kind of things give you the giggles? Can you think of an example?
- What sort of things make you laugh?
- Do the members of your group share the same sense of humour?
- What kind of things do people in your country find particularly funny?
- How do you feel when a friend doesn't find something as funny as you do?

INHUMAN NATURE

Rita Rudner

I try to be the best person I can be, but I'm constantly letting myself down. Human nature is largely something that has to be overcome. Lots of the little things in life that give me pleasure are usually connected with someone else's misfortune. Not big misfortunes, not even misfortunes, more inconveniences; little victories in my life that keep me going. Before you start to hate me, let me give you a few examples and see if they sound familiar.

1   You're standing on line for a very popular movie. You're warned about whether or not you will get in. You wait ten minutes. You turn around. You are no longer at the end of the line. There are now at least thirty people behind you who have less chance of getting in than you do, and if they do, you will almost certainly get a better seat. What is your reaction? Do you say to the people behind you, "Hey, you can all get in front of me, I can see this movie tomorrow night." No, you gloat – admit it, you gloat . . . or am I the only one?

2   I'm staying in a hotel, and while walking down the corridor I always peek in other people's hotel rooms to see if they are nicer than mine. If their room is nicer, I rationalize to myself, "It's just a room, I'm going to be sleeping in it most of the time." However, if my room is nicer, I think, "Ha ha, I got a better room, ha, ha, ha, ha, ha, ha, ha, ha." I revert to a three-year-old and say "ha" far too many times.

3   We all know that life isn't fair; but restaurant service should be. When I sit down at a restaurant and the people who sit down fifteen minutes after me get served first, I'm furious, unless I'm the later person who has gotten served. I don't wait and say, "I'm not eating until the people who got here before me are taken care of." I eat. I eat, and it's especially delicious.

4   There are few things that have given me more joy than Geraldo Rivera [*see below*] being hit in the nose by a chair. It still gives me the giggles when I think about the bandage. I don't like Geraldo Rivera, but I would never wish him harm. I just think it's the chair that makes the image special. A fist would have been too common and a blender too disturbing, but a chair and a nose coming together when the nose belonged to Geraldo Rivera, that was a delight.

5   This is something that must not go farther than this book. Sometimes, when I'm in an elevator and I see someone running toward it, I . . . I . . . I pretend I can't find the Open Door button. There, I said it. It has nothing to do with the character of the person who wants to come in. I don't even particularly want to be alone. I just don't want to press the button.

6   When I'm driving down the street and see someone else fixing a flat tire, I sit a little taller. I know someday that will be me out there, but it hasn't happened yet, so I'm still able to chuckle.

7   In traffic there is only one rule that is a constant. The lane of traffic that you are in is the lane of traffic that isn't moving. If I were in the lane of traffic that was moving, I'm sure I would be happy about it, but this personally has never happened to me.

8   I'm in the movie theater, a woman with an enormous head sits down directly in front of the person sitting next to me. I am amused, but only for a few seconds before she changes her mind and sits directly in front of me.

9   One of my very best friends who has never been able to gain weight (poor thing) recently gained ten pounds and had to go on a diet. Glee. I call her and laugh and hang up. (She does deserve it; all those years of complaining to me about the horrors of having to drink a chocolate shake every day.)

10 My husband found a gray hair on his head. He was upset. I had it framed.

There are more things about myself that I'm ashamed of but I'm going to stop here, just in case it's not really human nature . . . and I'm the only one.

from *Naked Beneath My Clothes* by Rita Rudner

The Geraldo Rivera Show is a US daytime talk show focusing on controversial and sometimes unpleasant topics. Geraldo often tries to provoke or humiliate his guests in front of the audience and this often makes them angry. There are dozens of less controversial daytime shows where ordinary people are famous for five minutes on television, often for having done something stupid or embarrassing. The most successful of these is the Oprah Winfrey Show.

(15.4) Mind control

Listening and Creative writing

A Before you listen to the interview, read this definition of a cult and then discuss the questions below.

> **The Cult Information Centre (CIC) defines a cult as a group having all of the following five characteristics:**
>
> **1** It uses psychological coercion to recruit and indoctrinate potential members ("mind control").
> **2** It forms an elitist totalitarian society.
> **3** Its founder leader is self-appointed, dogmatic, messianic, not accountable and has charisma.
> **4** It believes "the end justifies the means" in order to solicit funds or recruit people.
> **5** Its wealth does not benefit its members or society.

- How does a bona fide religion seem to be different from a cult, as defined above?
- What kind of people might be vulnerable to cults? What kind of people might be recruited?
- What cults have been in the news recently?

Ian Howarth

B You'll hear an interview with Ian Howarth, General Secretary of the Cult Information Centre.

1 Listen to the first part of the interview and complete these sentences with ONE word only.

Ian is concerned with a group's methods not its ₁ _____ .
The woman who approached Ian in Toronto was ₂ _____ .
She appeared to be doing some sort of ₃ _____ .
What the main speaker at the first meeting said seemed to be ₄ _____ .
He was approached by another woman when he left the room for a ₅ _____ .
The apparent purpose of the course was to help him to stop ₆ _____ .

Two and a half weeks later he read a(n) ₇ _____ about the group.
Luckily, the group had failed to ₈ _____ him against the media.
Cults tell their members that the media is full of ₉ _____ or run by the ₁₀ _____ .
It took him ₁₁ _____ months to recover.

2 Listen to the second part of the interview and fill the gaps.

₁₂ What kind of people are recruited by cults? Note down FOUR qualities or characteristics of a typical recruit, using a word or short phrase:

_____   _____   _____   _____

Fill each gap in these notes with ONE word only.

On 18 November 1978 at Jonestown, Guyana ₁₃ _____ members of a cult died.
Some cult leaders . . .
   want to make ₁₄ _____ ; programme their followers to think that they are ₁₅ _____ ;
   are crazy — they believe they are ₁₆ _____ ; do it for ₁₇ _____ purposes; want to take over
   the ₁₈ _____ ; just enjoy the ₁₉ _____ they have over innocent people.
There are over ₂₀ _____ cults in Britain.
The occult ranges from ₂₁ _____ at its worst to ₂₂ _____ at its most harmless.
The CIC looks at a group's ₂₃ _____ not its ₂₄ _____ .
Ian describes a letter from a family who had been reunited with their daughter after she had spent
₂₅ _____ years in a cult in Australia.

✒ **C**   Read this extract from a letter from your friend, Amy. Write a short note to your friend (about 50 words) and a letter (about 200 words) to Tim, Amy's cousin, advising him what to do.

> I'm afraid my cousin Tim may have become a victim of a cult. He has become very friendly with a woman he met at a café and she has persuaded him to go with her to several meetings. He won't listen to me, so could you please write to him?

15.5 *Day* and *time*
Idioms and collocations

A   Replace each expression in red with a synonym from the list below, making any necessary changes.

1   She hates having to do the same boring chores day in and day out.
2   OK that's enough, I think we'd better call it a day.
3   'Do you think you'll be boss one day?' 'Haha, that'll be the day!'
4   Today's a red-letter day: I take delivery of my new car this afternoon.
5   I wasn't paying attention because I was daydreaming about my holiday.
6   It'll make his day if she agrees to go out with him.
7   One of these days I'm going to go into my boss's office and tell her what I really think of her.
8   Today has been one of those days I'm afraid.
9   Watching that horror film on video scared the living daylights out of him.
10 I'm sorry I've made another mistake — it's not my day today.
11 Remember when we were at school together? Those were the days!

> a bad day   being unlucky   stop   every single day   make happy   eventually   terrify   special day
> that's very unlikely   that was a wonderful period   thinking pleasant thoughts

B   Fill the gaps in these sentences with one of the expressions below.

1   Legends have been told _____ and they are still being told today.
2   Folk stories often begin with the words: '_____ . . .'
3   I haven't received a reply from my friend, _____ he wrote back.
4   You only have to do two writing tasks in the exam but there's a two-hour _____ .
5   You can borrow the book, I don't need it _____ .
6   There's no quick and easy way to learn idioms, it's a _____ process.
7   I've warned him _____ that he should be more careful but _____ he just doesn't seem to take any notice. You know, _____ I feel that I'm _____ talking to him.
8   A good actor or comedian has to have _____ when on stage.
9   There's no hurry, so you can _____ and do the work _____ .
10 We didn't manage to get there _____ for the start of the meeting — it had already begun.
11 If you go to Disneyland I'm sure you'll have _____ .
12 Next time we'll try to be there _____ .

> at times   for the time being
> from time immemorial   good timing
> half the time   in time   in your own time
> it's about time/it's high time   on time
> once upon a time   take your time
> the time of your life   time and time again
> time-consuming   time limit   wasting my time

© 1994 H. L. SCHWADRON

SUPERSTITION RESEARCH PROJECT
SECRETARY WANTED.
No LEFT-HANDED CAPRICORNS, PLEASE!

SCHWADRON

Sixteen

Body and mind

16.1 **How are you?**
Vocabulary
and Listening

 A **Ask your partners these questions:**

● How are you?

● If you ask people in your country 'How are you?', do they usually tell you about their health
  – or do they usually say they're well?

● What are the most common illnesses that cause people to take days off work or school?

B **You'll need to use a dictionary to answer some the following questions. In each case,
one answer is given as an example.**

1 How many ways of keeping fit can you think of?   **e.g.** *Playing football*

2 How do the various people you know stay slim (or try to get slim)?   **e.g.** *By eating less*

3 How many different illnesses or diseases can you think of?   **e.g.** *Measles*

4 How do people tend to feel if they . . . ?
   don't take enough exercise – *unfit* *have drunk too much*   *have overslept*   *have had a bad night*
   have just run a marathon   *eat only junk food*   *have had a bad day*   *have had a busy day*

5 Who do you see if you . . .?
   have toothache – *a dentist*   *have sore feet*   *need an injection*   *are having a baby*
   need an operation   *have a sore throat*   *are having a nervous breakdown*

6 What would be the symptoms of each of these medical problems?
   measles – *spots or a rash*   *hay fever*   *flu*   *migraine*   *food poisoning*   *sprained ankle*   *schizophrenia*
   a cut finger   *a broken arm*

7 What would be the normal treatment for each of these ailments?
   a cut finger – *put a plaster on it*   *hay fever*   *a cold*   *a bruise*   *scratch*   *dog bite*   *headache*
   toothache   *graze*   *wasp sting*   *mosquito bite*   *aching back*   *sprained wrist*   *a bad cough*

8 Which of these people work in a hospital?
   anaesthetist ✓   *consultant*   *convalescent*   *matron*   *midwife*   *outpatient*   *porter*   *sister*
   specialist   *surgeon*   *vet*   *victim*

C **Ask your partners these questions:**

● What do you do if someone has hiccups?

● If you had a friend who takes no exercise at all, what advice would you give him or her?

● Do you trust or mistrust doctors, nurses and dentists? Why?

D 1 You'll hear five people speaking. Match the extracts to the people listed.

A a dentist
B a paramedic
C a nurse
D a pharmacist
E a psychiatrist
F a psychologist
G a fitness instructor
H a vet

1	
2	
3	
4	
5	

2 Listen to the extracts again. Match each extract to what the speaker is referring to.

I knee
J insomnia
K ear
L tail
M nose
N neck
O back
P throat

1	
2	
3	
4	
5	

(16.2) Prefixes
Word study

A **Use one of these negative prefixes to form the OPPOSITE of each of the adjectives below. Here are some examples:**

un helpful satisfactory stable

dis agreeable organised satisfied

in accessible accurate adequate

im mature moral patient perfect

il legal legitimate

> acceptable appropriate bearable compatible complete conscious contented convenient
> credible desirable discreet experienced flexible foreseen frequent grateful healthy
> hospitable legible literate logical mortal natural obedient personal polite probable
> respectful sane sociable sufficient visible willing

B **Look at these examples of prefixes that alter the meaning of verbs. Then use the prefixes to alter the meaning of the verbs listed below. (Some can be used more than once.)**

mis calculate spell understand
    = wrongly: *'Accommodation' is a word that is frequently misspelt.*

out grow live number
    = beyond, exceeding: *The girls outnumbered the boys at the party.*

re build use write
    = again: *I've rewritten the letter but I'm still dissatisfied with it.*

un button do tie
    = reversal of action: *This knot is so tight that I can't undo it.*

> consider count dress last load lock name open pack play print read record
> report roll screw sell sit an exam tell think unite wind zip

C Look at these examples of prefixes that alter the meaning of nouns, adjectives and verbs. Then use the prefixes with the words listed below.

mid- July way winter

= in the middle: *It's warmer in mid-July than in mid-February.*

over act cook polite ripe sensitive

= excessively: *Overripe fruit doesn't taste good and may not keep well.*

under charge powered staffed

= inadequately: *This car is so underpowered that it won't go up hills.*

self- control interest sufficient

= to, for, by oneself or itself: *The country is self-sufficient in oil.*

ultra- modern sensitive

= extremely: *I wouldn't like to work in an ultra-modern building.*

air catering cautious confident contained crowded defence discipline dose
enthusiastic estimate explanatory fashionable fast fifties loaded polite privileged
qualified react respect satisfied simplify twenties valued weight

D Fill each gap with a suitable word from **A**, **B** and **C**. Use only one word for each space.

1 An _____ new hospital is being built _____ between the two towns to replace the old ones which have _____ their usefulness.

2 She tends to get quite _____ when people _____ her.

3 I think he _____ when he got so angry — I only suggested he should _____ the last paragraph of the report because it was _____ .

4 Don't you think John and Mary are _____ ? He's so conceited and _____ , whilst she's so gentle and _____ .

5 It's _____ ! They've closed down the hospital because it's _____ . Apparently it won't be _____ till they've recruited more nurses.

6 You need a lot of _____ if you're working on your own, especially if you're a _____ kind of person.

7 When I got to my hotel room I _____ my suitcase and _____ my things. Then I _____ and had a shower.

8 I don't like big _____ hotels because they're much more _____ than small family hotels. But some people are more _____ than me: they prefer _____ accommodation, which has its own _____ kitchen, and where there aren't any staff to talk to.

"My spelling checker said everything was spelled incorrectly. It turned out I had the Portuguese version."

(16.3) Spelling
Word study

👥 Ⓐ 1 Read the first part of this article and then discuss the questions below.

Mirror, mirror

THESE drugs are meant to make you better. Not "well", you understand, but better – more attentive, more attractive, better in bed. Already many such drugs are being worked on in laborataries. The first to be released could be Johnson & Johnson's anti-wrinkle drug, called Renova, which is now awaiting regulatory approval. Such treatments – part drug, part cosmetic – have even been given their own name: "cosmeceuticals". These hybrids are a puzzle for regulators, for they fall under no definate rules. Until that is put right, the cosmeceutical industry cannot make money or, incidentally, enhance humanity.

The term "cosmeceutical" was coined in 1990 when the cosmetics industry had a brush with America's Food and Drug Administration (FDA). The FDA thought that sunscreen and sun-tanning lotions should be classified as drugs and subjected to rigorous tests. While cosmetics need be tested only for safety, drugs are actually required to work as described. Any product making a medical claim is, legally, a pharmaceutical.

- There were three spelling mistakes in the text – did you spot them?
- What's your opinion of people who use 'cosmeceuticals'?
- If there was a drug you could take to enhance your memory or help you to concentrate better, would you consider using it? Why/Why not?

2 Now read the continuation of the article. In *most* lines there is one spelling error. Write the correctly spelled word on the right, or put a tick if there are no mistakes.

0	Unfortunately, when it came to cosmeceuticals, nobody could agree what was	✓
00	meddical and what cosmetic. So it was proposed in 1990 that these chemicals should be	*medical*
1	in a category of their own – potent biological substances that do not seem to treat any	
2	disease – and that new rules should be drafted to deal with them. So far none has been.	
3	If Renova is approved, it will therfore have to be sold as a pharmaceutical rather	
4	than as a cosmetic. The disease it will be prescribed to treat is "apearance of fine	
5	wrinkling roughnes and hyper-pigmentation all associated with photo-damaged skin"	
6	(i.e. ageing). The absurdity is that Avon last year lunched a new potion that does much	
7	the same thing, but got it approved as a cosmetic.	
8	Regulaters willing to call products designed to rejuvenate "pharmaceuticals"	
9	nevertheless seem reluctant to regard memory-enhancers in the same way – even	
10	through memory-loss, like skin damage, is generally caused by ageing rather than	
11	ilness. Doctors have tried to devise a loophole – "age-associated memory-impairment	
12	disease", or AAMI – which they diganose in anybody over 50 not suffering from a	
13	mental disorder, but complaning of forgetfulness. AAMI has yet to gain official	
14	recognition.	
15	After this regulatory mess has ben sorted out, the cosmeceutical industry could	
16	be huge. Acording to Kline and Company, a consultancy based in New Jersey, new anti-	
17	aging lotions have helped boost 1992 sales of facial treatments in America by 7%, to $1.2	
18	billion. (That compairs with a rise of just 1–2% for other cosmetics.) As consumers	
19	grow elder, they want pills and ointments that will improve their health, fitness and	
20	appearance – and it seems they are going to get them.	

📼 Ⓑ 1 Listen to the recording and write down each of the 15 words you hear – you'll hear each one in a sentence to help you. The first one is: *handkerchief*

2 Cross out the words below that are spelled incorrectly.

~~accross~~ • across   agressive • aggressive   campaining • campaigning   diphthong • dipthong
disruppted • disrupted   enthusiastically • enthusiasticly   extinction • extincsion   foreign • foriegn
inconceivable • inconcievable   interrupted • interuppted   sanctaury • sanctuary   seize • sieze
seperate • separate   underdeveloped • underdevelopped   wierd • weird

3 Look at your own previous written work and see which words you spelt incorrectly. How many of these are words that you know you often get wrong?

16.4 Conditional sentences
Grammar

A **Discuss the differences in meaning between these sentences:**

1 *When it rains our roof leaks.*   *If it rains our roof leaks.*
   If it rains our roof will leak.   *If it rained our roof would leak.*
   When it rained our roof would leak.

2 *I'd go first class if I could afford to.*   *I'll go first class if I can afford to.*
   I go first class when I can afford it.   *I'll go first class when I can afford it.*
   I'd have gone first class if I could have afforded it.

3 *He could get a rise if he asked his boss.*   *He would get a rise if he asked his boss.*
   He might get a rise if he asked his boss.   *He might get a rise if he asks his boss.*
   He should get a rise if he asks his boss.   *He will get a rise if he asks his boss.*

4 *If you should see him, give him my love.*   *If you happen to see him, give him my love.*
   If you see him, give him my love.   *When you see him, give him my love.*

5 *You should save your money in case you want to go on holiday.*
   You won't be able to go on holiday unless you save your money.

6 *If only I hadn't spent all my money and had saved some!*
   If I hadn't spent all my money and had saved some . . .

B **Correct the errors in these sentences – one sentence contains no errors.**

1 If I were born rich I hadn't needed to work.
2 If you have been feeling unwell you should go to see the doctor.
3 He says that if it weren't for the tax system he'll be much better off.
4 There wouldn't be so much poverty when less money is spent on arms.
5 If you shouldn't arrive in time they won't let you into the concert.
6 If you would have bought it last week, the price didn't have go up.
7 If you'd let me know if you arrived I'd meet you at the airport.
8 I'll be surprised unless prices go up next year.

C 1 **Particularly in FORMAL style, the structures in red are sometimes used. Rewrite each sentence beginning with *If* . . .**

1 Were it not for his strict diet, he would have put on even more weight.
   If _____

2 Had he realised how long the exercise plan would take, he would never have started.
   If _____

3 Should you see her tonight, please remind her to get in touch with me.
   If _____

2 Fill the gaps in these sentences:

1 _____ the weather _____ more favourable,
   we _____ enjoyed our holiday more.

2 Should _____ enough space, continue your work
   on a separate sheet.

3 Were _____ disparity between our incomes,
   I _____ feel so envious.

4 Had they _____ that the exam _____ so
   difficult, they _____ more time revising for it.

5 _____ wish us to send you a sample, please enclose
   a cheque for £5.

6 I _____ have plenty of money now, _____ for having spent it all.

D **Read this informal note and use the information in it to complete the numbered gaps in the more formal letter. Use NO MORE THAN THREE WORDS in each gap — but don't use the same words that are in the informal note.**

INFORMAL NOTE

I've just heard from Tony about the fitness programme he's just finished at the Leisure Centre. He was really disappointed and I'd like you to write a letter to the manager, Mr Brittas, to complain about it.

These are the problems that arose:

There wasn't enough supervision in the fitness room. He didn't know how to work some of the machines and this could have been dangerous.

He had to queue up to use some of the machines – it wouldn't be so frustrating if there was a limit on the number of customers allowed in at one time.

They said he'd lose 10 kg in 10 weeks but he put on 2 kg! They shouldn't make claims like that if it's not possible.

They should have told him to spend longer in the fitness room and told him what diet to follow – then he could have lost some weight.

Tell him to get in touch with you if he has any questions.

FORMAL LETTER

Dear Mr Brittas,

I am writing to you on behalf of my colleague, Tony Harris, who has just
1 _____ an intensive fitness programme at Whitbury Leisure Centre and is very disappointed with it.

There was 2 _____ supervision in the fitness room, which could have been dangerous. If he 3 _____ instructed how to work each piece of equipment there 4 _____ less risk. Moreover, he frequently had to queue for some of the machines. If you 5 _____ the number of customers allowed in the fitness room, there 6 _____ frustration.

Despite your claim that he would lose 10 kilos in 10 weeks he in fact 7 _____ 2 kilos. I do not think you should make such extravagant claims 8 _____ they are 9 _____. If he 10 _____ to spend longer in the fitness room and if he 11 _____ a diet to follow, he 12 _____ able to lose some weight.

If my colleague 13 _____ how badly your leisure centre is run he would certainly not 14 _____ for the course.

I look forward to hearing your reply to these comments. 15 _____ you have any questions do please contact me.

Yours sincerely,

(16.5) Giving advice
Speaking

A 1 **Find out your partners' answers to these questions:**

The telltale signs of stress

- Do you feel guilty when relaxing – uneasy if not 'on the go'?
- Do you lie awake worrying about tomorrow?
- Are you tense ... does your neck feel 'knotted-up'?
- Are you impatient or irritable – do you interrupt when others are talking?
- Do you feel that you have a lot on your mind – have difficulty concentrating?
- Are you smoking or drinking more – do you eat in a hurry?
- Does life seem full of crises – are you always having rows?
- Do you find it difficult to make decisions?
- Do you feel frustrated when people don't do what you want?
- Do you frequently experience a butterfly stomach, a dry mouth, sweaty palms or a thumping heart?

If you've said yes to some of these, read on . . .

2 **What advice would you give to someone who answered Yes to each of the questions above? Here are some useful phrases:**

If I were you . . .	The best thing to do is . . .	If you don't . . . you'll . . .
It's a good idea to . . .	Have you tried . . . *-ing*?	Why don't you . . . ?
You could always . . .	Try . . . *-ing* instead of . . . *-ing*.	

3 **One of you should look at Activity 11, one at 15, and the other at 28. You'll each have two pieces of advice to pass on in answer to this question:** *What can I do to avoid stress?*

B 1 **Imagine that you have SOME of these problems. Take it in turns to ask your partners for advice, each time on a different problem.**

My problem is . . .

I can't sleep.	I keep oversleeping.	I always wake up early.
I keep waking up in the night.	I snore.	I'm always tired.
I need to lose weight.	*I need to get fit.*	*I keep getting headaches.*
I keep getting backache.	*I can't stop smoking.*	*I lose my temper a lot.*
I can't concentrate on my work.		I don't have time to revise or do homework.
I can't remember vocabulary.		I always panic when I have to take an exam.
I don't have time to take exercise.		*When I get home I just flop in front of the TV.*
It's too much trouble to prepare healthy food.		*It's easier to drive or go by bus so I never walk.*

. . . What should I do?

You can react to your partners' advice by saying:

That's easier said than done.	That sounds like a good idea, but . . .
That's all very well, but . . .	Hmm, I'm not sure that would work.

2 **Imagine that a friend has written to you saying that he or she has ONE problem from EACH group of problems above. Write a letter in reply giving your advice (about 250 words).**

(16.6) First aid
Creative writing

A 1 Note down the things you **WOULD** do and **WOULD NOT** do if you were first on the scene in each of these these cases:

> **Snake bite** – in Britain the adder (viper) is the only poisonous snake and its bite is rarely fatal (there may be more poisonous snakes in your country)
>
> **Epileptic seizure** – 10% of people have some form of epilepsy and a fit can be dangerous if not handled properly
>
> **Shock** – all major injuries can bring about shock, a medical condition where the heart and circulation progressively lose power

2 Student A should look at Activity 9, B at 16 and C at 31. Read the suggested treatment and then explain it to your partners in your own words.

B 1 Decide how you would treat:

someone with a suspected broken/fractured arm or leg

someone who has bumped their head and feels dizzy

someone who has been rescued from drowning

2 Write instructions on how to treat TWO of the patients described in B1 to be included in a first-aid manual for staff at your college or place of work (about 250 words).

(16.7) *Hearts, hands, legs* and *feet*
Idioms and collocations

Fill the gaps in these sentences with suitable forms of heart, hand, leg, foot **or** feet.

1 Even if it's hard to keep up your exercise programme, don't lose _____ .

2 You can trust her, I'm sure she has your interests at _____ .

3 If he's in hospital I'm sure he's in good _____ .

4 A lot of the staff are off sick, so we're rather short- _____ .

5 Ask someone who's been working here for years — one of the old _____ .

6 We had to learn the words by _____ .

7 You can do it by yourself, I'm sure you don't need me to hold your _____ .

8 My new job was hard at first, but I eventually found my _____ .

9 I used to really enjoy keeping fit but now my _____ isn't in it.

10 The new manager was given a free _____ to restructure the company.

11 It's you that must decide — the decision is in your _____ .

12 I know you're upset but try not to take it to _____ .

13 They refused to help us, but in the end they had a change of _____ .

14 What he did was quite unjustified — he hasn't got a _____ to stand on.

15 We decided not to enter for the competition because we had cold _____ .

16 I used to play a lot and I still play occasionally to keep my _____ in.

17 If you need help, let me know and I'll give you a _____ .

18 Don't worry, leave it to me — I have the matter in _____ .

19 I didn't mean what I said, I was only pulling your _____ .

20 We all had to do as we were told when she put her _____ down.

21 I shouldn't have mentioned his ex-wife — I think I put my _____ in it.

22 Don't take it seriously, it was only a light- _____ remark.

23 When you've finished this work you'll be able to put your _____ up.

24 When she told him she was leaving him, it almost broke his _____ .

Seventeen

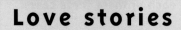

Love stories

(17.1) **What do you enjoy reading?**
Vocabulary

A **Ask each other these questions:**

- What were the last two books you read? What were they about? Did you enjoy them?
- How much time do you spend reading ... during the week? ... at weekends? ... on holiday?

B **In these sentences tick the words and phrases that make sense in the gaps, and <u>underline</u> the ones that you think DON'T fit. When <u>would</u> you use the ones you've underlined?**

1 It's such a(n)   book you won't be able to put it down.

   amusing ✓ <u>*best-selling*</u> *entertaining* ✓ *gripping* ✓ *literary* *poetic* *popular* *predictable* *thought-provoking* *well-written* *clear* *complex* *hard to understand* *lucid* *readable* *simple*

2 Have a look at this   in the book — it's really amusing.

   appendix *bibliography* *blurb* *chapter* *character* *dustjacket* *extract* *footnote* *foreword* *index* *page* *paragraph* *passage* *preface* *quotation* *section* *title* *unit*

3 There are many genres of literature, but my favourite kinds of bedtime reading are   .

   autobiographies *bestsellers* *biographies* *classic novels* *comic novels* *crime stories* *drama* *historical novels* *mysteries* *non-fiction* *poetry* *propaganda* *romances* *science fiction* *thrillers* *Westerns* *whodunits*

(17.2) **Small World**
Reading

A **1 Read the passage opposite.**

2 Discuss these questions about the text:

1 Is this the kind of book you'd like to read more of? Why (not)?
2 Do people read 'Bills and Moon' romances (or photo romances) in your country?
3 How do you predict the story that Cheryl was reading will end?
4 How do you predict Cheryl's own story will end?
5 Do you think Cheryl's job sounds 'dull and monotonous'? In what way?
6 What kind of person do you imagine Cheryl to be?
7 Give some examples of jobs generally regarded as 'glamorous' or 'satisfying'.
8 What is the difference between a *proposition* (line 32) and a *proposal*?
9 What did you enjoy most in this passage?

DAVID LODGE

Small World

THE job of check-in clerk at Heathrow, or any other airport, is not a glamorous or particularly satisfying one. The work is mechanical and repetitive: inspect the ticket, check it against the passenger list on the computer terminal, tear out the ticket from its folder, check the baggage weight, tag the baggage, ask Smoking or Non-smoking, allocate a seat, issue a boarding pass. The only variation in this routine occurs when things go wrong – when flights are delayed or cancelled because of bad weather or strikes or technical hitches. Then the checker bears the full brunt of the customers' fury without being able to do anything to alleviate it. For the most part the job is a dull and monotonous one, processing people who are impatient to conclude their brief business with you, and whom you will probably never see again.

Cheryl Summerbee, a checker for British Airways in Terminal One at Heathrow, did not, however, complain of boredom. Though the passengers who passed through her hands took little notice of her, she took a lot of notice of them. She injected interest into her job by making quick assessments of their characters and treating them accordingly. Those who were rude or arrogant or otherwise unpleasant she put in uncomfortable or inconvenient seats, next to the toilets, or beside mothers with crying babies. Those who made a favourable impression she rewarded with the best seats, and whenever possible placed them next to some attractive member of the opposite sex. In Cheryl Summerbee's hands, seat allocation was a fine art, as delicate and complex an operation as arranging blind dates between clients of a lonely hearts agency. It gave her a glow of satisfaction, a pleasant sense of doing good by stealth, to reflect on how many love affairs, and even marriages, she must have instigated between people who imagined they had met by pure chance.

Cheryl Summerbee was very much in favour of love. She firmly believed that it made the world go round, and did her bit to keep the globe spinning on its axis by her discreet management of the seating on British Airways Tridents. On the shelf under her counter she kept a Bills and Moon romance to read in those slack periods when there were no passengers to deal with. The one she was reading at the moment was called *Love Scene*. It was about a girl called Sandra who went to work as a nanny for a film director whose wife had died tragically in a car accident, leaving him with two young children to look after. Of course Sandra fell in love with the film director, though unfortunately he was in love with the actress taking the leading role in the film he was making – or was he just pretending to be in love with her to keep her sweet? Of course he was! Cheryl Summerbee had read enough Bills and Moon romances to know that – indeed she hardly needed to read any further to predict exactly how the story would end. With half her mind she despised these love stories, but she devoured them with greedy haste, like cheap sweets. Her own life was, so far, devoid of romance – not for lack of propositions, but because she was a girl of old-fashioned moral principle. So she was still waiting for Mr Right to appear. She had no very clear image of what he would look like except that he would have a hard chest and firm thighs. All the heroes of Bills and Moon romances seemed to have hard chests and firm thighs.

5

10

15

20

25

30

35

from *Small World* by David Lodge

▼ B **Highlight these words and phrases in the text and try to deduce their meanings from the context (the line number is given beside each word). Underline the words or phrases that help you to deduce the meanings.**

a technical hitch	6	a lonely hearts agency	18	slack periods	24
the full brunt	6	by stealth	18	a nanny	25
to alleviate	7	instigated	19	keep her sweet	29
accordingly	13	made the world go round	21	devoid of	32
blind dates	17	did her bit	22	not for lack of	32

(Use a dictionary to look up any phrases you couldn't deduce the meanings of.)

C **Find an example in the text of each of the following:**

1 HUMOUR — something that made you smile

2 INFORMATION — something you didn't realise or know before

3 OPINION — a point of view expressed by the writer

4 SOCIAL COMMENT — a comment on the way people behave

5 EMPATHY — something that made you share the writer's or Cheryl's feelings

A Read this article and fill each gap with one suitable word.

In her arms, he melted . . .

FOR something that money can't buy, love sells well. Harlequin Enterprises, a subsidiary of Torstar, a Canadian publisher, knows that better than ₁ _____ . A mix of lush locations ("from the ₂ _____ she felt herself lifted on to Rodrigo Aviles's saddle, Rebecca Harper knew she had definitely wandered off the tourist trail in Baja"), and lusher characters ("Arminel knew that her holiday friendship with Rhys Beringer was no more than that, a friendship"), Harlequin's simple ₃ _____ last year produced C$348m ($300m) in sales and C$58m in operating profit. British and Australian pulp-passion readers know them under the Mills & Boon imprint.

Harlequin works more like a periodical publisher than a ₄ _____ publisher. Over 60 new ₅ _____ appear each month. Distributed through newsstands and mail-order rather than ₆ _____ , all go out of print within weeks. Priced at under $3 and fewer than 200 pages long, the books are cheaper than most magazines, and take no ₇ _____ to read.

To keep the titles flowing, Harlequin maintains a vast stable of regular ₈ _____ . Around 600 are managed from the firm's Toronto and New York offices, 350 from London. Few contributors write full-time: one of the most popular started ₉ _____ as a bank cashier; most are housewives or slumming journalists. To keep their output consistent, Harlequin issues them with ₁₀ _____ instructions on characterisation and plot. The hero must be "overwhelmingly attractive – that means he probably isn't bald, short or fat," suggests an introductory tape. Happy endings are ₁₁ _____ .

Harlequin's marketing strategy is as simple as its editorial one. Different sub-brands aim at different ₁₂ _____ of reader. The relatively explicit Temptation series, launched six years ago, aims at younger women. Harlequin's Medical Romances ₁₃ _____ in war-time love stories about injured soldiers and caring nurses. Latest in the series: Starsign Romances ("too late for her to avert her ₁₄ _____ now, she decided, holding her aloof Virgo stare on his smiling face"). Harlequin also has a series celebrating that most romantic of unions, the single European market. Each book's ₁₅ _____ will be from a different EU country. Yes, even Belgium.

B 1 Look at this blurb from the cover of a Mills & Boon Enchanted® romance. Discuss what happens if the roles are reversed (i.e. man falls in love with his mother's daughter).

2 Draft a blurb (about 100 words) for the back cover of another romantic novel.

3 Look at each other's blurbs.

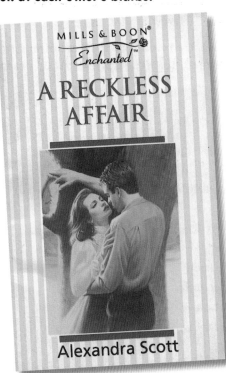

MILLS & BOON®
Enchanted™
A RECKLESS AFFAIR
Alexandra Scott

A forbidden love?

Ginny has flown off to the United States expecting to find the father she never knew. Instead she finds Jake Vanbrugh – his son! Jake is the most arresting man, and when Ginny discovers the instant attraction is mutual, she knows she's in deep trouble.

Jake doesn't know that she's Hugo Vanbrugh's daughter, and things are going to have to stay that way until Jake leads Ginny to him.

But in the meantime how can Ginny control her own feelings and keep Jake's avid attentions at bay? It seems impossible and also imperative – but, then, Ginny doesn't know the truth about Jake...

Romance
UK £2.20
ISBN 0-263-80369-4

9 780263 803693

C 1 You'll hear nine people answering this question: 'Do you believe in love?' Count up the number who give (or imply) the answer Yes or the answer No.

Yes	
No	

2 Listen to the recording again and discuss these questions:

- To what extent do you share the views of each speaker?
- Which speakers do you agree with and disagree with? Why?
- Which speaker would you most (and least) like to meet in person?

- What is your own definition of 'love'?
- What is the difference between 'being in love' with someone and 'loving' someone?
- Are you a romantic person? What are your reactions to the image of romance in the photo on the right?

Preparation

Find a cassette of a favourite British or American love song – or, if you prefer, a song about something else. Write down the words so that the others in your group can see them.

D Present your song to the others in your group and explain why you like it – what makes it special? Show them the words and point out your favourite lines.

17.4 First meetings
Speaking and Listening

A Discuss these questions:

- In your country/city where do young people meet to spend time together?
- At what age do people usually get married and how long do engagements usually last?
- How have romantic relationships changed since when your parents were young?

B We asked some people to describe their first meeting with their present partner. This is how their replies began:

I was on my way home from junior high school . . .
I'd arranged to have a drink with a friend of mine . . .
We met at a fancy-dress party . . .
I was going out to the cinema with a group of friends . . .
I first met him when he was on a boat and I was on the river bank . . .

1 Use your imagination to work out how TWO of the stories might have continued.

2 Tell your stories to each other.

3 Now listen to the real stories – how close were your ideas to what really happened?

(17.5) First paragraphs
Reading and Speaking

A These are the opening paragraphs of five well-known books. Note down what kind of book each extract seems to be from.

▼ Highlight TWO phrases in each extract that intrigue you and encourage you to read on.

a

> EMMA WOODHOUSE, handsome, clever, and rich, with a comfortable home and happy disposition, seemed to unite some of the best blessings of existence; and had lived nearly twenty-one years in the world with very little to distress or vex her.

b

> THERE were four of us – George, and William Samuel Harris, and myself, and Montmorency. We were sitting in my room, smoking, and talking about how bad we were – bad from a medical point of view I mean, of course.
> We were all feeling seedy

c

> Last night I dreamt I went to Manderley again. It seemed to me I stood by the iron gate leading to the drive, and for a while I could not enter, for the way was barred to me. There was a padlock and chain upon the gate. I called in my dream to the lodge-keeper, and had no answer, and peering closer through the rusted spokes of the gate I saw the lodge was uninhabited.
> and the little lattice

d

> IT was a bright cold day in April, and the clocks were striking thirteen. Winston Smith, his chin nuzzled into his breast in an attempt to escape the vile wind, slipped quickly through the glass doors of Victory Mansions, though not quickly enough to prevent a swirl of gritty dust from entering with him.

e

> I was three or perhaps four years old when I realized that I had been born into the wrong body, and should really be a girl. I remember the moment well, and it is the earliest memory of my life.
> I was sitting beneath my mother's piano, and her music was falling

B One of you should look at Activity 13, the other at 21. You'll each have more information about the books to share with your partner.

C 1 Make notes on a favourite book of yours. Explain why you liked the book, what it is about and why you recommend it to other readers. Try to cover these aspects:

- Style – how well-written and readable it is
- About the writer – his or her background and other books
- The characters – what kind of people they are
- Plot – what happens in the story
- Setting – where the action takes place
- Why you enjoyed it – and why other people would enjoy it

2 Prepare a short talk about it to give to the other members of your group or the whole class.

3 Give a presentation about the book and answer questions about it.

D 1 Write an article (about 250 words) for a student magazine, describing the book and persuading others to read and enjoy it.

2 Show your article to two or three other people and read their work too.

(17.6) Expressing feelings
Effective writing

A In a conversation we often show our attitude or feelings through smiles, frowns, sympathetic expressions, etc. In writing we have to express these feelings in words.

Add three more words that express each of these feelings. Use a dictionary, if necessary.

How marvellous! → I was delighted	*pleased*	*thrilled*	....
Oh dear! → I was dismayed	....	....	....
What a surprise! → I was amazed	....	....	....
How annoying! → I was annoyed	....	....	....
How strange ! → I was puzzled	....	....	....

B 1 Imagine that you've just received this card from Pam and Max, two former classmates of yours. It's quite a surprise because you didn't even know Pam and Max were seeing each other.

> *Sandra and Rupert Dupont*
> are pleased to announce the engagement
> of their only daughter
> *Pamela*
> to
> *Max Steiner*
> eldest son of Maria and Richard Steiner
> of Geneva, Switzerland

The last time you heard from Pam was in 1997 when she sent you this note:

The last time you heard from Max was in 1998 when he sent you this letter:

> 4 April 1997
>
> Dear Chris,
> It's been a long time since we heard from each other. Guess who I met the other day: Max who was in our class! He hasn't changed at all – still the same clumsy, inconsiderate person. He asked me out for dinner but I said no thanks (obviously). He asked about you and sent his love.
> Let me know how you're getting on,
> Love,
> Pam

> 12 May 1998
>
> Dear Chris,
> I just had to write to tell you that I've got engaged! My fiancée's name is Kate and she works in one of the offices at the university. She's a wonderful person and we get on really well. Although we haven't fixed a date for the wedding yet, I won't forget to invite you when we do.
> Send me a card with your news!
> Love,
> Max

2 Write one **letter** (about 100 words) to Pam, and another **letter** (about 100 words) to Max, and a **note** to Pam's parents (about 50 words), thanking them for sending you the card.

(Look at **Activity 33** for some useful phrases that can be used when you're sending someone greetings or congratulations.)

Four weddings and . . .
Listening and Creative writing

A 1 You'll hear Karen, Michael, Ishia and Tim describing weddings they have attended. Match the names of the speakers to the points they made.

Write K, M, I or T beside the comments – or N if nobody mentioned a point.

1	
2	
3	
4	
5	
6	
7	
8	

1 Everyone gave the newly-weds money.
2 The best man wore a black suit.
3 The live band was terrible.
4 The reception was not much fun.
5 The speaker's brother was dressed like the other guests.
6 The wedding ceremony is not as important as the reception.
7 The wedding took place in Turkey.
8 There was a civil ceremony, not a religious one.

2 Discuss these questions:

● What aspects of each wedding was different from your own experiences of weddings in your country?
● Which of the weddings sounded the most fun?

3 Find out if your partners have ever attended a wedding and get them to describe it to you. Find out how the guests at the wedding felt – was everyone happy?

B 1 Read the first paragraph of this account of a wedding on the left. What improvements have been made in the second version?

> It began with a civil ceremony at the registry office. Not many people came to that. Then the close family had lunch at the Royal Hotel. The main reception was in the evening. They invited all their friends to the party and there was a live band and lots to eat and drink.

> All weddings are different — but in some ways they're all the same. This one started with a civil ceremony, attended only by the couple and their parents, who went on from there to the Royal Hotel for lunch. Then they all had a break before the reception, which <u>everyone</u> had been invited to!

2 Look at the second and third paragraphs and suggest how they can be improved. Then write a fourth, concluding paragraph.

> The party itself was wonderful. Everyone was there: all the couple's friends from work, the people they knew at college and even some old school friends had been invited. It started at 8pm and went on till midnight. At exactly 10pm the band stopped playing and the couple cut the wedding cake. We all got a piece.
>
> Then it was time for the speeches. The bridegroom was awfully nervous and his speech was disappointing, but then the best man made his speech and it was hilarious. He told us all about the groom's childhood and student days because he was his best friend. Then he got the giggles and couldn't go on, but everyone clapped for ages.

C Write an account (about 250 words) of either:

a wedding in your own country that you have attended

OR a family event that you have participated in (a birthday celebration, anniversary party, christening, funeral, etc.)

When you're writing an account of your personal experiences, in real life you'll tell the truth — but in an exam you can use your imagination and invent fictional experiences. In real life too an account can be more interesting if you exaggerate a little, focus on the most exciting or amusing events and don't mention the routine or boring things that happened.

17.8   Head over heels . . .
Idioms and collocations

A   **Number these expressions, grading them according to their meanings:**

1 **loves** → 2 **likes**   3 **dislikes** → 4 **hates**

HE/SHE . . .

fancies	can't bear	is crazy about
is devoted to	can't live without	doesn't think much of
is indifferent to	is fond of	is keen on
thinks the world of	is incompatible with	detests
doesn't get on with	loathes	gets on really well with
can't stand the sight of	is attracted to	has gone off
has fallen out with	is head over heels in love with	adores

. . . HER/HIM

B   **Fill the gaps in these sentences with a suitable form of head, brain or mind.**

1   She's very good at maths – she has a good .... for figures.
2   They were in two .... whether to get married.
3   If there's an emergency, don't panic – try to keep your ....
4   We couldn't solve the problem, but suddenly I had a .... wave.
5   I'll spin a coin to see – do you want to call .... or tails?
6   That's too difficult for me to follow – it's over my ....
7   He can't climb a ladder because he has no .... for heights.
8   They were .... over heels in love.
9   A good book can help to take your .... off your troubles.
10   When it comes to politics, I try to keep an open ....
11   I'm sorry I didn't make that phone call, it slipped my ....
12   If there's a problem to solve, two .... are better than one.

C   **Fill these gaps with a suitable form of face, eye, nose, or ear.**

1   I can't tell you exactly what to do – you'll have to play it by ....
2   I tried to catch the waiter's .... but he didn't look my way.
3   I have to go away for a while, can you keep an .... on them for me?
4   They normally see .... to .... but in this case they disagreed.
5   During the wedding someone started giggling and I couldn't keep a straight ....
6   When they said they'd got engaged I couldn't believe my ....
7   She's such a snob – she looks down her .... at everyone.
8   Don't bother to tell me how to get there – I'll follow my ....
9   You can't support both sides at once – don't be so two-............... .
10   If you admit to making such a serious mistake you may lose ....
11   He knew the risks and went into it with his .... open.
12   Anything you say to them goes in one .... and out the other.

"Forsake all others! That's a bit drastic, isn't it?"

Eighteen

THE NATURAL WORLD

(18.1) FAUNA AND FLORA
Vocabulary and Listening

A 1 Ask your partners:
- what kinds of creatures are popular as pets among their friends
- why they believe it's important to protect the environment

2 Note down FIVE environmental issues that are in the news at the moment.

B Identify these animals and plants and make sure you can both spell and pronounce their names correctly. Then add two more species to each group.

1 Mammals

2 Birds

3 Insects and invertebrates

4 Reptiles and amphibians

5 Flowers

6 Trees and plants

7 Sea creatures

C One of you should look at Activity 5, the other at 24. When you've read the short passage there, tell your partner about it and then discuss these questions:

● Whose situation would be worse: Gregor's or Eric's? Why?

● What do you think might have happened next in each story?

● If you could be an animal, what kind of animal would you *most* like to be and why?

D You'll hear ten extracts from conversations – the last word or phrase of each clip is not audible. Write down the missing word or phrase.

1	*giraffes*
2	
3	
4	
5	

6	
7	
8	
9	
10	

(18.2) Compound words
Word study

> As a rule of thumb, the most common short compound nouns tend to be written as single words. If you're unsure you should consult an up-to-date dictionary. If in doubt, write a compound noun as two words, without a hyphen.

A 1 Compound nouns

There are no hard-and-fast rules about whether the two elements of a compound noun are written as one word or two words. Look at these examples:

one word	*blackbird bookcase bookseller breakdown classroom girlfriend greenhouse headache lighthouse railway raincoat rainforest sightseeing wildlife*
two words	*breakdown service bus driver bus station bus stop greenhouse effect headache tablets power station railway station sightseeing coach station manager toy shop wildlife reserve*
hyphen	*do-it-yourself great-grandmother make-up two-thirds*

2 Match each of the words in the first group with words in the second group to form compound nouns:

acid rain   chain reaction   coal mine   coffee break

acid ✓   chain ✓   coal ✓   coffee ✓   charter   committee   computer   drinking   flight
food   holiday   language   meeting   ozone   palm   pet   post   pressure   progress
safety   steering   telephone   traffic   typing   video   waiting   washing   wastepaper
water   window   zoo

attendant   basket   break ✓   brochure   call   chain   cleaner   flight   food   group   keeper
layer   lights   machine   meeting   mine ✓   office   paper   point   precautions   pressure
rain ✓   reaction ✓   recorder   room   screen   teacher   test   tree   water   wheel

B 1 Compound adjectives

Most compound adjectives are written with a hyphen. Look at these examples:

*user-friendly   well-known   self-satisfied   self-employed   state-of-the-art   second-hand
up-to-date*

But some are written as one word:

windproof   suntanned   breathtaking   homesick

2 Match each of the words in the first group with words in the second group to form compound adjectives.

broad-minded   duty-free   energy-efficient   environment-friendly

broad ✓   duty ✓   energy ✓   environment ✓   good   green   hard   hard   heart   home
ill   loose   narrow   quick   record   self   short   time   under   user   well   well

behaved   breaking   broken   consuming   efficient ✓   employed   fingered   fitting   free ✓
friendly ✓   friendly   hearted   informed   looking   made   meaning   minded ✓   minded   paid
staffed   witted   working

(18.3) Protecting the environment
Reading and Listening

**1 Choose the best phrase given opposite to fit in each of the numbered gaps.
Two of the phrases don't fit at all.**

PLANET EARTH IS 4,600 MILLION YEARS OLD

If we condense this inconceivable time span into an understandable concept, we can liken Earth to a person of 46 years of age.

Nothing is known about the first seven years of this person's life, and whilst only scattered information exists about the middle span, we know that only at the age of 42 did the Earth begin to flower.

Dinosaurs and the great reptiles 1 _____, when the planet was 45. Mammals arrived only 8 months ago; in the middle of last week manlike apes 2 _____, and at the weekend the last ice age enveloped the Earth.

Modern Man has been around for four hours. During the last hour Man 3 _____. The industrial revolution began a minute ago.

During those sixty seconds of biological time, Modern Man 4 _____.

He has 5 _____, caused the extinction of 500 species of animals, ransacked the planet for fuels and now stands like a brutish infant, gloating over this meteoric rise to ascendancy, on the brink of a war to end all wars and of effectively destroying this oasis of life in the solar system.

GREENPEACE

Against all odds, Greenpeace has 6 _____ to the attention of caring people. Terrible abuses to the environment, often carried out in remote places or far out to sea have 7 _____ and in the press.

Greenpeace began with a protest voyage into a nuclear test zone. The test was disrupted. Today, the site at Amchitka in the Aleutian Islands is a bird sanctuary.

Then Greenpeace sent its tiny inflatable boats to protect the whales. They took up position between the harpoons and the fleeing whales. Today, commercial whaling is banned.

On the ice floes of Newfoundland, Greenpeace volunteers placed their bodies between the gaffs of the seal hunters and the helpless seal pups. The hunt 8 _____.

In the North Atlantic, Greenpeace drove its inflatables underneath falling barrels of radioactive waste. Now nuclear waste dumping at sea has been stopped.

In the North Sea, Greenpeace swimmers 9 _____ carrying chemical wastes. New laws to protect the North Sea have been promised.

Peaceful direct action by Greenpeace 10 _____, which in turn has forced changes in the law to protect wildlife and to stop the pollution of the natural world.

A appeared eight years ago

B brought the plight of the natural world

C did not appear until one year ago

D evolved into ape-like men

E has made a rubbish tip of Paradise

F turned back dump ships

G been headlined on television

H continued despite their efforts

I discovered agriculture

J has invoked the power of public opinion

K multiplied his numbers to plague proportions

L was subsequently called off

 2 Discuss your reactions to what you've read in the passages opposite.

B You'll hear an interview with Cyril Littlewood, who runs the Young People's Trust for the Environment and Nature Conservation. Choose the best answer to questions 1–5.

1 Why did the poachers show Cyril and his friends where to watch badgers?
   A They didn't want to trouble them.
   B They wanted them to help them catch rabbits.
   C They didn't want to get caught.
   D They were hungry.

2 Why does Cyril run courses in Dorset?
   A Local schools invite him to talk to the pupils.
   B So that pupils discover more about nature.
   C The scenery is beautiful.
   D To teach the pupils about the archaeology of the county.

3 Why are many schoolteachers pleased with the courses?
   A The pupils behave better than they do in school.
   B The pupils start to take nature for granted.
   C They get a break from the classroom.
   D The pupils learn more on Cyril's course than they do at school.

4 What should you do when approaching giraffes?
   A Don't get too close.
   B Don't let them see you.
   C Let them see you.
   D Talk in a whisper.

5 What has been the problem with saving the tiger?
   A Money can't stop poachers killing tigers.
   B Not enough money has been raised.
   C The money hasn't been spent on the right things.
   D Too much money has been raised.

Cyril Littlewood

6–12 Fill each gap in this summary with a number:

> Every minute $_6$ _____ babies are born (= $_7$ _____ per day).
>
> Net population growth: $_8$ _____ per day (= $_9$ _____ million per year).
>
> $_{10}$ _____ % of the Earth is covered by the oceans, $_{11}$ _____ % is land.
>
> Only $_{12}$ _____ % of the land surface is available for agriculture to feed the world.

13 In one word, how does Cyril feel about the future? $_{13}$ _____

C Ask your partners:

- how they feel about the future of our planet
- how 'green' they are
- what they do to protect the environment
- what they recycle

 D Write a report about what is being done to protect the environment in your country or region – and recommending what more should be done (about 250 words).

The future and degrees of certainty
Grammar

A **Discuss the difference in meaning between these sentences:**

1 *I'll write to her tomorrow.*   *I will write to her tomorrow.*
   I'm going to write to her tomorrow.   *I'm writing to her tomorrow.*
   I was going to write to her tomorrow.   *I'll have written to her tomorrow.*
   I'll be writing to her tomorrow.   *I'll have to write to her tomorrow.*

2 *Are we going to make the first move?*   *Do we make the first move?*
   Shall we make the first move?   *Will we make the first move?*

3 *I'm just going to phone them now.*   *I'm phoning them now.*
   I'm about to phone them now.   *I've phoned them now.*
   I was just about to phone them now.   *I'll phone them now.*

4 *Will you help us later?*   *Are you helping us later?*
   Are you going to help us later?   *Were you going to help us later?*
   Will you be helping us later?   *Won't you help us later?*
   Won't you be helping us later?   *Aren't you going to help us later?*

B **Spot the errors in these sentences – some contain NO errors.**

1 Will I help you to carry the shopping?
2 What time does the flight land?
3 I'll have a drink while I'm going to wait for his plane to land.
4 The meeting shan't begin until everyone will have arrived.
5 I probably won't have finished my work by the time you arrive.
6 I'm sure it doesn't rain tomorrow.
7 I'll be glad when it will be time to go home.
8 I know you'll be angry when I tell you you've got to rewrite the letter.

C **Fill the gaps in these sentences, using the verbs below. All the sentences refer to FUTURE events.**

1 Fifty hectares of jungle _____ during the next minute.
2 Next year another 250,000 square kilometres of tropical rainforest _____ .
3 Soon most of the world's jungles _____ .
4 Toxic wastes _____ in the oceans more and more in the future.
5 A complete, permanent ban on whaling _____ eventually.
6 Many species of plants and animals _____ extinct next year.
7 The use of pesticides _____ to the evolution of chemical-resistant pests.
8 Pollution _____ still _____ damage to the environment in the 21st century.
9 Governments _____ more notice of environmental pressure groups.
10 Energy conservation measures _____ into effect.

| accumulate   become   cause   come   cut down   devastate   destroy   impose   lead   take |

"Negotiate? What is there to negotiate?"

D Match each sentence in the first column with one in the second column that means the same.

1 I don't think he'll be here on time.
2 He's very unlikely to be on time.
3 I'm sure he'll be late.
4 He'll probably get here on time.
5 He may get here on time.
6 I know he'll get here on time.
7 I expect he'll be here on time.
8 I'm almost certain he'll be on time.

a He can't possibly arrive on time.
b I doubt if he'll be late.
c He's not going to be late.
d I don't know if he's going to be late.
e I think he'll be late.
f There's a slim chance he'll be late.
g I'm pretty sure he'll be late.
h He's unlikely to be late.

E This chart shows various people's predictions about the effects of global warming.
Decide where the sentences in red below fit into chart, according to their meanings.

100% ↑	Temperatures will rise. I'm sure that temperatures will rise.	= I'm certain they will
	Temperatures will probably rise.	= probable
↑ 50% ↓	Temperatures may rise. I'm not sure whether temperatures will rise or not. Temperatures may not rise.	= I'm uncertain
	Temperatures probably won't rise.	= improbable
↓ 0%	I'm sure that temperatures won't rise. Temperatures won't rise.	= I'm certain they will not

It looks as if it will get warmer.
I'm fairly sure it won't get warmer.
I doubt if it will get warmer.
It's going to get warmer.
In all probability it will get warmer.
I'm absolutely sure it will get warmer.
I wouldn't be surprised if it got warmer.
I suppose it might get warmer.
There's not much chance that it will get warmer.
There's a very good chance that it will get warmer.

I bet it will get warmer.
I guess it might get warmer.
I'd be surprised if it got warmer.
It's likely to get warmer.
Of course it won't get warmer.
It's sure to get warmer.
It's bound to get warmer.
I don't think it will get warmer.
There's no likelihood that it will get warmer.
In all probability it's going to get a great deal warmer.

F Find out if your partners are optimistic or pessimistic about the 21st century by discussing these questions:

● How much of the damage caused to the natural world is likely to be controlled or reversed during the 21st century?
● What scientific and medical discoveries will be made? How are they likely to affect YOU?
● What technological breakthroughs and inventions will be made?
● What political and cultural changes will there be? How might these events affect you?
● What will your OWN lives be like in the 21st century?

Spelling and pronunciation 2 – Vowels
Pronunciation and Word study

> Although there are only five vowels in the alphabet, there are over 24 vowel and diphthong sounds in English.

A **Write down another word that RHYMES with each of the words below:**

vowels	æ	e	ɑː	ɔː	ɜː	iː	ɪ	ɒ	ʊ	ʌ	uː
	bad	end	calm	caught	bird	sleep	slip	pot	look	lunch	cool
	sad	*friend*	....	....	....	....	....	....	....	....	....

diphthongs	aɪ	aʊ	ɔɪ	eə	ɪə	eɪ	əʊ	ʊə	aɪə	aʊə	ɔɪə	eɪə	əʊə
	bite	now	toy	there	here	make	note	fuel	tired	tower	royal	player	lower
	....	....	....	....	....	....	....	....	....	....	....	....	....

B 1 **Remember that the weak vowel sounds /ə/ and /i/ occur in _unstressed_ syllables. Look at these examples and listen to the recording.**

This kind of thing happens again and again.   ðɪs kaɪnd əv θɪŋ hæpənz əgen ənd əgen

All of us thought it was a pretty good party.   ɔːl əv əs θɔːt it wəz ə prɪti gʊd pɑːti

2 **Underline the unstressed weak vowels in these sentences – imagine they're spoken at normal conversational speed. Then listen to the recording to check.**

1 We all enjoyed your talk very much – the subject was very interesting.

2 The damage caused to the environment by industry is often overlooked.

3 Against all odds, Greenpeace has brought the plight of the natural world to the attention of caring people.

C **Look at these words that are pronounced the same but spelt differently. Take it in turns to explain the differences in meaning between them, like this:**

> A BAND is a group of musicians.
> 'DAMN!' is what you might say if you're annoyed.

> If a film is BANNED it can't be shown.
> A DAM holds back the water in a lake or reservoir.

æ	band · banned damn · dam
e	red · read weather · whether bred · bread lent · leant scent · sent · cent sell · cell
ɑː	passed · past draught · draft
ɔː	bored · board nor · gnaw or · awe · ore · oar sawed · sword stalk · stork
ɜː	heard · herd colonel · kernel fur · fir
iː	piece · peace be · B · bee he'll · heel · heal key · quay read · reed steel · steal
ɪ	mist · missed which · witch
ɒ	not · knot what · watt
ʊ	wood · would
ʌ	one · won none · nun some · sum son · sun
uː	root · route dew · due flew · flu queue · cue
aɪ	right · write die · dye high · Hi hire · higher isle · I'll · aisle mind · mined sighed · side site · sight tire · tyre
aʊ	allowed · aloud bough · bow flour · flower
ɔɪ	boy · buoy
eə	fair · fare there · their · they're air · heir bear · bare hair · hare mayor · mare
ɪə	here · hear cereal · serial deer · dear peer · pier
eɪ	break · brake vain · vein wade · weighed whale · wail
əʊ	nose · knows groan · grown rode · road · rowed rose · rows soul · sole so · sew · sow toes · tows

D Put the words in each group into pairs, according to the way the vowels in red are pronounced. Look at the examples first:

i	mile film fright firm title sir island kitchen
	mile + title film + kitchen fright + island firm + sir
a	watch father bald share ache hand says castle yacht scarce factory any vague yawn
ea	bear team break threat hearty fear search weak jealous earnest pear dreary sweetheart steak
au	sausage naughty laugh daughter draught cauliflower (*note also:* gauge)
ei	receive weight leisure their height perceive heir either neighbour Leicester (*note also:* foreign)
ie	chief fierce friendship die pier pliers believe unfriendly (*note also:* ancient)
u	bury bullet butter business refuse murder flute butcher burst guess busy mustard
o	monkey lose folk crowd orange boy ordinary frontier joyful shower glorious soften ghost movement
ou	enough found bought cough dough through should thorough rough although could trough court plough throughout borough
oo	food flood floor foot book loose door blood

18.6 *Keep, hold, stand* and *turn*
Verbs and idioms

Fill the gaps with the appropriate form of keep, hold, stand or turn.

1 The children were misbehaving, but their uncle .... a blind eye to it.

2 They had to .... back before reaching the summit of the mountain.

3 If you can't do it on Friday, the work can be .... over till next week.

4 Make yourself at home — there's no need to .... on ceremony.

5 If you want to succeed in our office, you have to .... in with the boss.

6 Everyone else was against him, so we decided to .... up for him.

7 The college .... a record of every student's attendance.

8 Concorde .... the world record for the fastest round-the-world flight.

9 While on holiday I always .... a diary to help me to remember it later.

10 He's feeling lonely and upset, will you be able to .... him company?

11 The day he met Maria was a .... point in his life.

12 We were disappointed when they .... down our offer.

13 I've been trying to get .... of her on the phone, but there's no answer.

14 .... it! It's not time to start yet.

15 I knew the bad news would upset them, so I .... it back from them.

16 Bob is Mrs Reed's assistant: he .... in for her when she's on holiday. If he's away then someone else has to .... the fort.

17 In an emergency, try to .... your head — i.e. don't panic.

18 She can do fantastic somersaults and she can even .... on her head.

19 If you really want to do that, I won't .... in your way.

20 This new fabric can .... up to very heavy wear.

Nineteen

What's in the news?

(19.1) ### In the headlines
Vocabulary and Speaking

A **Ask your partners:**
- which newspaper they normally read and why — or why they don't normally read one
- which sections they normally read and if they ever read the editorial (leader)
- if they prefer a tabloid (e.g. *The Sun*) or a quality daily (e.g. *The Guardian*)

B **Look at these newspaper headlines, which appeared on successive days in a newspaper. Can you explain what happened each day?**

M   Bus fares set to rise says report *A report has been published saying that bus fares are going to rise.*

Tu   "BUSES TO BE AXED IN BID TO CUT COSTS" SAYS BUS CHIEF

W   Clash over threat to axe buses – passengers slam bus chief

Th   MINISTER BACKS BUS CHIEF

F   Bus chief quits over bus battle

S   MINISTER AXED AFTER CABINET SPLIT OVER BUS ROW

C **1** **Match these verbs which are often found in newspaper headlines with the more common verbs below:**

axe/scrap   back   call   clash   curb   grab   loom   oust   quit   slam   soar   swoop   vow/pledge

be imminent   confiscate   criticise   disagree   promise   raid   reduce/dismiss   replace   request
resign   restrict   rise   support

2 **Now do the same with these nouns which are used in newspaper headlines:**

battle/clash/feud/row   bid   blaze   chief   drama   fury/outrage   link   riddle   split   threat   war

anger   attempt   connection   disagreement   division   fire   happening   mystery
person in charge/leader   possibility   rivalry

D **1** **Can you guess what was the amusing story that followed each of these headlines?**

1	**Wife attacks husband**	7	Bird starts blaze
2	Bird's unlucky escape	8	Burglar washes up
3	Burglar interrupts TV	9	**Son has Dad arrested**
4	Greetings card drives couple from home	10	*'Sorry, wrong country!'*
5	NO MONEY IN THE BANK	11	Short-sighted robber arrested
6	**Dad sends son to jail**	12	A GENEROUS TIP

2 **One of you should look at Activity 17, one at 30 and one at 36. Tell your partners the real stories — and find out if you guessed right!**

Preparation ✂   **Find an English-language newspaper and read it before the next lesson. Choose one article and make notes on the main points (or use a highlighter). Get ready to tell the rest of your group about your article in the next lesson.**

(19.2) Don't believe everything you read . . .
Reading

A 1 Read this newspaper article and find out what mistake *The Sun* made.

2 Note down your answers to these questions:

Was it Dr Heinz Wolff (*Dr*), Prof Heinz Wolff (*Prof*) or both of them (*Dr + Prof*) who . . .

1 died, according to *The Sun*?
2 is/was a bio-engineer?
3 is/was 61?
4 once lived in Hampstead?
5 presented a television programme?
6 studied at University College Hospital?
7 came to live in London?

8 was in Holland yesterday?
9 is/was a doctor?
10 is/was 73?
11 was born in Berlin?
12 really died on Monday?
13 studied at University College, London?

Sun tribute cried the wrong Wolff

Ed Vulliamy

PROFESSOR Heinz Wolff, the distinguished director of the Brunel Institute for Bio-engineering, whose tragic death was reported in *The Sun* last Monday, spoke cheerfully enough to *The Guardian* yesterday, using not a ouija board or spirit medium but a telephone from a Dutch seaside town called Noordwijk.

"Great Egg Race Prof Dies at 61," announced *The Sun*, referring to Professor Wolff's role in what the paper called the "loony inventions series" on BBC TV – and sparked off a bizarre chain of events throughout which Professor Wolff remained alive and well.

Within days of *The Sun's* story, two obituaries appeared in *The Times* and *The Independent*, detailing the career of a Dr Heinz Wolff a leading psychodynamic psychiatrist, who had died at 73.

Dr Wolff had, sadly, died –

but *The Sun* had got the wrong Heinz Wolff.

Professor Heinz Wolff was in Holland yesterday to make a presentation to a research laboratory. "I have started to receive cards in the post saying, 'I'm glad you are still alive'," he said. "The main thing has been the tremendous number of phone calls I've had to make – family, friends, people who ask me to lecture to them or make videos; I'm still doing it."

When his death was announced, organisers of a meeting he was due to attend decided to cancel, out of respect, and telephoned his home to offer condolences. His wife, Joan, said yesterday:

"The switchboard at Brunel was jammed with people ringing up on Monday morning. But our first thoughts were for the family, and the terrible worry that people would hear secondhand – I mean, most of our friends don't read *The Sun*."

Both Professor Heinz Wolff and Dr Heinz Wolff were born in Berlin and settled in London. At one time, when Professor Wolff lived in Hampstead Garden Suburb and Dr Wolff lived in Hampstead, their telephone numbers differed by one digit.

Professor Wolff is a graduate of University College, London; Dr Wolff trained, and later became a department head, at University College Hospital. "We have been confused before," said Professor Wolff, "but never in such a horrifying way."

Several famous names have read of their own deaths in the newspapers, the most celebrated being Mark Twain, who complained that "reports of my death are grossly exaggerated". George Bernard Shaw read his own obituary and Ernest Hemingway was killed in print twice before he died. *The Guardian* also paid last respects to the writer Ngaio Marsh before she was quite ready to accept them.

B Tell each other about the newspaper articles you've read and made notes on. Then discuss these questions:

● Why did you choose that particular article to tell the others about?
● Do you believe everything you read in the newspapers? Give your reasons.
● What makes an event newsworthy?

Danger – Hippies!
Reading and Listening

 30 May You'll hear the early evening radio news. Listen to the recording at least twice.

1 Decide what is the attitude of the broadcaster to the travellers.

2 What actually happened? Note down what you consider to be the THREE most important points.

3 Compare your notes with a partner.

31 May Now read the press report of the same events.

1 Decide what is the attitude of the writer to the travellers.

2 Note down what you consider to be the THREE most important points made in the article.

3 Compare your notes with a partner.

4 What are your reactions to the points of view expressed by Tony?

Travelling tribe of 300 individuals tries to leave 'rubbish society' behind

Andrew Moncur

Home for Tony and his four-year-old daughter, Emma, is a tarpaulin tent, now packed into a Jaguar with chronic engine fatigue.

It, and possibly 99 other irregular mobile homes, were in the process of eviction from a Somerset farmer's land yesterday. Tony and Emma were resuming their barefoot journey through the byways of an England whose conventional society they reject. Society has returned the sentiment, in full measure, since they took to the road two years ago.

This mutual antipathy had its expression yesterday when the convoy's children, who have

shocked local people and been widely criticised, took the chance to throw a little mud (literally) at the local Tory MP, who came to inspect the site of their mass trespass. Mr Robert Boscawen, MP for Somerton and Frome, was not greatly put out.

Tony is not typical of the 300-odd travellers whose sojourn in farmer Les Attwell's grass field at Lytes Cary near Somerton has been front page news this week.

This is because the typical traveller does not really exist. The convoy consists of disparate groups.

The age of the adults ranges from 16–60; backgrounds are

widely varied, from the painfully respectable to the more painfully deprived.

Tony, aged 23, was set on a life of utter normality in a North Wales town before he gave up his shoes and his trade as a time-served plumber.

"I saw what society was, just rubbish. You could say it's a paranoid view but I don't think so – George Orwell's 1984 has happened already," he said yesterday.

"This is my family. Where else can you go where there are 300 members of a family all in one place? It is a lot closer than it is in the city, where you never get close to anybody."

"In my bender I have probably got everything you have in your house; gas cooking, heating, even a kitchen table. I prefer it to living in a house. I believe in doing what I want to do.

"Put Emma with a kid in London who might be three or four times as old as her, and she's the same age as them. She learns what she wants to learn, what she needs to learn.

"It is like a tribe, if you like. She can read and write. She has been on the road since she was two and she is healthier here than she was anywhere else.

"I don't wear shoes and she doesn't either. One day there was snow and I took about four steps outside and bloody felt it. She was out there, sitting in the snow and making a snowman. She doesn't feel it.

"I think we are people who have seen society for what it is. It takes a lot of courage to make that move, to give up everything you know. It takes about three days to adjust."

31 May to 9 June   You'll hear a sequence of early evening radio news broadcasts for each day between 31 May and 9 June.

1 As you listen, mark the ROUTE that the 'peace convoy' took by joining up the places on the MAP.

2 Note down what you consider to be the SINGLE MOST IMPORTANT EVENT reported on each day. Compare notes with a partner halfway through the sequence and again at the end.

3 Find out how your partners would feel if the Peace Convoy had set up camp in THEIR fields or in a field next door to THEIR home. Discuss these questions:

- Do you approve or disapprove of what the police did on 9 June?
- What do you think the police (or government) should have done sooner?

10 June and 12 June

1 Read the two texts on the next page: one is the editorial from *The Guardian* and the other a letter to the Editor of *The Guardian* from the late John Duke, Chief Constable.

2 Decide on your answers to these questions:

1 What is *The Guardian*'s attitude to the Convoy members?

2 What, according to *The Guardian*, were the three main mistakes of the police operation?

3 What does *The Guardian* think should be done?

4 Why, according to John Duke, did the police move in at 4am?

5 What is John Duke's attitude to the 'hippies'?

6 What is the main point of John Duke's letter?

7 Whose views do you side with and why?

3 Write your seven answers in no more than ONE sentence each.

Operation Overkill

Nothing better illustrates the bizarre pointlessness of the current persecution of the Peace Convoy than the sight of dozens of police marching dozens of hippies along the A31 in the drizzle yesterday after the Stoney Cross campsite was broken up at first light. Sure, the Convoy members are not all sweetness and light, free love and lentils. Sure, they leave a lot of litter and they drink too much. Sure, they have messed up some fields and a disused airfield and blocked some roads for a while. But that hardly makes the Convoy the public enemy that it has now become, commanding headlines, parliamentary statements and emergency ministerial committees.

It doesn't make Stoney Cross "the world's most famous blot on the landscape," as one tabloid had it yesterday. And it doesn't justify the absurd waste of police time and public money (500 police officers on overtime at four o'clock in the morning don't come cheap) that was involved in ludicrous Operation Daybreak launched yesterday.

Nothing that the police either did or said yesterday was remotely proportionate to the problem posed by the Peace Convoy. First, there was no need to go in at 4am, rather than in mid-morning. It wasn't as though the hippies were planning on going anywhere; on the contrary. Second, there was no need to have so many officers, drawn from four different forces. The country is supposed to be short of police in the war against crime. The Convoy has consistently acquiesced when it has been evicted in the past and there was no reason to suppose that this time would be any different; nor was it. Third, it is clear that the main object of the operation was to separate the hippies from their vehicles, thus in the words of the Hampshire chief constable "neutralising" and "decommissioning" the Convoy. Fine – but then what? People don't just disappear, however much you may want them to. Given the importance of the summer solstice to this particular group, it is obvious that they will soon be back in some way. Does that mean that hundreds of police are to spend the next fortnight marching around the lanes of southern England in case someone makes a fraudulent social security claim or someone else steals some firewood? Chief Constable Duke talked yesterday as though he had solved the problem. Alas, he has merely displaced it.

Sooner or later, someone is going to have to be a bit sensible. The Peace Convoy is an environmental problem, it is true, but is it really as great an eyesore or disruption as all the Ministry of Defence's convoys, ranges and no-go areas? Has the Peace Convoy destroyed rural England on a scale to match the grain baron farmers? Are all the road traffic, drugs and criminal damage offences that have piled up around the Convoy really so overwhelmingly serious that everyday crime prevention across large tracts of the south-west needs to be suspended to deal with it? If there was one person in Whitehall with a fraction of the public spirit of the Cornish landowner who has now offered asylum to some of the Convoy, then the whole problem could have been solved weeks ago by the provision of a site. Instead Government seems much happier aimlessly stoking up a mood of intolerant over-reaction which does no credit to anybody and which ensures that the trouble and expense of this whole pathetic business is perpetuated far longer than it ever needed to be.

Why the police officers of Stoney Cross deserve bouquets from the convoy

IN THE interests of accuracy about our operation at Stoney Cross, I feel bound to take what is for me a most unusual step in writing to you.

The previous violence of the convoy when its members drove heavy goods vehicles and coaches at police officers endeavouring to enforce the law, when vehicles from the convoy were driven forcefully at police road blocks, have in the past led to scenes that I would certainly not like to see repeated.

It was for those reasons that such a large number of officers was drawn together so early in the morning, to ensure a peaceful containment of the site without risk of further violence which would have required a police response. That no injuries or damage occurred during the taking of the site is clear justification for that decision.

Recognising that at the end of the operation a large number of people, including children, would be effectively displaced, it was police officers who took the initiative to draw together the relevant groups of the social services in order that those caring agencies, including police, could play their part in taking care of members of the convoy.

Police officers laid on coaches to provide transport to the social services; *police officers* offered and provided refreshment to members of the convoy; *police officers* persuaded members of the convoy to take the obvious advantage of the caring agencies.

Police did not march dozens of "hippies" along the A31; the "hippies" themselves decided to set off in that direction without any consultation with or direction from the police. The police officers went with them to ensure their safety and that of other road users.

As to your frivolous comment (Leader, June 10) about fraudulent social security claims and the theft of firewood, I am sure you realise that the unlawful behaviour of the convoy is far greater than this.

Yes, of course the convoy is a social and environmental problem, as well as a legal one. For my part I have no hesitation in applying the law to ensure the safety and protection not only of the public but also of the convoy members themselves.

As for the order of the High Court, are you really suggesting that it should be ignored, or would you expect me to sit back and contemplate another series of offences and disruption for other communities? I am confident that the firm, caring operation by the police, coupled with its shared and overtly caring aspect, was justified and proper.

John Duke,
(Chief Constable).
Hampshire Constabulary,
Winchester.

(19.4) Connecting words
Effective writing

(A)1 Look at *Operation Overkill* again and highlight the following words and phrases in it:

Sure, . . . Sure, . . . Sure, . . .	= anticipating objections
But . . .	= counter-argument
It doesn't . . . And it doesn't . . .	= adding further points
First, . . . Second, . . . Third . . .	= list of points
Sooner or later . . .	= time relationships

2 Highlight the rhetorical questions that were used in the editorial. What answer (if any) is expected to each question?

(B)1 These expressions can be used (rather like 'signposts') to connect the ideas in a piece of writing and show the reader which way you're heading:

Anticipating objections
While it is true that . . .   Although it must be admitted that . . .
Certainly . . .   Although . . .

Counter-argument or contrast
On the other hand . . .   Nevertheless . . .   Nonetheless . . .
In spite of this . . .   All the same . . .   After all . . .
At all events . . .   In any case . . .

Adding further points
Furthermore . . .   Moreover . . .   Besides . . .   What is more . . .

List of points
Firstly . . .   First of all . . .   In the first place . . .   To begin with . . .
Secondly . . .   In the second place . . .

Time relationships
Meanwhile . . .   At the same time . . .   In the meantime . . .   For the time being . . .
Eventually . . .   One day . . .   Until then . . .

Giving reasons
The reason for this is . . .   The cause of this is . . .

Stating or anticipating consequences
As a result of this . . .   Consequently . . .   Because of this . . .   And so . . .
This means that . . .   Therefore . . .   That is why . . .   It follows that . . .
If this happens . . .   If this happened . . .

Summary or conclusion
To sum up . . .   In other words . . .   In short . . .   After all . . .
When all's said and done . . .

2 Decide which of the expressions you could use in place of the phrases you highlighted in the editorial.

(C) Fill the gaps in this article and then continue it with your own ideas (about 150 more words), beginning like this: *Secondly . . .*

_____ hard drugs can never be totally eradicated, there are a number of steps that should be taken to reduce their use. _____ these steps must be taken at once – before it is too late. _____, national governments throughout the world must control the use and supply of drugs within their borders. _____ international organisations must coordinate individual states' policies. States which 'supply' drugs may be pursuing contradictory policies to states that 'consume' them and _____ time and effort is frequently wasted.

Crime and punishment
Vocabulary and Speaking

A 1 Fill each gap in this description of the English legal system with one of the words below. Put a ring round the letter beside the correct answer.

> The underlying ₀ _____ of English justice is that everyone is ₁ _____ until proved guilty.
> In England and Wales, if a person is ₂ _____ of a serious ₃ _____, he (or she) is
> ₄ _____ and then ₅ _____ by the police and ₆ _____ with the crime. Then he may
> be held in ₇ _____ or released on ₈ _____ until his case is heard first at a Magistrates'
> Court, where he is represented by a ₉ _____. He may then have to wait some time before his
> case is heard in the local Crown Court or the Central Criminal Court (The Old Bailey) in London, where
> the ₁₀ _____ is represented by a ₁₁ _____ and the case is heard by a ₁₂ _____ and
> a ₁₃ _____ of twelve men and women. At the end of the ₁₄ _____ he may be found not
> guilty and ₁₅ _____ or he may be found guilty and ₁₆ _____. He may be sent to jail,
> given a ₁₇ _____ sentence or put on ₁₈ _____, or perhaps made to pay a ₁₉ _____.
> If he feels he has been wrongly convicted, he may ₂₀ _____ against his sentence.

0	A principal	B principle	C rule	D practice
1	A harmless	B innocent	C virtuous	D blameless
2	A convicted	B accused	C suspected	D suspicious
3	A sin	B offence	C wrong	D injury
4	A arrested	B handcuffed	C tortured	D caught
5	A examined	B asked	C questioned	D queried
6	A accused	B framed	C blamed	D charged
7	A cells	B probation	C police station	D custody
8	A security	B bail	C freedom	D liberty
9	A notary	B solicitor	C representative	D deputy
10	A gangster	B criminal	C crook	D defendant
11	A barrister	B champion	C assistant	D supporter
12	A referee	B judge	C examiner	D justice
13	A group	B jury	C panel	D committee
14	A trial	B experiment	C process	D search
15	A acquitted	B excused	C forgiven	D pardoned
16	A committed	B sentenced	C executed	D blamed
17	A suspended	B hypothetical	C conditional	D theoretical
18	A trial	B probation	C parole	D report
19	A penalty	B fine	C forfeit	D damages
20	A protest	B grumble	C complain	D appeal

2 Describe the legal process in your own country, beginning like this:

In my country, if a person has committed a serious crime . . .

*"Did Esme Draycott really go to her lover that
night? Is Selwyn Plunkett dead, or alive and well in
Peru? Was Melanie Frayle asleep or drugged? Who
was the man in the green Lagonda? Stay with us for
Part Two, after the break."*

B 1 Look at the pictures below. One of you (student A) should talk for one minute about them. Compare and contrast them and say what you think the people might be feeling. Student B should listen carefully (see B3 below).

2 Look at the pictures below. Student B should talk for one minute about them – see B1 above. Student A should listen carefully (see B3 below).

3 Explain to what extent you agree or disagree with what your partner said and explain why.

C 1 Consider these situations, all of which involve people breaking the law. Number them in order of seriousness (1 = least serious, 11 = most serious). Discuss how the perpetrators should be dealt with in each case.

2 Think of one even more serious crime to add to the list – and one less serious offence.

> A gang member is shot and injured by a member of his own gang.
> A husband beats up his wife.
> A mother beats up her children.
> A motorist drives at 100km/h in a 60km/h zone.
> A motorist who has been drinking hits a cyclist.
> A person throws away an empty cigarette packet on the pavement.
> A person travels on the bus without a ticket.
> A person finds someone's wallet in a phone box and takes the money from it.
> A wealthy business person doesn't pay his or her taxes.
> An office worker takes some pens and stationery home after work.
> A shopkeeper sells alcohol to children.

D Spend about five minutes discussing these questions:

- Why do you think the crimes you numbered 10 and 11 are so serious?
- Some people say, 'Lock them all up and throw away the key.' What do you think?
- Some people say, 'Society is to blame.' What do you think?
- What would you do if a close friend of yours stole some money?
- What more should be done to prevent crime?

(19.6) **Reports and opinions**
Creative writing

A 1 Look at each of the photos below and discuss these questions:
- What has just happened — and what do you imagine is going to happen later?
- Why are such events considered to be 'newsworthy'?
- What can be done to prevent such things happening?

2 Make notes.

3 Share your ideas.

B Choose ONE of the photos above and, using the notes you made in A2, write TWO articles (each about 120 words) about it:

1 An **account** by a person who was there, describing what happened and how you felt.

2 A **letter to the editor** of a local newspaper, giving your views on what should be done to prevent this kind of thing happening again.

In an **account**, you can show what the people involved said, and how they felt, if you include direct speech.

"Each new speaker's words should begin on a new line."

(19.7) Presenting a radio show
Listening

JoAnne Good

 A You'll hear an interview with JoAnne Good, a radio presenter. Match the reasons on the right to the questions on the left and complete the answer box.

1	Why did she mention so many traffic jams?	A	Listeners made their own personal contributions
2	Why did her early morning travel bulletins become a cult?	B	One of the callers used bad language on air
3	Why was she given a four-hour show?	C	Presenting a phone-in is easier than giving traffic reports
4	Why does she enjoy the first hour of her show?	D	She can't play any music
5	Why does a red light flash on her desk?	E	She had become popular with the listeners
6	Why was she happy to talk to Dorothy from Eastbourne?	F	She had interesting questions to ask the expert
7	Why did she have to cut Dorothy off?	G	She represents the listeners
8	Why do callers on mobile phones take risks?	H	She was an old lady
9	Why did one call kill the show one night?	I	She was boring
10	Why is it better to cover a single topic rather than several?	J	The managing editor wants to speak to her
11	Why is it not a good idea to ask your friends to phone in?	K	There were no other callers that evening
12	Why is it worrying if there are no callers?	L	There will be a much better discussion during the show
		M	They can't be traced
		N	They don't sound like real callers
		O	To please listeners in each county
		P	To show that a caller is waiting to talk
		Q	The traffic was very bad every morning

1	
2	
3	
4	
5	
6	
7	
8	
9	
10	
11	
12	

B Discuss these questions:

● Could you do JoAnne's job? Why (not)?
● What kind of people take part in phone-ins?
● Have you ever listened to a phone-in? What was the topic of the discussion?

(19.8) *Back*, *front* and *side*
Idioms and collocations

Fill the gaps in these sentences with back, front or side.

1 I don't like it when people criticise me behind my _____.
2 The interviewer tried to find out more about the candidate's _____ground.
3 He is a civil servant but he moonlights as a plumber on the _____.
4 They are such good friends that they always sit _____ by _____.
5 The Peace Convoy was _____-page news for two weeks.
6 The Vice-President is the _____-runner in the Presidential contest.
7 If you need some support, let me know and I'll _____ you up.
8 They were going to take part in the scheme but they've _____ed out of it.
9 Computers can crash, so always keep a _____-up copy of your data.
10 We were scared when the car started moving _____wards down the hill.
11 A _____ bencher is an MP who isn't a minister or a shadow minister.
12 Drowsiness is a _____ effect of taking these tablets.
13 I didn't realise that I had my jumper on _____ to _____.
14 The laundry business was a _____ for the gang's criminal activities.
15 A reference book has its contents in the _____ and an index in the _____.
16 We all felt sick as the train moved from _____ to _____.
17 When I challenged him, he _____ down and changed his mind.
18 What was I talking about before I got _____tracked?

Twenty

The real world . . .

(20.1)   **Earning a living**
Vocabulary and Speaking

ii Ⓐ **Write down TEN words that come to mind when you consider the jobs shown above. Then discuss:**

- which of the jobs looks the most appealing, and why
- what jobs you've done, including holiday jobs
- what kind of work you're likely to be doing five years from now
- what kind of job you'd LEAST like to have

iiii Ⓑ 1 **Discuss which of the descriptions on the left best describe the jobs or professions listed on the right:**

strenuous glamorous undemanding	a ski-teacher an airline pilot a market trader
challenging repetitive unpredictable	a bus driver a fisherman a nurse
low-paid highly-paid unpleasant	a soldier a receptionist a telephonist
best done by women	a prime minister or president a truck driver
best done by men	a managing director a merchant seaman

2 **Make a list of FIVE MORE jobs that match the descriptions on the left. Compare your list with another group's list.**

ii Ⓒ 1 **Choose one of the photos above. Then use your imagination to answer these questions:**

- What kind of person does he or she seem to be? What's his or her name?
- What does he or she do on a typical day? What kind of day do you think he or she has had today?
- What happened to him or her today that was unusual or strange?

2 **Write an account of your character's day at work (about 120 words):**

Either a story from your character's point of view, beginning like this:

It was 5.30 on Friday afternoon and I was on my way home after . . .

Or a story about the character (as if in a novel or short story) beginning:

(s)he had had a hard day at work that day . . .

(20.2) **A satisfying job**
Reading

Rosalyn Clark

A Read this interview with Rosalyn Clark. In most
lines of the article there is one unnecessary
word. Write the unnecessary word in the spaces
below. Some lines are correct – indicate
these lines with a tick (✓).

Rosalyn Clark, bus driver

0   I'VE always loved the driving. For some reason I find it relaxing, so driving a bus is ideal. Some
00   of the male bus drivers were a bit funny at first and I think it took them a while to get used to the
1   fact that I was a woman. I could see it in their faces that they were a bit shocked. Bus driving is
2   very male dominated which did make me a bit nervous at the first.
3   When passengers will get on the bus, they sometimes look at me as if to say, "Oh my God, it's a
4   girl, what's she doing?" but when they get off they usually say thank you. My friends and family
5   do think it's weird that I'm a bus driver conductor – and sometimes they get on as I live locally.
6   I like being in control of a big vehicle, perhaps it's the power. I don't find in London traffic
7   stressful, and I don't let anyone get to me. I've learned to switch off when people start being abusive.
8   I think I'm quite a good driver, although on some days are better than others. Switching back to
9   driving cars when I'm not working was a bit difficult at first – I was kept forgetting how wide the
10   car was, but I'm used to it now. I don't know too much about the mechanics of the bus. We don't
11   mess about with the engines or anything. It's not much fun when it breaks down and I have to tell
12   everyone how to get off.
13   I've had a couple of accidents, but fortunately nothing too serious. I've never taken the roof
14   off the bus or anything. I clipped a BMW recently, as he was overtaking past, but that was his fault.
15   I don't work through out the night, but we have to do shift-work, so I might start at 4am and
16   finish at 2am. They don't make any special allowances for females, so sometimes I'm being on my
17   own at night alone. But we have radios which go straight through to the police so I've never
18   felt too threatened. People try and get away without paying, and I sometimes get an abuse, but I've
19   got the assault alarm, which usually gets rid of them away.
20   I get letters sometimes from a bloke called Alan. But then he writes to everyone, specially
21   the girls. He bought for everyone Easter eggs and Christmas presents.

0	*the*
00	✓
1	
2	
3	
4	

5	
6	
7	
8	
9	
10	

11	
12	
13	
14	
15	
16	

17	
18	
19	
20	
21	

⋔ B **Discuss these questions about the article:**

- What are the things Rosalyn enjoys most about her work?
- What are the things she doesn't enjoy?
- If you had her job what would you enjoy and not enjoy about it?

Satisfaction and success
Speaking

A The class is divided into two groups. Group A will carry out a survey based on Questionnaire A and group B on Questionnaire B. Each group should follow this procedure:

1 Interview the members of the other group and find out how they rate the following aspects. Note down their responses.

2 Return to your group. Collate your findings and produce a table summarising the results of your survey. Prepare a presentation of your findings.

3 Give a presentation of your findings to the whole class.

B Write a report of your findings (about 250 words).

A   JOB SATISFACTION

1   How important are the following to you in giving you job satisfaction?

VERY IMPORTANT   IMPORTANT   NOT IMPORTANT   NOT RELEVANT

being popular with colleagues	being asked for advice
being part of a team	being praised by your superiors
being promoted	being successful
challenge	exercising power
giving advice	helping others
increased responsibility	influencing people
learning new things	making money
personal freedom	respect of colleagues
security	seeing the results of your actions
setting up a new system	solving problems
starting a project	completing a project
status	working conditions

2   Which of the features exist in the job you're planning to do one day (or your present job)?

B   SUCCESS IN YOUR CAREER

1   How important are the following attributes in helping someone to be successful in their career?

VERY IMPORTANT   IMPORTANT   NOT IMPORTANT   NOT RELEVANT

a practical mind	ability to delegate
ability to express yourself	ability to think on your feet
ability to work fast	ability to write well
being good at giving orders	being good at flattery
accepting responsibility	ambition
being good with figures	being good with people
concentration	good "connections"
experience	popularity with colleagues
good education	patience
physical and mental toughness	ruthlessness
good social background	willingness to take risks

2   Which of the attributes do you have yourself?

(20.4) **Word order**

Effective writing

Ⓐ **Rearrange these words to make sensible sentences. There are several possible arrangements for each group of words.**

1 a business find hard I it letter to usually write

    I usually find it hard to write a business letter.

  OR   *Usually I find it hard to write a business letter.*

2 get in should as soon as possible them touch We with

3 a fax immediately send should them We

4 a also letter send ought them to We

5 an every day send shouldn't e-mail them We

6 in morning never phone should the them We

7 have letter long really to reply shouldn't so taken their to We

8 completely finished have will When you?

Ⓑ **Rearrange these words to make complete sentences, beginning with the words on the right.**

1 ~~a~~ block brand busy downtown ~~have~~ heart in Manhattan new of office the ~~They~~
                                                  They have a . . .

2 a an company computer ~~has~~ ~~got~~ in job new ~~She~~ software splendid up-and-coming well-paid
                                                  She has got . . .

3 early is taking member most of our permanent reliable retirement staff ~~The~~
                                                          The . . .

4 a a always beautiful beside family hotel + in little lovely mountain stay traditional lake
                                                              I . . .

5 a an and then ~~attended~~ business call committee ~~First~~ + I important long-winded made meeting monthly phone staff
                                            First I attended . . .

Ⓒ **Read the notes below and expand each set of notes into one sentence only, using connecting words and phrases as appropriate, but without adding any extra information.**

A BRIDGE IN THE DESERT

1 River Thames, London: over 20 bridges – Tower Bridge (1894) most famous

2 London Bridge 1st stone bridge 1209 – lasted 600 years – only bridge until 1750

3 1968: Robert McCulloch (US millionaire) found out London Bridge to be demolished (new one to be built)

4 Decided buy it – ship to USA – rebuild bridge in desert – Lake Havasu, Arizona – tourist attraction

5 Offer: $2.4 + $60,000 (extra $1,000 for each of his 60 years) – offer accepted

6 Later: realised slight mistake

7 Assumed buying Tower Bridge – London Bridge ordinary 1908 stone bridge, not landmark – disappointed

8 Now visit Lake Havasu – see London Bridge – impressive!

20.5 Great business deals?
Reading and Listening

 A 1 Choose a suitable title for each of the three passages from this selection:

| A great bargain | He needed the money | Nice ice at a reasonable price |
| Striking gold | Not again, Josephine! | The best real estate deal in history |

2 Find the answers to these questions in the three texts. Each answer is a number.

1	How much was paid for the whole of Manhattan Island in 1626?	$
2	How much does an offfice block in New York cost now?	$
3	How much did Napoleon sell the Mississippi Valley for in 1803?	$
4	What was the price per hectare? (2.5 acres = about 1 hectare)	cents
5	How big was the United States before this deal?	sq. miles
6	How big was the United States after this deal?	sq. miles
7	How much did the Tsar of Russia sell Alaska for in 1867?	$
8	What was the price per hectare?	cents
9	How much gold has Alaska yielded?	$
10	How much coal is there in Alaska?	tons

1

Even in the days when America was known as the New World, it was a country with a reputation for its spirit of enterprise and the ability of its people to make a good deal.

When the settlers started negotiating, the natives hardly knew what had hit them – and in the summer of 1626, probably the most spectacular real estate coup in history took place.

Governor Peter Minuit of the Dutch West India Company had the job of buying Manhattan Island from the Native Americans.

After some haggling with Chief Manhasset, the price was agreed at 24 dollars' worth of kettles, axes and cloth.

Today, $24 would not buy one square foot of office space in New York City, and an office block in central Manhattan changes hands for around $80 million. Even allowing for inflation, Minuit got himself a real bargain.

2

You would think that the Manhattan deal would remain a one-off for ever. But less than two centuries later the loser was Napoleon, Emperor of France and (in his early years, at least) a brilliant military tactician.

In 1803, Napoleon had his mind on European affairs (in particular, an invasion of Britain), so he decided to dispense with France's American possessions.

He sold the entire Mississippi valley, an area of 828,000 square miles extending from Canada down to the Gulf of Mexico and westwards to the Rockies, for just over 27 million dollars.

Through this deal, known as the Louisiana purchase, President Thomas Jefferson doubled the size of the United States for only around 5 cents per acre.

The judgement of the Emperor, on the other hand, never seemed to be quite the same again.

3

Napoleon did just manage to reach Moscow in his ill-fated invasion of 1812 – but it would seem that news of his poor American deal did not.

For, astonishingly, the Russians went on to become the *third* victims of major land deals with America.

On March 30th 1867, the U.S. Secretary of State, William Seward, bought Alaska from Tsar Alexander II for a mere $7.2 million – thereby acquiring another 586,000 square miles of territory for less than 2 cents per acre.

The Tsar presumably thought that this remote, frozen and virtually uninhabited piece of land had nothing at all to commend it – and at first, the American people agreed with him, for Alaska was known as 'Seward's folly' and 'Seward's ice box' for years.

In 1896, however, gold was struck at Klondike in the Yukon, and since then, over 750 million dollars' worth has been mined.

In 1968, black gold was discovered – and an estimated 100 billion tons of coal are also lying underground, just waiting to be dug up.

 B   Now listen to the recording: you'll hear about three businessmen and some of the deals they made. Fill each of the 20 gaps below with one or two words, or a number.

1933

Seller: THE CANADIAN NATIONAL ₁⬚ COMPANY

Place	Product	Price	Purchaser
Canada	Ten vessels	$ ₂⬚ per ship	₃⬚

Outcome: Shipping began to boom when the world ₄⬚ ended and he became a ₅⬚.

1923–5

Seller: ARTHUR FURGUSON

Place	Product	Price	Purchaser
London	Trafalgar Square	₆⬚	an American
London	₇⬚	£1,000	a tourist
London	Buckingham Palace	£ ₈⬚ deposit	another tourist
Washington	The White House	$ ₉⬚ a year	a Texan
New York	₁₀⬚	$100,000	an ₁₁⬚

Outcome: Arthur Furguson was identified, recognised, arrested and imprisoned for ₁₂⬚ years. After his release he retired to ₁₃⬚ and lived a life of luxury.

1925–34

Seller: 'COUNT' VICTOR LUSTIG

Place	Product	Price	Purchaser
Paris	The Eiffel Tower: as 7,000 tons of ₁₄⬚	(not known)	André Poisson
USA	A machine to print ₁₅⬚	$ ₁₆⬚	a millionaire
Chicago	A 'system' to double money on Wall Street	$5,000	₁₇⬚

Outcome: Victor Lustig was imprisoned in 1934 – but he escaped and was rearrested in ₁₈⬚ and found guilty of printing $ ₁₉⬚. He died in prison in ₂₀⬚.

Abbreviations and acronyms
Word study

Abbreviations made up of initial letters, like EU, NB and USA, are spoken with the stress on the last letter: /iːˈjuː/ /enˈbiː/ juːesˈeɪ/

A If you're reading a textbook or a reference book you'll come across abbreviations like these. Match them to their meanings below:

i.e.   e.g.   fig   pp   qv   cf   ch   ed   para   NB   intro   cont'd

important note   pages   see another entry   edited by   that is   for example
introduction   continued   chapter   paragraph   figure   compare

B Work out the meanings of the abbreviations in red, which are used in business situations. Use a dictionary if necessary.

Many frequently used abbreviations may be written with or without full stops:
i.e. or **ie**
a.m. or **am**
p.m. or **pm**
U.S.A. or **USA**

1 I heard my name called out on the PA system.   *public address*
2 May I introduce Kay, who is Ms Brown's PA.
3 Salary up to £15K p.a.
4 If you're filling in a form, put N/A if the question doesn't apply to you.
5 encl. CV & photo
6 Ask them to reply ASAP.
7 Thank you for your letter ref. 4352.
8 We can supply 15 packs @ £19.99 (incl. VAT) per doz, with the usual 15% discount.
9 Marks and Spencer Ltd became Marks and Spencer plc on 1 Jan 1985.
10 My tel. no. is 518362 ext. 414
11 K. Wells p.p. Angela Brown, Export Dept.

C Rewrite each sentence using abbreviations and contractions (*isn't, can't,* etc.) where possible:

1 Doctor Brown does not live at thirteen Saint Albans Avenue any more – she has moved to number thirty, has she not?
2 This Video Home System video cassette recorder can record near-instantaneous companded audio-multiplex stereophonic broadcasts in high-fidelity sound, and it can also play either National Television System Committee or Phase Alternation Lines system videos.
3 The United States of America is over nine million square kilometres in area: it is thirty-eight times larger than the United Kingdom.
4 This compact disc read only memory player operates at two hundred and twenty volts alternating current, not direct current.
5 At the end of the talk there was not time for a question and answer session.

D 1 Look at an English-language newspaper and highlight the abbreviations you find. If necessary, check their meanings in a dictionary.

2 Note down ten common abbreviations that are used in your own country. Explain each one and, if possible, translate them into English.

3 Write a message to the members of another group, including six abbreviations.

We use *the* when referring to *the* EU, *the* USA, *the* UN, but not with acronyms like UNESCO, UNICEF, OPEC.

(An acronym is an abbreviation that is spoken as a single word: AIDS, QANTAS, SABENA, etc.)

(20.7) -ing and to . . .
Grammar

A Discuss the difference in meaning (if any) between these sentences. Then decide how each sentence might continue . . .

1 *We stopped to eat our sandwiches when* . . .
We stopped eating our sandwiches when . . .

2 *I won't forget to meet her because* . . .
I won't forget meeting her because . . .

3 *He'd like to study alone because* . . .
He likes studying alone because . . .
Studying alone is what he likes because . . .

4 *I used to write a lot of 250-word essays but* . . .
I usually write a lot of 250-word essays but . . .
I'm used to writing a lot of 250-word essays but . . .

5 *Sometimes she didn't remember to hand in her work because* . . .
Sometimes she doesn't remember to hand in her work because . . .
Sometimes she doesn't remember handing in her work because . . .

6 *The lecturer went on to tell the audience about* . . .
The lecturer went on telling the audience about . . .

7 *We tried to get through to her on the phone but* . . .
We tried getting through to her on the phone but . . .

8 *I regret to tell you that your application was unsuccessful because* . . .
I regret telling you that your application was unsuccessful because . . .

B 1 Decide in which of these sentences the verbs below can be used – the verbs in red can be used in two of the sentences. Write down the PAST FORM of each verb as well.

Anne (A)	....	to fill in the application form.
Bill (B)	....	me to write a letter of application.
Cathy (C)	....	reading the Situations Vacant ads.
Dennis (D)	....	me writing my CV.
Elaine (E)	....	that we were looking for new jobs.

> **admit** *admitted – C + E* **advise** *advised – B* **agree** *agreed – A + E*
>
> allow appreciate arrange ask assume attempt avoid begin choose consent consider
> continue decide deny discover dislike encourage enjoy expect fail feel like find
> find out finish forbid force forget get give up guess happen hear help hesitate
> imagine intend invite know manage mean notice order persuade postpone
> pretend promise propose realise recommend refuse see spend some time suggest
> tell think try understand want watch wish

2 Highlight TEN verbs in B1 which you found difficult or made mistakes with.

3 Write sentences to illustrate the verbs you highlighted. Try to illustrate more than one use if necessary. For example, with *imagine*, you might write these examples:

In my dream I imagined myself being chased down a long dark corridor.
I can imagine her finding out about the mistake and being really angry.
I imagine that they were very pleased to pass their exams.

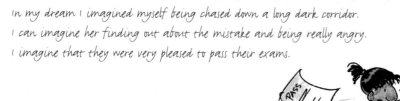

C Correct the errors in these sentences:

1 Although I was looking forward to meet her, I was afraid to make a bad impression.
2 To smoke is not allowed in the office but employees are permitted smoking in the canteen.
3 Everyone was beginning getting nervous before the exam, but once we began realising that we were all in the same boat we began to feel better.
4 The man denied to have committed the crime but he failed convincing the magistrate.
5 They made me to sit down and wouldn't let me leaving without to apologise for being rude to them.
6 To get a good job you have to having the right qualifications.
7 Don't forget making notes before you start to write the essay, and remember checking your work through afterwards.
8 You can't expect achieving success without to work hard.

20.8 Applying for a job
Creative writing

A Look at these two job ads and discuss these questions:

● Which of the jobs appeals to you more? Why?
● What kind of person is the advertiser looking for? To what extent are you that kind of person?
● What would you say about yourself if you wanted to apply for the job you prefer?

Part-time hosts/guides

ACME Travel International organize personalized world tours for small groups of people (up to ten), mainly from North America. We are looking for men and women who speak good English to act as local hosts and guides to accompany our clients during their time in your city.

The work involves accompanying guests at weekends and evenings as well as during the day on weekdays.

Excellent hourly rates, plus a monthly retainer. Generous expenses.

Write me now: tell me about yourself, why you think you would be suitable and when you are available.

Please enclose your resumé.

**Elliot Western, ATI Inc,
Suite 777, 454 Diamond St,
Philadelphia, PA 19107, USA**

International educational exchange coordinator

We are looking for a lively self-motivated person to act as LOCAL COORDINATOR for our expanding programme of educational visits and exchanges. Your duties will include corresponding with schools, colleges and individuals in Britain and the USA, liaising with similar institutions and interviewing prospective students in your own country. There will also be an expenses-paid two-week follow-up visit each year to Britain and/or the USA.

Salary to be negotiated, depending on experience, qualifications and the amount of work involved.

Please reply by letter, explaining why you would be suitable for this work, enclosing CV, to:

Mrs Lena Taylor, Educational Director-General,
International Visits and Exchanges plc,
144 London Road, Ipswich IP3 4JT

B 1 Write a letter (about 250 words) applying for one of the jobs.

2 Read your partner's letter. If you were Mr Western or Mrs Taylor, would you invite your partner to come for an interview?

> Read a job ad carefully to find out what kind of person they're looking for, and make sure that what you tell them is relevant to their requirements.
>
> (In an exam, you can bend the truth about yourself – but this may be risky in real life, where you could get caught out at the interview!)

(20.9) *First, second, third . . . and last*

Idioms and collocations

†† A **Discuss the difference in meaning (if any) between these phrases and sentences:**

1 *Max arrived late.*   *Max arrived last.*

2 *I decided to catch a late train.*   *I decided to catch the last train.*
   I decided to catch the first train.   *I decided the train was late.*
   I decided to catch the early train.   *I decided to catch an early train.*

3 *A second-hand watch*   *The second hand on a watch*

4 *Her first husband*   *Her second husband*
   Her last husband   *Her late husband*
   Her latest husband   *Her former husband*
   Her ex-husband   *Her husband is late.*

B **Fill the gaps in these sentences with suitable forms of first, second, third, last or late:**

1 If this awful weather ⬜⬜⬜⬜ till the weekend it will be the ⬜⬜⬜⬜ straw.

2 Right, ⬜⬜⬜⬜ things ⬜⬜⬜⬜: when shall we meet tomorrow? I think I'd better call for you ⬜⬜⬜⬜ thing in the morning. No, on ⬜⬜⬜⬜ thoughts, it's better if you call for me by 8 o'clock at the ⬜⬜⬜⬜.

3 There are only a few left unsold, so it's ⬜⬜⬜⬜ come, ⬜⬜⬜⬜ served.

4 They didn't get on very well at ⬜⬜⬜⬜ but by the end of the course, which ⬜⬜⬜⬜ six months, they were the best of friends.

5 It seems to be ⬜⬜⬜⬜ nature to many American people to be on ⬜⬜⬜⬜ name terms with everyone.

6 I expected there would be a lot of ⬜⬜⬜⬜-minute preparations to make but ⬜⬜⬜⬜ on I found that nothing at all needed doing.

7 Well, I haven't dealt with ACME plc at ⬜⬜⬜⬜ hand but they have a ⬜⬜⬜⬜-rate reputation. You should certainly apply for the job.

8 On the other hand, Zenith International are a ⬜⬜⬜⬜-rate company – I'd only apply for a job with them as a ⬜⬜⬜⬜ resort.

9 He's never satisfied unless he has the ⬜⬜⬜⬜ word in an argument.

10 Everyone is entitled to one mistake, please give me a ⬜⬜⬜⬜ chance.

11 The doctor wasn't sure what to do, so she asked for a ⬜⬜⬜⬜ opinion.

12 My aunt's children are my ⬜⬜⬜⬜ cousins but my mother's cousin's children are my ⬜⬜⬜⬜ cousins.

13 The ⬜⬜⬜⬜ news is that, at long ⬜⬜⬜⬜, the problems have been solved.

14 I attended a ⬜⬜⬜⬜ aid course the week before ⬜⬜⬜⬜.

15 Most novels are written in the ⬜⬜⬜⬜ person but some, where the narrator is the main character, are written in the ⬜⬜⬜⬜ person.

16 ⬜⬜⬜⬜ but not least, I'd like to wish you every success in the future – I hope you've enjoyed using this book!

"Sorry, I should have knocked."

Communication Activities

1 Spend a few minutes studying this summary and then tell the story. DON'T just read the summary aloud — try to MEMORISE the main points. Refer back to the summary only if you lose track of the story.

THE BLUE LAGOON by H. de Vere Stacpoole (1909)

Dick (age 9) + Emmeline (age 8, his foster sister) + Paddy Button (sailor) — shipwrecked on desert island

Island had fresh water + bananas + fruit — Paddy warned them not to eat red berries — they 'would send them to sleep'

Passing sailors landed on island — children afraid + hid — sailors took Emmeline's box

Paddy drowned — Dick learned to find food + catch fish

Years passed

One day, Emmeline went off into forest — next day (to Dick's surprise) came out with baby

Made boat to go round island — current carried boat away from the island — ate red berries — went to sleep, expecting never to wake up

Meanwhile Dick's father — living in San Francisco — bought Emmeline's box from a sailor — found out where he had got it — set sail to find them

Found young couple + baby in tiny boat apparently dead

But, happily, not dead — just sleeping!

2 Read the continuation of 'Japanese beach lovers bask in their artificial all-weather paradise'. Highlight the most interesting or amusing pieces of information in the article. Then, in your own words, tell your partners what you've found out.

"It's the instant noodles of beaches," explains Rie Kato, as she lies under a sun lamp at a £190 million indoor beach park in Yokohama. "Real noodles are great, but instant noodles can be filling, too."

Sunbathing is one way of spending the day at Wild Blue, an enormous structure accommodating 4,000 people on an average Saturday.

Inside, simulated fog is sprayed into the temperature-controlled 32°C environment, as artificially created waves crash on to simulated sand. A few scant rays of real sunshine filter down from skylights to mingle with illumination providing simulated midday light.

"Why on earth would anyone have this indoors when you can go to the ocean?" says John Hamilton, whose company builds indoor parks. "The simple answer is, they can't go to the ocean so they create an alternative using technology and design. We build nature ourselves."

The concept is not that radical in Japan: attempts to improve on the environment have a long history. Japanese gardens, and the miniature bonsai trees, are supposed to be cultivated and trimmed into perfection. Nature is not expected to happen naturally.

Wild Blue seems to have succeeded by creating the least wild environment possible. Tattoos, nudity, swimming clothes or picnics are not permitted. And it does not come cheap: up to £29 to get in plus £7.50 for a beach chair, and £15 for the one-day rental of a body board.

Eriko Shimomato and Akihito Nakayama have picked a choice spot between fake rocks near a fake stream on top of fake earth.

"It's artificial, that's why we like it," says Mr Nakayama. "You open the door and find this — summer all the time, any time, under a nice palm tree."

3

4

Study this information about graphology.

THE RUDIMENTS OF WISDOM

☆ HANDWRITING ☆
COMPILED & DRAWN BY HUNKIN

THE ANCIENT ROMANS WROTE MAINLY IN CAPITAL LETTERS. LOWER CASE LETTERS CAME INTO USE TOWARDS THE END OF THE ROMAN EMPIRE (400AD) & THE FIRST JOINED-UP WRITING APPEARED SOON AFTERWARDS.

JOINED-UP WRITING

M·AGRIPPA
FECIT

GRAPHOLOGY

A SYSTEM FOR ANALYSING ASPECTS OF HANDWRITING (SEE EXAMPLES BELOW & RIGHT) WAS DEVISED IN 1875 BY A FRENCHMAN CALLED ABBE MICHON & IS USED BY MOST MODERN GRAPHOLOGISTS. ALTHOUGH INDIVIDUAL ASPECTS CAN BE MISLEADING, GRAPHOLOGISTS CLAIM THAT ALL THE ASPECTS TAKEN TOGETHER CAN ACCURATELY PORTRAY PERSONALITY.

LOOPS
PRONOUNCED LOOPS BELOW THE LINE EXPRESS AN INTEREST IN MATERIAL WELL-BEING (FOOD, MONEY, SEX, POSSESSIONS ETC).

PRONOUNCED LOOPS ABOVE THE LINE EXPRESS IDEALISM, MORAL VALUES, RELIGION ETC.

JOINS

SMOOTH JOINS BETWEEN LETTERS INDICATE ADAPTABILITY & IMPRESSIONABILITY. ANGULAR JOINS INDICATE GREAT WILL POWER & LACK OF ADAPTABILITY.

SLOPES
AN EXTREME FORWARD SLOPE INDICATES AN OBSESSIVE & AMBITIOUS NATURE. BACKWARD SLOPES INDICATE SHYNESS.

5

When Gregor Samsa awoke one morning from troubled dreams he found himself transformed in his bed into a monstrous insect. He was lying on his hard shell-like back and by lifting his head a little, he could see his curved brown belly, divided by stiff arching ribs, on top of which the bed-quilt was precariously poised and seemed about to slide off completely. His numerous legs, which were pathetically thin compared to the rest of his bulk, danced helplessly before his eyes.

'What has happened to me?' he thought. It was no dream. His room, an ordinary human room, if somewhat small, lay peacefully between the four familiar walls.

from *The Transformation* by Franz Kafka

(6)

How the soundtrack on a movie film works

A stripe along the edge carries the soundtrack. The width of this sound stripe varies according to the sound signals produced during the recording.

1 Light shines through the sound stripe. Because of the varying width of the stripe, a varying amount of light passes through to a photoelectric cell.

2 The photoelectric cell converts the light back into sound signals which are identical to the original sound signals.

3 The sound signals travel down a cable to the cinema's loudspeakers. These convert them into sound waves.

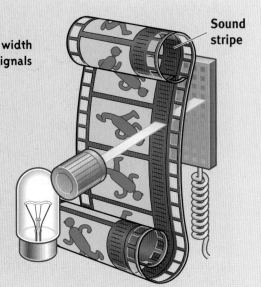

Sound stripe

Did you know . . . ?

● Before sound films took over from silent movies in the 1930s, very large cinemas often employed a symphony orchestra to accompany each performance.

● A film is shown in the cinema at 24 frames per second. On TV the same film is shown at 25 frames per second — a two-hour cinema film only lasts about 1 hour 55 minutes on TV.

(7) **1 Rewrite this passage as reported speech. Your friend Max spoke to you on the phone last Wednesday and this is what he said:**

> It's my birthday today. I got a card from my uncle in Australia yesterday and one from my aunt in Canada today. I know you can't come to my party tomorrow, so would you like to join me for a drink now or maybe we can meet later this evening?

2 Now rewrite this passage using the exact words Susan used.

Last Wednesday, my friend Susan spoke to me on the phone and told me that she wouldn't be able to see me this week. She had had a call from her brother ten minutes earlier and had found out that her grandfather would be arriving there at the end of the week and this would be the first time she'd have seen him since he went to New Zealand in 1990. She hoped I wouldn't mind if we changed our meeting from this week to next week.

3 Compare your versions with what the students in the other pair have written — and with the passages in Activity 26.

(8) **Tell this story to your partner:**

9

Snake bite

1   DON'T cut the wound.

2   DON'T suck out the poison.

3   Encourage the patient to rest, lying down.

4   Wash the wound and apply a clean dry dressing.

5   Bandage firmly with a soft pad pressing on the wound.

6   Prevent the patient from moving the affected part — this reduces the spread of the poison.

7   In Britain and Northern Europe: Reassure the patient that a snake bite is painful but not fatal (unless you are a very small child or animal).

8   You can give aspirin to reduce the pain.

9   Get the victim to hospital as soon as possible.

10

Here are some more points that distinguish rapid conversational style from formal written style:

1   Stress, intonation, pauses in speech
    – help to make message clear
    – in writing only punctuation and layout: bold letters, italics, underlining, etc.

2   Vocabulary
    – use of words like 'nice'
    – listener can ask questions

3   Writing has to be clearer and less ambiguous than speech.

4   It doesn't take as long to speak as it does to write — but listener receives information more slowly.

11

Read these pieces of advice. Then pass on the tips in your own words.

1   How much exercise do you get? Gentle rhythmic cycling, jogging or swimming are ideal ways of reducing the tension caused by stress. They help release all that pent up energy and will encourage deep refreshing sleep. Yoga, body conditioning classes or relaxation techniques may also be helpful.

2   Try to cut down on drinking and smoking. If you use these to 'unwind', the relief can only be temporary. They will not solve the problems that make you tense.

12

This is the second part of the article on page 49. Read it and then tell your partner about it IN YOUR OWN WORDS.

Jane Martin, a spokesman for the district, said: "A six-year-old kissing another six-year-old is inappropriate behaviour. Unwelcome is unwelcome at any age."

She said the rules on sexual harassment were clearly set out in a handbook. Parents signed a form saying that their children would abide by them.

Johnathan's mother, Jackie Prevette, said she would be asking for the rules to be applied only to children aged 10 or older.

She said that if her son were caught holding hands with or kissing another child again, he could be suspended.

"This seems awfully harsh for babies. What can a child of six understand about sexual harassment?"

13 Share this information with your partner. Don't read the summaries aloud — use your own words.

> **Paragraph a is from *Emma* by Jane Austen (1816)**
>
> The delightful Emma's mismanagement of other people's affairs leads to consequences she could not have foreseen. A comedy of self-deceit and self-discovery. Jane Austen's elegant, gently ironic style makes her one of the greatest English novelists, whose work still appeals strongly to the present-day reader. Most of her books have been made into movies.

> **Paragraph d is from *Nineteen Eighty-Four* by George Orwell (1949)**
>
> This futuristic story tells of one individual's fight against a totalitarian State, where the Party controls everything in everybody's lives — even the way they think. A nightmarish vision of a totalitarian world. Many of the book's phrases ('Big Brother is watching you', 'the Thought Police', etc.) have passed into the English language.

> **Paragraph e is from *Conundrum* by Jan Morris (1974)**
>
> The story of how James Morris, a well-known writer and married man with children, became Jan Morris. This is an honest and moving account of the problems she faced during her life and how she eventually overcame them by having a sex-change operation. Full of surprising humour, wit and warmth.

14 **1 Study this information before joining your partner.**

> ### ★ Marilyn Monroe ★ (1 June 1926 – 5 August 1962) ★
>
> * Star sign: Gemini.
> * Born Norma Jean Mortensen, raised by foster parents and in orphanages. Began modelling in 1945, signed up by 20th Century Fox in 1946. First starring role in *Niagara* 1952.
> * Married 3 times: at 16 to aircraft worker Jim Dougherty 1942 , for 9 months to baseball star Joe DiMaggio 1954, to intellectual writer Arthur Miller 1956.
> * Affairs with Marlon Brando, Frank Sinatra, Charlie Chaplin Junior, Yves Montand, John F. Kennedy, Robert Kennedy – and many others.
> * Most famous films: *Gentlemen Prefer Blondes* 1953, *How to Marry a Millionaire* 1953, *The Seven-Year Itch* 1955, *Some Like It Hot* 1959 – her films earned Fox over $100 million.
> * Created and destroyed by the Hollywood star system.
> * Committed suicide (overdose of sleeping pills) at the age of 36 after being fired from her last film – though some believe she was murdered.
> * Reasons for her appeal even today: the ultimate embodiment of the desirable woman, a sex symbol who was vulnerable. She had real talent as well as sex appeal.
> * Quotes: 'Everyone is always tugging at you. They'd all like sort of a chunk of you.' 'A sex symbol becomes a thing. I hate being a thing.'

2 Note down FIVE QUESTIONS you want to ask your partner about James Dean. Then join your partner to share information.

15 Read these pieces of advice. Then pass on the tips in your own words.

> 1 Remember your 'stress situations' and when you get caught up in one, use it as a cue to relax. When the traffic is making you 'tense up', do the opposite. Give your arms and neck a stretch — try smiling at someone else caught in the jam.
>
> 2 When the phone is engaged, or the taxi ignores you, take a deep breath and exhale slowly — think how silly it seems that minor hassles like these made you uptight.

16

Shock

1 Move the patient as little as possible. Call for a doctor or ambulance.

2 Position the patient with his or her head low and feet raised — do not move any part that may be fractured.

3 Loosen tight clothing.

4 Keep the patient warm — cover them with a coat or blanket.

5 Reassure the patient by being calm, sympathetic and confident. Even if the patient appears to be unconscious they may be able to hear any unfavourable comments you make.

6 DON'T give the patient anything to drink, not even water and definitely not alcohol.

7 DON'T give the patient anything to eat.

17

2
Firefighters spent 24 hours hacking through a cavity wall to save a trapped sparrow in South Shields. The sparrow was put in the back garden where it was immediately eaten by a neighbour's cat.

8
A burglar who spent the night in an empty students' flat in Liverpool tidied up the mess and washed up the dirty plates before stealing the television and the video.

5
Robbers took weeks to build a 20-foot tunnel under a busy road to reach the Yorkshire Bank in Cross Gate, Leeds. On arrival they discovered that the bank had been shut down for renovations.

10
An American pilot had to make a grovelling apology after landing 200 miles off course. "Gee! Sorry, wrong country," he told the 241 passengers after landing in Belgium instead of Germany. The cabin crew on the Northwest Airlines flight from Detroit knew they were off course, but they did nothing because they assumed they were being hijacked.

18

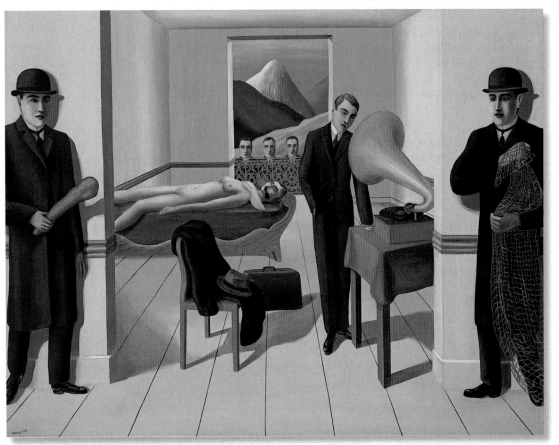

The Threatened Assassin, 1926, by René Magritte

19 Spend a few minutes studying this summary and then tell the story. DON'T just read the summary aloud — try to MEMORISE the main points. Refer back to the summary only if you lose track of the story.

THE SWISS FAMILY ROBINSON
by J.R. Wyss (1813)

Father, mother + 4 sons: Fritz, Ernest, Jack, little Francis

shipwrecked on deserted island — + dogs, sheep, cows, hens

Called island New Switzerland — built tree house

Found gunpowder, clothes, books, mirrors, chairs washed up on beach

Pineapples, sugar cane + fruit growing — salmon in river — fish + oysters in sea

One day found albatross with message tied to leg — from Jenny, a girl shipwrecked on nearby island — Fritz rescued her — fell in love

Years passed — ship came to island

Fritz, Jenny + little Francis went back to Europe — Father + Mother + Jack + Ernest stayed — 3 passengers on ship liked New Switzerland — decided to stay there!

20 Read the continuation of 'Push-button lover'. Highlight the most interesting or amusing pieces of information in the article. Then, in your own words, tell your partners what you've found out.

Japanese vending machines are also more productive. Sales per machine are almost two-thirds higher than in America, because the Japanese machines sell high-value products, like whisky, as well as the usual CocaCola and gum.

Craving a cigarette or a bar of chocolate? In America or Britain the nearest vending machine is probably vandalised, empty, or accepts only the right money in the wrong coins. Thanks to its low crime rate and sophisticated electronics, Japan's vending machines are much more reliable. They are also less likely to run out, thanks to on-line monitoring of stocks.

Despite what looks like saturation by anyone else's standards, the number of vending machines in Japan is set to grow, predicts a recent report from Jardine Fleming Securities, a Tokyo stockbroker. This is because the labour-saving advantages of vending machines have yet to be fully exploited. Declining birth rates, an ageing population and tight controls on immigration are creating a shortage of low-wage workers in Japan and boosting the demand for ever cleverer machines. One of the fastest-growing sectors is heated food such as pizzas. A vending machine can replace waitresses in hamburger joints, ticket vendors in cinemas and counter staff in all-night stores.

The latest craze is vending machines that sell love. Men looking for a girlfriend pay to have their vital statistics fed into the love machine — including their name, telephone number and, most important of all, the kind of car they drive. Women drop in a few coins, then choose the take-away man of their dreams.

21 Share this information with your partner. Don't read the summaries aloud — use your own words.

Paragraph b is from *Three Men in a Boat* by Jerome K. Jerome (1889)
Three friends decide to go for a holiday on the River Thames in a boat, taking with them plenty of food, a tent and a dog. A series of hilarious mishaps occur during the trip.
One of the funniest books in the English language.

Paragraph c is from *Rebecca* by Daphne du Maurier (1931)
This outstanding romantic novel tells the story of an innocent young woman who marries a sophisticated aristocrat, Max de Winter, and goes to live in a remote country house called Manderley, with its sinister housekeeper, Mrs Danvers. Here she is caught up in the mystery of Rebecca, Max's beautiful first wife who died in mysterious circumstances.

22

23 **Study this information about graphology.**

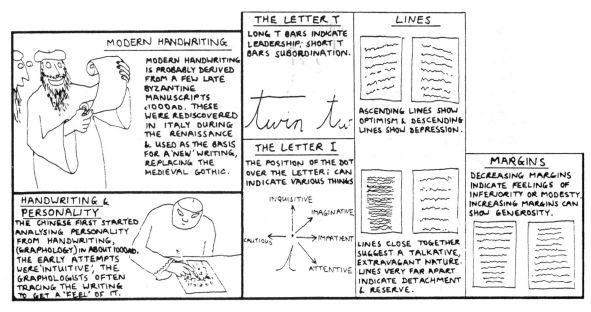

MODERN HANDWRITING

MODERN HANDWRITING IS PROBABLY DERIVED FROM A FEW LATE BYZANTINE MANUSCRIPTS c1000AD. THESE WERE REDISCOVERED IN ITALY DURING THE RENAISSANCE & USED AS THE BASIS FOR A 'NEW' WRITING, REPLACING THE MEDIEVAL GOTHIC.

HANDWRITING & PERSONALITY

THE CHINESE FIRST STARTED ANALYSING PERSONALITY FROM HANDWRITING, (GRAPHOLOGY) IN ABOUT 1000AD. THE EARLY ATTEMPTS WERE 'INTUITIVE', THE GRAPHOLOGISTS OFTEN TRACING THE WRITING TO GET A 'FEEL' OF IT.

THE LETTER T

LONG T BARS INDICATE LEADERSHIP; SHORT T BARS SUBORDINATION.

THE LETTER I

THE POSITION OF THE DOT OVER THE LETTER i CAN INDICATE VARIOUS THINGS

INQUISITIVE
IMAGINATIVE
CAUTIOUS
IMPATIENT
ATTENTIVE

LINES

ASCENDING LINES SHOW OPTIMISM & DESCENDING LINES SHOW DEPRESSION.

LINES CLOSE TOGETHER SUGGEST A TALKATIVE, EXTRAVAGANT NATURE. LINES VERY FAR APART INDICATE DETACHMENT & RESERVE.

MARGINS

DECREASING MARGINS INDICATE FEELINGS OF INFERIORITY OR MODESTY. INCREASING MARGINS CAN SHOW GENEROSITY.

24

He felt a curious tingling in his hands and feet. He felt his nose becoming cold and wet, his ears becoming flappy.

Eric is a perfectly ordinary boy. Perfectly ordinary that is, until the night when, safely tucked up in bed, he slowly but surely turns into a dog!

What becomes of Eric – the adventures he has with his best friend Roy, and their joint efforts to puzzle out the *reason* for his transformation – makes a very funny and entirely believable book.

from *Woof!* by Allan Ahlberg

Allan Ahlberg

WOOF!

Illustrated by Fritz Wegner

(25)

How a movie projector works

1 Feed reel feeds film into the projector. The scene is recorded as a series of pictures taken rapidly one after the other.

2 Gate. Each frame, or picture, is pulled down one by one into the gate and held for a fraction of a second.

3 A shutter behind the gate opens as each frame is stationary in the gate. It closes while the film is moved on to a new frame.

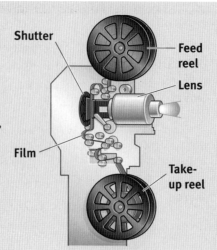

Shutter

Feed reel

Lens

Film

Take-up reel

4 Light shines on to the film when the shutter is open.

5 The lens enlarges the picture on the film and focuses it on the cinema screen.

6 A take-up reel collects the film at the end.

Did you know . . . ?

● A two-hour movie consists of 172,800 frames. Even a five-minute cartoon film consists of 7,200 separate drawings.

● Most films are shot on normal 35mm film but projected in the cinema with the top and bottom of the frame cut off to give a wide-screen effect. On TV the whole frame is usually shown – if you watch carefully, you can sometimes spot the microphone at the top of the screen.

(26) **1 Rewrite this passage using the exact words Max used:**

Last Tuesday my friend Max told me that it was his birthday that day. He had had a card from his uncle in Australia the day before and one from his aunt the same day he spoke to me. He knew I couldn't go to his party the next day, so he invited me for a drink then or suggested I could meet him later that evening.

2 Now rewrite this passage as reported speech. Your friend Susan spoke to you on the phone last Wednesday and this is what she said:

I won't be able to see you next week. I had a call from my brother ten minutes ago. I've heard from him that my grandfather will be arriving here at the end of this week and this will be the first time I'll have seen him since he went to New Zealand in 1990. I hope you don't mind but I'd like to postpone our meeting from next week to the week after.

3 Compare your versions with what the students in the other pair have written – and with the passages in Activity 7.

(27) **Tell this story to your partner:**

28 **Read these pieces of advice. Then pass on the tips in your own words.**

> **1** Stop trying to do more than one thing at a time. Take jobs in order of importance and try to plan ahead. Take control and have a positive action plan. You'll soon find that instead of doing everything at the last minute, you can get things done at a relaxed pace.
>
> **2** Instead of talking at other people, try having conversations with them and listen to what they say. Over lunch, eat more slowly, savour your food, forget work problems and have a good look around.

29 **Here are some more points that distinguish formal written style from rapid conversational style:**

1 Showing feelings + attitude — tone of voice
  – in writing you can't tell if writer is angry, happy or sad
  – use of special words in novels to show feelings: 'whispered', 'sarcastically', etc.
2 Grammar and style
  – unfinished sentences in speech
  – less complex style in speech
3 Hesitation gives you time to think and decide what to say.
4 It takes longer to write than to speak — but reader receives information more quickly.

6

30 3

A burglar climbed through the window of an 85-year-old pensioner's home in Marsh Farm, Luton, and stole her television set while she was watching it.

A 23-year-old man was rumbled during an armed robbery on a bank after calling the cashier Dad. His amazed father, who worked at the branch in Lyons, France, ripped his mask off and identified him. He was jailed for 25 years.

9

4

In Germany, a greetings card has driven a young couple from their home. When the musical card slipped behind a cupboard and into the wall cavity, it played its tune round the clock for four months until Anneliese and Axel Probst leapt into action and consulted a builder. The quote to knock down the wall was £1,200, so they moved in with relatives instead and are waiting until the electronic chip runs out of power.

A Missouri man was arrested for mowing the carpet in his son's bedroom at 6am because the boy had refused to mow the lawn.

31 Epileptic fit (major convulsive seizure)
1 Keep calm.
2 Support the head with hands/forearms if nothing else is available.
3 If possible turn person onto his/her side.
4 Stay until recovery is complete.
5 NEVER put anything in the mouth.
6 NEVER try to restrict movements or move to another place unless in danger.
7 If seizure lasts more than five minutes, call an ambulance.

32 This is the first part of the article on page 49. Read it and then tell your partner about it IN YOUR OWN WORDS.

A BOY of six has been punished by his school in America for sexual harassment after giving a girl classmate a peck on the cheek.

His defence – that she had asked for a kiss – was not accepted.

Johnathan Prevette was ejected from his class at Lexington primary, North Carolina, forcing him to miss a painting lesson, playtime and an ice cream party for children with good attendance records.

The headmaster decided that he had breached the school district's rules on sexual harassment, which apply to all pupils up to 18.

He was made to spend the day working alone in a separate room.

33 Here are some phrases that can be used when you're sending someone greetings or congratulations:

Dear ...,

Congratulations to you (both) on your ...

... engagement / exam success / new job / promotion / wedding, etc.

I was ... to hear that ...

I really must apologise for not having kept in touch with you.

Since we were last in touch, a lot of things have happened: ...

You'll never believe what has happened to me ...

Please give my love / regards / best wishes to ...

My very best wishes for the future.

All my love,

My very best wishes,

All the very best,

34

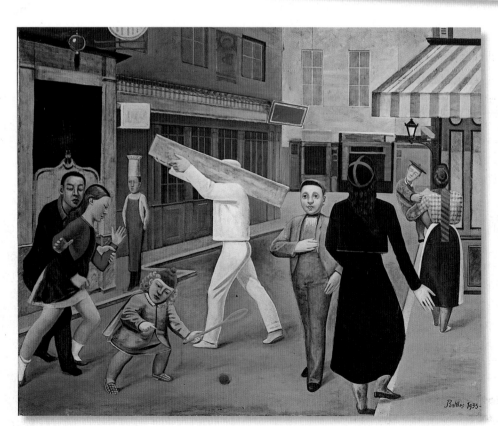

The Street, 1933, by Balthus

35 Spend a few minutes studying this summary and then tell the story. DON'T just read the summary aloud – try to MEMORISE the main points. Refer back to the summary only if you lose track of the story.

ROBINSON CRUSOE
by Daniel Defoe (1719)

Robinson Crusoe shipwrecked alone on desert island

Got food, rum, guns from wrecked ship + dog + 2 cats

Made furniture – wrote diary. Shot birds + wild goats for food. Planted seeds from old sack – grew corn + made bread

Years passed – found a footprint on beach – but no people

Years later – one Friday – saw natives on beach with two prisoners – one ran away – Crusoe shot some natives – others escaped

Found escaped prisoner – called him 'Friday' – trained him as servant – taught him English

Years later – ship came to island – Crusoe + Friday back to England – famous!

36

I Mrs Gunn, a German housewife, attacked her husband with an egg whisk after an argument about how much sugar she'd put in her coffee. Luther Gunn, 52, of Dortmund, is obsessive about money. "He wouldn't let us flush the toilet," his wife said. "And we only had one light bulb in the house, which we moved from room to room depending on where we needed it." When he told her off for using 53 sugar grains in her coffee instead of 45, she finally lost control.

II A thief who took off his glasses to avoid being recognised as he robbed a bank in Madrid stumbled into furniture and was arrested after fleeing into the arms of the police.

7 Salesman Bob Sharland had his house set on fire by a starling. The bird took a lit cigarette end back to its nest inside a wall and started a huge blaze.

12 Harrison Clamp, 48, is suing a waitress in Oregon for a $1,000 dollar tip he gave her when he was drunk, claiming he only meant to give her a dollar. Clamp paid $1,004 by credit card for a gin and tonic. The waitress, Ruth Bullis, 37, has since spent the money.

37 1 **Study this information before joining your partner.**

★ James Dean ★ (8 February 1931 – 30 September 1955) ★

- ★ Star sign: Aquarius.
- ★ First words spoken to him in his first film: 'Hello, pretty boy.'
- ★ Symbolised tormented, rebellious middle-class youth.
- ★ Famous for his looks: his slouch, the glance from beneath his hair, his vulnerable eyes.
- ★ Only starred in three films: of which only *East of Eden* 1955 had been shown before he died. *Rebel Without A Cause* 1955 and *Giant* 1956 both released after his death.

- ★ Killed in a crash in his new Porsche at the age of 24.
- ★ Mass grief at his death – huge posthumous box office success of all his films.
- ★ Reasons for his appeal even today: epitome of moody, vulnerable young man. Attractive to young women and men. Charismatic screen performances. He died so young that he remains a mystery.
- ★ Quote: 'To me the only success, the only greatness is immortality.'

2 **Note down FIVE QUESTIONS you want to ask your partner about Marilyn Monroe. Then join your partner to share information.**

The publishers are grateful to the following for permission to reproduce copyright material. It has not been possible to identify the sources of all the material used and in such cases the publishers would welcome information from the copyright owners.

p.8 Victor Gollancz Ltd for the extract from *Castaway* by Lucy Irvine; pp. 12–13 Adrian Mitchell for 'The Castaways or Vote for Caliban', reprinted by permission of The Peters Fraser and Dunlop Group Ltd on behalf of Adrian Mitchell, © Adrian Mitchell, 1991, available in *Heart on the Left: Poems 1953–1984*; pp.17, 21, 26 and 58, 60, 76, 78, 98, 104–5, 106, 109 The Guardian for articles by Lucy O'Brien, Thomas Easton, Christopher Reed, Philip Elmer-DeWitt, Anna Tomforde, Joanna Moorhead, Lawrence Donegan and Andrew Culf, Michael White, Tom Smithies, Toby Young; pp.21, 130, 139, 146, 186 The Economist for articles in *The Economist* of 16 November 1991, 13 June 1992, 17 April 1993, and 31 August 1991, © The Economist, London; p.30 Punch for the review; pp.33 and 81 Richard Brautigan for the extracts from *The Tokyo-Montana Express*; p.42 The Guardian Weekend and Polly Pattullo for the article; p.46 The Harvill Press for the extract from *For Love and Money* by Jonathan Raban, first published in Great Britain by Collins Harvill in 1981, © Jonathan Raban; pp.49, 50, 183, 190 The Daily Telegraph for the articles; p.57 Blackwell Publishers for the extract from *Coping with Japan* by Randall and Watanabe; pp.59, 120 Cambridge University Press for the extracts from *The Cambridge Encyclopedia of Language* by David Crystal, 1987; p.61 Claris for the advertisement; p.62 Working Software Inc. for the *QuickLetter* advertisement; pp.66–67 Dorling Kindersley Publishers Ltd for the extract from *Chronicle of the Twentieth Century*; p.67 Chambers Harrap Publishing Ltd for the extract and cover blurb from *Dreams for Sale*; pp.74–5 Sonia Beesley and *The Listener* for the article; p.83 Anuradha Vittachi and *New Internationalist* for the review; p.85 Mr J. Rodengen for the advertisement; p.94 Alexander Walker for the article; p.103 Hogarth Press for the extracts from *Cider with Rosie* by Laurie Lee; p.103 The Peters Fraser and Dunlop Group Ltd for the extract from *Decline and Fall* by Evelyn Waugh, © 1928 the Estate of Evelyn Waugh; pp.114–5 Desmond Morris and Random House UK Ltd for the extracts from *Manwatching*; p.116 HarperCollins Publishers Inc. and HarperCollins Publishers Ltd for the excerpt from Chapter 1 from *Men Are from Mars, Women Are from Venus* by John Gray, © 1992 by John Gray; p.117 Little Brown and Virago Press for the extract from *You Just Don't Understand* by Deborah

Tannen; p.118 US Council for Energy Awareness for the advertisement; p.129 W.W. Norton & Company Inc. for the extract from *The Vanishing Hitchhiker* by Jan Harold Brunvand, © 1981 by Jan Harold Brunvand; p.133 Viking Penguin, a division of Penguin Books USA Inc. for the extract from *Naked Beneath My Clothes* by Rita Rudner, © 1992 by Rita Rudner Enterprises Inc.; pp.142, 183, 184, 189 Van den Bergh Foods for the extracts; p.145 Curtis Brown Ltd and Martin Secker & Warburg for the extract from *Small World* by David Lodge, © 1985 David Lodge; p.146 Harlequin Books for the cover of *A Reckless Affair* by Alexandra Scott; p.148 Curtis Brown Ltd for the extract from *Rebecca* by Daphne du Maurier on behalf of the Estate of Daphne du Maurier, © 1938 by Daphne Du Maurier Browning; p.148 Martin Secker & Warburg and A.M. Heath & Co. Ltd for the extract from *Nineteen Eighty-Four* by George Orwell, © Mark Hamilton as the Literary Executor of the estate of the late Sonia Brownell Orwell; p.148 The Julian Bach Literary Agency Inc. for the extract from *Conundrum* by Jan Morris, © 1975 by Jan Morris; p.154 Greenpeace UK, Canonbury Villas, London N1 2PN for the extracts; p.164 Hampshire Constabulary for the letter by the late Chief Constable John Duke; p.174 Epson UK Ltd for the extract from an advertisement; p.181 Penguin books for the extract from *The Transformation and Other Stories* by Franz Kafka (Translation copyright © Malcolm Pasley 1992); pp.185, 189, 191 The Week Ltd for the articles; p.187 Allan Ahlberg for the text from *Woof!* (Viking Kestrel, 1987), © Allan Ahlberg, 1986 and for the blurb of *Woof!* (Puffin, 1987), © Penguin Books, reproduced by permission of Penguin Books Ltd.

The publishers are grateful to the following for their permission to reproduce copyright material and photographs:

Key: *t* = top, *m* = middle, *b* = bottom, *l* = left, *r* = right

Penguin UK on pp.9*tm*, 103*t*, 144*b*, 148*r*, *mr* /Puffin Books on pp.9*bm*, 187*b*, /Atkinson Art Gallery, Southport, Lancs/Bridgeman Art Library, London/New York on p.9*br*, /Lee Miller Archive on p.103*b*, /Christie's Images/Bridgeman Art Library, London/New York on p.148*l*, /Gavin Graham Gallery, London/Bridgeman Art Library, London/New York on p.148*ml*; Ronald Grant Archive on pp.9*tl*, 25*br*, 26*tl*, *br*, *bl*; Addison Wesley Longman on p.9*bl*; Pen Hadow on p.14; Punch Ltd on pp.15, 20, 27, 38, 41, 80, 151, 156, 166; ©Huis Ten Bosch on p.21; The Image Bank/Stephen Wilkes on p.24*t*, /Alvis Upitis on p.48(g), /Barros & Barros on p.48(i), /ADEO on p.48(a), /L.D. Gordon on pp.48(k), 147, /Peter Hendrie on p.112, /Michael